Elephants in the Room

**Evolution
Versus the
Message of Scripture**

Robert J. Koester

GWA
Books

ELEPHANTS IN THE ROOM
EVOLUTION VERSUS THE MESSAGE OF SCRIPTURE

© 2020 Robert J. Koester

Cover Design: Pamela Clemons
Copy Edit: Lisa Miller
Cover Art: Images by InspiredImages from Pixabay
Center image by Gordon Johnson from Pixabay

GWA Books
gwabooks@midco.net
09-21-3

ISBN: 978-1-7344319-0-2
Library of Congress Control Number: 2019921020

Contents

The foundation of Scripture and evolution is their teaching about the history of the universe from beginning to end. This chapter explores both foundations and shows that Scripture cannot rest on the foundation of evolution and vice versa.

This chapter explores God's goodness and love. It contrasts Scripture's description of God with what theistic evolutionists must conclude about these qualities because of their belief in natural selection.

We can understand the message of Scripture only if we understand who we are. This chapter begins with how Jesus and the New Testament writers described who we are. It continues with a description of the distinct nature of mankind's body, spirit, creation in God's image, and role in creation.

Evolution forces us to understand mankind's origin in a completely different way than Scripture does. This fact has a profound influence on how we understand our relation to God and our salvation in Christ.

Chapter 6—Right and Wrong. Sin, Death, and Judgment

In the context of evolution, these topics are understood much differently than they are in Scripture. The message of God's salvation in Christ makes little sense if these topics are products of evolution.

Chapter 7—What Jesus Did for the World

The message of Scripture is that Jesus came to save the world from the guilt and power of sin, from Satan, and from the curse of death. Theistic evolutionists turn Christ from a Savior into an example to follow.

List of Clichés

(Clichés are statements often found in theistic evolutionary writings. Additional clichés and responses to them are included in the second book of this set: *One More Elephant: Evolution Versus the Text of Scripture.*)

Introduction

The gospel is at stake

A bad start leads to problems that in the end are almost impossible to fix. It's like shooting an arrow. The tiniest fluctuation at the beginning will translate into the arrow going wide of its mark.

Genesis 1 and 2 tells us how the universe began. Genesis 3 describes Adam and Eve's fall into sin. Reading those chapters is like pulling back on the bow string. By chapter 4 of Genesis, the arrow is already in the air.

The teaching of evolution also sets the arrow in motion, but in a different direction. In the 17th century, natural philosophers began studying geological formations. They concluded that it took a long time for those formations to have been laid down, much longer than the time afforded by Scripture. When the study of biology came into its own, many agreed that animals and mankind too must have come into being over long periods of time. Since that time, philosophers and theologians have been struggling to combine the two accounts of origins. The struggle continues.

What's at stake is not just Scripture's teaching about creation. At stake is everything Scripture teaches, up to and including the purpose of Jesus' life and death. This book compares the major teachings of Christianity as taught in Scripture with how those teachings must be reinterpreted if one accepts the theory of evolution.

Each chapter begins with an overview of what Scripture teaches on an important topic. I will not just describe what Scripture teaches in my own words and offer a few verse references. Most often, the text of Scripture will be included in full. Please read through the Scripture sections carefully, especially if you are new to Scripture or to the Christian faith. A good understanding of what Scripture teaches on a topic will provide a striking contrast to what evolutionists *must* teach if they are to maintain their belief in evolution.

The topics chosen for this study are not side issues. They are the major teachings of the Christian faith. The way the topics are taught in this book will be familiar and acceptable to anyone whose religious roots are in the Protestant Reformation.

Quotations from Scripture will be followed by quotations from those who want to combine Scripture and evolution. Their strategies will be described in some detail, in most cases with quotations from a variety of theistic evolutionist authors. In general, the theistic evolutionists quoted are in the mainstream of the debate.

My approach is based on the conviction that Christians treasure the Bible so greatly that if they are convinced that its teachings are compromised, they will choose what Scripture says.

Elephants in the room

You have heard the phrase: "There are elephants in the room." In a marriage, this means you are making small talk, but you know you are avoiding the big issues. In business, it might mean you are arguing vehemently how the shelves should be arranged, but everyone realizes that the problems go deeper; the business may be failing.

There are many detailed arguments for and against evolution. Many of them are based on the meaning of individual words or concepts found in Scripture. For example, there is the debate about the length of the days of creation in Genesis 1. One side points out that the days of creation were 24 hours long—which should be obvious if Genesis is read in a straightforward way.[1] If that is so, the debate is over; evolution could not have happened. But the other side demonstrates that in Scripture the word "day" can also mean a long period of time and that Genesis, therefore, can arguably be read in a more figurative manner. Both sides leave the table feeling they have proven their point.

All the while, however, there are elephants in the room—unseen or undiscussed ideas that stand opposed to the basic teachings of the Christian religion, up to and including the work of Christ. Amidst all the discussion over the details, as important as those discussions might be, those who want to accept evolution must allow beasts into the room of their Christian faith, that is, errors which simply cannot be reconciled with the message of Scripture.

This book will isolate thirteen elephants created by the theory of evolution. One after another we will watch them lumber into the room of Scripture's message about Jesus Christ. Once you see the elephants clearly, you will realize the affect they will have on a person's faith and eternal life.

---

[1] The phrase "a literal reading of Scripture" is often used in a derogatory sense. It is confused with "literalistic." A literalistic reading disregards the fact that language uses various kinds of literature, such as narration, symbolism, and poetry. In this book, we will use the word "straightforward" in place of literal. It is meant to emphasize that we understand the various kinds of literature found in Scripture and interpret them accordingly—in a straightforward way—just as one might read the Sunday newspaper, which also uses narration, symbolism, and poetry. This is in contrast with the various "higher critical" methods of interpretation, which encourage us to interpret Scripture through the lens of an idea or ideas not found in the words of Scripture itself. In the case of theistic evolutionists, that lens is the assumption that the theory of evolution is true.

You may be in the middle of your personal struggle on the matter of origins. This book will give you a clear view of the major issues and of the decisions every believer must make in this era of evolutionary science. My prayer is that seeing the elephants clearly will help you stop agonizing so much over the details of the debate, and recognize the dangerous teachings that are easily seen and understood. Then you can answer for yourself if the elephants of evolution leave room for Jesus in your Christian faith.

I encourage you to aim well—with Scripture—and you will hit the bullseye every time and retain the blessings God's Son has won for you.

Chapter 1

The Big Picture

Introduction

I went to a Lutheran high school where my faith was nurtured by teachers who believed in God's six 24-hour-day creation as described in Genesis 1 and 2. It was a sheltered environment, I confess. But it was not so sheltered that I didn't understand the claims of evolution and realize that they went counter to Genesis as I was taught to understand it.

This was back in the 1960s. In our school library were copies of *Genes, Genesis, and Evolution* by Henry Morris and of *The Genesis Flood* by Morris and Whitcomb, both of which had recently been published. I read them and appreciated what the authors had to say. At that point in my life, all I needed to know was that evolution didn't have a corner on interpreting the data and that there were other ways of understanding it.

But my Lutheran high school in the 1960s and a present-day high school, sometimes even a Christian high school, are two very different environments. I can't fully relate to the pressure faced by many of today's Christian students. Those interested in the beauty and complexity of the world and who want to engage in scientific research have it the hardest. The higher up the academic ladder they climb, the more even taking a mild stand against evolution is considered taking a stand against knowledge itself and setting up a roadblock to academic research.

What is a Christian to do?

Forty years ago, one author predicted:

> The day will come when the evidence consistently accumulating around the evolutionary theory becomes so massively persuasive that even the last and most fundamental Christian warriors will have to lay down their arms and surrender unconditionally. I believe that day will be the end of Christianity."[2]

In the years since that statement was made, Christianity hasn't come to an end. Some claim that belief in a six-day creation is currently held by only a minority

---

[2] G. Richard Bozarth, "The Meaning of Evolution," *American Atheist* (20 Sept. 1979), p. 30. This often-quoted statement was found on http://www.skeptictank.org/hs/evoquote.htm. Accessed October 30, 2012.

of Christians in a few backwater denominations that are still living in a more naïve age. But that is simply not true. The number of Christians who accept a six-day creation and who don't accept evolutionary interpretations is high.

The sheer number of arguments claiming to prove evolution has indeed become overwhelming, or so it seems. There can be little doubt that the Christian's struggle will grow as confidence in evolution grows. What are average believers to do, especially when it is beyond their ability to answer evolutionary interpretations of the data? Creation scientists present alternate ways of understanding the data, and this helps. But what if an argument for evolution cannot be overcome easily? What happens when pieces of evidence for evolution come too quickly to sort out and deal with adequately? What happens if the pressure to conform becomes too great for a Christian to resist?

In this regard, Christian author R. T. Kendall makes an important statement: "Every generation of Christians has its own stigma by which the believer's faith is severely tested."[3] No generation of Christians has the luxury of living in an age when all the challenges to the Christian faith can be overcome easily by the power of reason. The arguments of Greek philosophers, the early attacks against Jesus' divine nature that came from within the Christian church itself, and the seemingly unshakable logic of Enlightenment rationalism—all seemed nearly insurmountable in their day.

Years down the road, evolution may be supplanted by another seemingly unanswerable proof against Scripture. But for now, evolution is it. At any given point, Christians will likely find various evolutionary claims unanswerable, even with the help of creation scientists. But if you are willing to think through the issues on the basis of Scripture, you will find certainty—the certainty provided by God in his Word.

Little help from mainstream Christianity

Much of today's religious community offers little support to those who are wrestling with the issue of Scripture and evolution. A hundred years ago, most mainstream Protestant[4] denominations, colleges, and seminaries in America taught a literal six-day creation. Today, Christians who accept this view are considered to be on Protestantism's right wing.

---

[3] R. T. Kendall, "Faith and Creation," in *Should A Christian Embrace Evolution*, ed. Norman C. Nevin (American Edition: Phillipsburg, NJ: P&R Publishing, 2009), p. 109.

[4] *Protestantism* is sometimes used as a term for the non-Lutheran churches of the Reformation. In this book, *Protestant* will refer to all the churches of the Reformation.

The 1950 papal encyclical *Humani Generis* opened the door for Roman Catholics to discuss evolution as a method God might have used to create the world.[5] In recent years, Catholic leadership has virtually closed the door to Catholic scholars who take a stand against evolution.

The largest Lutheran church body in America, the Evangelical Lutheran Church in America (ELCA), refuses to issue pronouncements on scientific findings and believes that God's creative activity could have stretched over millions of years.[6] As recently as 1980, the American Lutheran Church, one of the church bodies that merged to form today's ELCA, could choose material for its adult instruction students that assured them:

> The story of how God created the world is told in the first two chapters of the Bible.... In six successive days... by His almighty word God brought forth the world and all that therein is.... There is no materialistic philosophy of evolution that can make God superfluous or unnecessary as the Creator of the universe. On the contrary, the design seen everywhere in nature, and the laws of nature point unmistakably to such a Creation as the Bible reveals.[7]

But today few college or seminary teachers in that denomination would agree with that.

Even the more conservative Assemblies of God, long-time defenders of the traditional interpretation of Genesis 1-3, said in a 2010 statement on evolutionary theory: "In attempting to reconcile the Bible and the theories and conclusions of contemporary scientists, it should be remembered that the creation accounts do not give precise details as to how God went about His creative activity."[8]

In their official statements of belief, some conservative denominations claim that they accept a six 24-hour-day creation week. But they are finding that what might be taught about creation in their seminary doctrinal classes is not the same as what is taught in the science departments of their church-run colleges.

For the past 50 years, large formerly conservative evangelical publishers have followed suit. Zondervan, Inter-Varsity, Eerdmans, and others are now

[5] Pius XII, Humani Generis, para. 36. http://w2.vatican.va/content/pius-xii/en/encyclicals/documents/hf_p-xii_enc_12081950_humani-generis.html. Accessed April 27, 2019.

[6] http://www.elca.org/What-We-Believe/Social-Issues/Faith-Science-and-Technology/Ask-a-Scientist.aspx#anchor5. Accessed August 12, 2012. http://www.elca.org/What-We-Believe/Social-Issues/Faith-Science-and-Technology/Ask-a Scientist.aspx #anchor14. Accessed August 12, 2012.

[7] Martin Anderson, The Adult Class Manual, Minneapolis: Augsburg Publishing House, 1938 (Fifty-sixth Printing, 1980), p. 12.

[8] http://ag.org/top/beliefs/Position_Papers/pp_downloads/PP_The_Doctrine_of_Creation.pdf. Accessed August 12, 2012.

sources of books on theistic evolution. To find books whose authors believe in a six 24-hour-day creation, one must turn to the relatively few small publishing houses associated with conservative Protestant denominations,[9] as well as those associated with creationist groups.

Theistic evolutionists appeal to prominent church leaders

Well-known and highly respected Christian leaders in the Evangelical world are being quoted by theistic evolutionists to support their ideas. My purpose in mentioning these men is not to disparage their conservative stance on many issues, but to illustrate the challenge to those who believe in a six 24-hour-day creation coming from within the Christian church itself. I don't know if these leaders ever changed their minds, but what they wrote about evolution, at least at one point in their lives, is supporting the theistic evolutionists' cause.

C. S. Lewis accepted theistic evolution and taught it. There is evidence that Lewis began to question his position on evolution in the 1950s. [10] But his published views, especially as he articulated them in the popular *The Problem of Pain*, are regularly used by theistic evolutionists to support their claims. In *The Problem of Pain*, Lewis described his version of how humans evolved from animals:

> For long centuries God perfected the animal form which was to become the vehicle of humanity and the image of Himself. . . . Then, in the fullness of time, God caused to descend upon this organism, both on its psychology and physiology, a new kind of consciousness which could say "I" and "me."[11]

Billy Graham kept the door open to evolution. There is only one statement attributed to him on the subject, but it is used regularly. In *Doubt and Certainties*, a book Graham wrote in 1964, he said the following:

> I don't think that there's any conflict at all between science today and the Scriptures. I think . . . we've tried to make the Scriptures say things they

---

[9]Northwestern Publishing House of the Wisconsin Synod and Concordia Publishing House of the relatively large Lutheran Church—Missouri Synod produce only material that teaches a six-day creation.

[10]"Though he may have privately come to struggle with this position by the late 1950s, his publications remained unchangeably imbued with this concept." Gheorghe Razmerita, *Theistic Evolution's Struggle for Survival: An Analysis and Evaluation of the Appeal of Theistic Evolutionist Systems to Dual Anthropology* (Saabrucken, Germany: VDM Verlag Dr. Mueller Aktiengesellschaft & Co., 2009), p. 80. Also see the article by John G. West, "Darwin in the Dock: C. S. Lewis on Evolution," in *Theistic Evolution: A Scientific, Philosophical, and Theological Critique*, ed. J. P Moreland et al. (Wheaton: Crossway, 2017), pp. 755-779.

[11]C. S. Lewis, *The Problem of Pain,* (Harper Collins e-books), p. 73.

weren't meant to say. . . . The Bible is not a book of science. The Bible is a book of Redemption, and of course I accept the Creation story. . . . I believe that God created man, and whether it came by an evolutionary process . . . makes no different as to what man is and man's relationship to God.[12]

Theistic evolutionists find this quotation quite useful. For example, in a 2012 *Christianity Today* reader comment column, the author was describing how she convinced her son that it was okay to believe in evolution. Her more conservative son was objecting to his mother's position until she pointed him to the Billy Graham quote. This was enough to convince her son that his mother "was not a total heretic."[13] Considering the coverage of *Christianity Today*, it likely convinced others as well.

Consider Wayne Grudem's *Systematic Theology*, written especially for lay audiences. Grudem confesses the inerrancy of Scripture. He believes the creation of Adam and Eve as described in Genesis 2. And he has written a number of prefaces to books that oppose evolution. I don't know if his views have changed since he wrote *Systematic Theology*, but this book is still very influential.

In *Systematic Theology*, Grudem leaves the door open for the "day-age theory," that is, that the days of Genesis are not solar days of 24 hours but long periods of time. Grudem claims that Genesis can be read to support both interpretations of the word *day*: "Both views are possible, but neither one is certain. And we must very clearly say that the age of the earth is a matter that is not directly taught in Scripture."[14] On that basis he forges a combination of possibilities based on old-earth science. It is possible, he writes, that "15 billion years is just the right amount of time to take in preparing the universe for man's arrival and 4.5 billion years in preparing the earth."[15]

Since the age of the earth is not discussed in Scripture, a Christian's answers will have to come from science: "It is likely that scientific research in the next ten or twenty years will tip the weight of evidence decisively toward either a young-earth or an old-earth view, and the weight of Christian scholarly opinion (from both biblical scholars and scientists) will begin to shift decisively

---

[12]Graham wrote this in 1964 in *Doubt and Certainties*. It is cited in *Billy Graham: Personal Thoughts of a Public Man*, 1997, pp. 72-74. This latter book was based on interviews by David Frost.

[13]Carolyn Arends, "God Did It," *Christianity Today* (November, 2012), p. 66.

[14]Wayne Grudem, *Systematic Theology: An Introduction to Biblical Doctrine* (Grand Rapids: Zondervan, 1994), p. 307, Kindle.

[15]Wayne Grudem, *Systematic Theology*, p. 297.

in one direction or another."[16] Grudem's speculations make it impossible for him to describe how God made the universe. He writes: "God may not allow us to find a clear solution to this question before Christ returns." But perhaps we can expect "that there will be further progress in scientific understanding of the age of the earth." [17]

Compared to other contemporary Christian writers, Grudem's position is relatively mild. But his opinion about the lack of clarity of Genesis 1 and 2 regarding the age of the earth leads his readers into the world of speculation. Grudem himself may not believe in theistic evolution, but his "day-age" speculations cannot help but lead some of his readers in that direction.

Theistic evolution

This book is about "theistic evolution," a term used for various methods to wed God (*theos* is the Greek word for God) and the theory of evolution. Theistic evolutionists teach that the world and the creatures living in it evolved over millions of years through a process God created and with God's guidance and help.

Theistic evolution has been around in some form since the early 1700s when natural philosophers (whom we today call scientists) began to speculate about how the earth came into being. Their conclusions—which at first centered on geology and later included biology—required much more time for the world to take shape than provided by a straightforward reading of Genesis 1 and 2. Most early natural philosophers believed that God created the world, and they tried to keep God in the picture, just like theistic evolutionists do today. But already in the first half of the 1700s, it was becoming clear that their views could not be reconciled with Scripture.

Theistic evolution in the narrow and broad sense

"Theistic evolution" is sometimes used in a narrow sense. The claim is made that God created the world by letting the process of evolution work on its own, or at least without his performing miracles to help evolution along. God is said to have given matter the built-in potential to organize itself (evolve) into the precise creation he envisioned. Some claim that the creation is the result of a seemingly random process. Others admit to miracles, but only when evolution needed help, for example, when it was time for life to appear.

---

[16]Wayne Grudem, *Systematic Theology*, p. 308.

[17]Wayne Grudem, *Systematic Theology*, p. 307.

Sometimes theistic evolution is used in a broader sense—in reference to any theory in which evolution is considered either in whole or in part to be the tool God used to create the world. *That is how the term is being used in this book.*

Some of the positions I am lumping together under the term theistic evolution go by other names, such as the "God-of-the-gaps" theory,[18] the "day age" theory, or "old earth creationism." These theories will differ from "theistic evolution" in the narrow sense. But they all claim that in some way God created the universe using the process of evolution. None of these variations is exempt from forcing Christians to face *all* the problems associated with trying to merge Scripture and evolution.

The theistic evolutionary landscape

Imagine you are beginning a study of theistic evolution and are trying to sort out the various authors and their positions. You scour local bookstores and internet booksellers for books on the topic. You find it difficult to determine the content of the books you come across. Titles provide some help, but they are often too general and don't reveal the author's position. Online book sellers often let you read the table of contents, which is a big help. But finding books that are helpful for your purpose is still somewhat hit and miss.

You begin to realize that one could spend a lifetime tracing the debate. It started long before Charles Darwin published his ideas. You also sense that you are living at a unique point in the history of the debate. Most of the books you come across in favor of theistic evolution were written since the turn of the 21st century.

During the 1950s and 1960s, the creation science movement began challenging evolutionary claims. Creationists became skilled debaters and would often win debates against evolutionists on secular university campuses. Evolutionists—both secular and theistic—knew they had to rise to the challenge. During the past 30 years or so, they have begun to push back, explaining their position in terms the average person can understand, and making a better showing in the public forum. Hence the large number of theistic evolutionary books in the last three decades.

You assemble a large stack of books, but your stack is rather disorganized. It is clear that theistic evolutionists have not arrived at a single, coherent approach

---

[18]This is not to be confused with the "gap theory," which teaches a gap of time between the creation of two universes. The "God-of-the-gaps" theory teaches that there were major periods when evolution could not have progressed unless God stepped in and created what needed to be in place for evolution to proceed. It also answers a major argument against evolution, irreducible complexity, with the claim that God created certain organisms fully mature.

to the subject. As you read, however, you find your books falling into distinct groups. So you clear some room on a bookshelf and begin to organize your pile of books.

Some of your books are by creation science authors. They are defined variously as "young earth" or "creationist" authors. There is no theistic evolutionism in these books. They attempt to show that the so-called unshakable scientific evidence for evolution is not really that unshakable. In these books Scripture is read in much the same way as you read the Sunday newspaper. Narratives are taken to be accurate descriptions of events that actually happened. Poetry is read as poetry, and its figurative language is recognized and interpreted accordingly. You group these books on the right side of your shelf.

Some of your books are by secular Darwinists like Richard Dawkins or Carl Sagan. These authors accept pure Darwinism, namely, that organic matter evolved by small mutations over huge amounts of time. In their systems, the mutations are completely random. There is no theistic evolution here, no hint of divine intervention. You file these books on the far left side of your bookshelf.

Among your books you find a few written by Christians who are convinced that evolution is true, or at least want to leave open the possibility. But these Christians also want to take seriously the *words* of Scripture. Collectively, they are called "old-earth creationists." They believe that with a few tweaks to the traditional interpretation of the words of Scripture, the teachings of evolution and Scripture can be harmonized. Perhaps the most the well-known tweak is the "day-age" claim, namely, that the "days" of Genesis are not necessarily 24-hour days. Rather, they are long periods of time during which living creatures evolved. You file these books on the right side of your bookshelf, next to the books by creationists. You will not be dealing with old-earth creationist views, but you realize that much of what you know about theistic evolution also applies to them. [19]

You may have purchased a few books from authors in the "intelligent design" movement. These books were written by scientists who question current evolutionary thinking but who do so from a purely scientific standpoint. Their research convinces them that pure Darwinism is wrong. The facts, they believe, can lead to only one conclusion, namely, that evolution was helped along by an intelligent being. You welcome their insights. But you realize that these authors are evolutionary scientists simply trying to base their conclusions on what they observe in nature. They have no interest in helping Christians wrestle with the implications of evolution for their faith. You put these books on the left side

---

[19] Among early old-earth creationist views are "gap creationism," the "day-age theory," and "progressive creationism." See Appendix 1 for more information on these theories.

of your bookshelf, next to the pure Darwinists. You realize that these writers are different from men like Dawkins and Sagan, but they are still working on the basis of scientific observation without any concern for what Scripture says about origins.

The remaining books in your stack belong solidly in the category of "theistic evolution." The authors of these books are all attempting to combine divine creation with the science of evolution. These books will be placed in the middle of your bookshelf. But before you put them there, you realize you must make one further distinction. Some will have to be placed further to the left and others further to the right.

On the left side (of your middle section), you place books by liberal Protestant and Roman Catholic authors. These authors are members of denominations that for decades have held to the historical-critical method of interpreting Scripture (which is the topic of the second book in this set). These authors have little concern for reading the Bible in a straightforward way. Often, their views on God's role in evolution sound more philosophical than scriptural. If you come from an evangelical background that still defines the gospel as the good news that Jesus died for the world's sin and rose to show his victory over death, you likely will find little satisfaction in these books. You put these in the center section of your bookshelf, but to the left, next to the intelligent design books.

That leaves one final group of books. These books are by authors who grew up in denominations that accept the traditional Protestant understanding of Christianity. Their upbringing and education includes the historic Reformation approach to sin and forgiveness and to the text of Scripture. These authors are more sensitive to the questions asked by Christians trying to base their beliefs on Scripture alone. You sense that some of these authors are still struggling in their own minds—even as they write—to reconcile their childhood beliefs about creation with the teaching of evolution. Sadly, a few of these authors—who have recently experienced a personal conversion from belief in a literal six-day creation to belief in evolution—take every opportunity to mock those who accept a literal reading of Genesis.

Somewhat unexpectedly, however, you realize that your more conservative authors are not that much different from your liberal authors. Both sides use historical criticism. And both use similar arguments for reconciling Scripture and evolution. You put these books on the right side of the middle group on your bookshelf, but you realize that the difference between them and their liberal neighbors is not always that apparent.

Your bookshelf is full. Going from right to left, it looks like this: On the right side are books that teach a literal "young earth" reading of Scripture. Next are books by those who claim to read the words of Scripture in a straightforward way, but who have tried to adjust the traditional meaning of Scripture's words and phrases in order to make Scripture and evolution compatible. Next come books by theistic evolutionists from denominations with a closer connection to historic Protestantism. Next come books by theistic evolutionists from within liberal Protestant denominations and the Catholic Church. To the left of them are books by intelligent design authors. At the extreme left are books by pure Darwinists, who remove God from the picture entirely.

What you will find in this book

The chapters in this book contain the following elements:

1. Each chapter begins with what Scripture says about the topic of the chapter. Scripture will speak for itself. The many passages cited might seem overwhelming at times. But the sheer number of statements, which are located all over the Bible, will provide the foundation on which to evaluate theistic evolutionary statements.

2. Quotations from theistic evolutionists will come next. We will see in their own words how they approach each of the topics. These quotations will be taken primarily, but not exclusively, from theistic evolutionists who come from denominations that until recently have confessed the traditional view of creation. But, as mentioned above, conservative and liberal positions are merging. Also, I have tried to use quotations from authors who are in the mainstream of theistic evolutionary thought and have tried to avoid citing authors who are on the fringe.

3. Scattered throughout the book are short articles that evaluate arguments that appear regularly in theistic evolutionary books. I'm calling these articles "clichés" because that is what they have become in the literature. Some authors understand these topics better than others as is evident by their more nuanced treatment. Sometimes, however, the arguments appear with little scholarly thought, research, or explanation. They sometimes seem to be thrown in just to score an easy point. I'll include one of these at the end of this chapter to give you an idea of what these clichés are like.

4. Each topic will conclude with a description of the elephants theistic evolution has allowed to enter the room of the Christian faith.

A note on something that will *not* be covered in this book. One elephant in the room needs its own treatment. The presence of this elephant is usually recognized, and it is often discussed. In fact, most theistic evolutionists, especially those who come from historically conservative Christian denominations, realize they themselves must introduce this elephant before they attempt to give their position on Scripture and evolution. The topic is this: How should we read and interpret Scripture? This elephant is covered in the second book in this set: *One More Elephant: Evolution Versus the Text of Scripture.*

Here is a sample cliché. It addresses a common theistic evolutionary way to dismiss the teaching of Genesis 1 and 2.

> **Cliché: Genesis was not intended to be a *science textbook* but rather a *book of theology*.**
>
> There certainly is a difference between the Bible and the "scientific" books we have all used, like a high school introduction to science or a college book on anatomy. We agree that Scripture is not like that kind of science book.
>
> But the logic in this cliché forces the reader into a false antithesis. (A false antithesis contrasts one statement with another and forces a person to choose between them. It fails to reveal other options.) This false antithesis is often stated like this: "The Bible teaches us how to go to heaven but not how the heavens go."
>
> Consider the following illustration:
>
> My son sends me a letter about a Green Bay Packers' football game. He describes the block that sprung the runner open for a big gain. He describes the fingertip reception in the end zone that brought the crowd to its feet. He describes how tired the defense looked after it had been on the field through six first downs.
>
> Now, if the head coach of the Packers ran across that letter, he wouldn't say, "This is not a scientific description of the game. It does not include a thorough treatment of what went on in the locker room at halftime, nor does it include the reasoning behind our fourth quarter defensive strategy. This letter has no value to help a person understand the game as it really happened."
>
> An accurate description of a football game is not a matter of who wrote it or what method of analysis they used. To make that claim is to set up a false antithesis. True, my son's letter is different than a coach might write. But it is a no less accurate description of what actually happened in the game. And perhaps the head coach forgot to mention a key aspect of the game so evident to the fans in the bleachers, which actually makes his very deep and technical description less accurate than my son's letter.
>
> Questions about theology and science are not resolved by creating a false antithesis based on differing types of literature or focus. They can only be resolved by carefully studying what each teaches and deciding which is correct.

Chapter 2

The Universe from Beginning to End

According to Scripture

Introduction

The Bible's account of creation and evolution's account of the Big Bang are not two fuzzy views of origins that can easily be combined through a little sleight of hand. Both are well-defined systems. Each contains a central core and individual teachings that are consistent with that core.

In this chapter we will discuss the central core of Scripture and of evolution, the "framework" of our universe, that is, the history of the universe from beginning to end.

Scripture's framework

The first two chapters of Scripture and the last two chapters of Scripture describe a perfect world. The chapters in between tell about a terrible change that took place in our world and what God did to remedy that change. The basic events recorded in Scripture—namely, the creation of a perfect world, our first parents' fall into sin, the changes that came into the world after that event, and God's promise to change the world back to what it was at the beginning—form the framework of our universe as described in Scripture.

The beginning as described in Scripture

A finished world

The framework of our existence hinges on how and when our universe began. The Bible begins with the words, "In the beginning, God created the heavens and the earth" (Genesis 1:1). Before God created the world nothing existed, but when his creation was finished, a world filled with beauty and life lay before him.

> Thus the heavens and the earth were finished, and all the host of them. And on the seventh day God finished his work that he had done, and he rested on the seventh day from all his work that he had done. So God

blessed the seventh day and made it holy, because on it God rested from all his work that he had done in creation" (Genesis 2:1-3).

According to Scripture, how the universe began is not something that can be discovered by human reason. The writer of Hebrews tells us: "By faith we understand that the universe was created by the word of God, so that what is seen was not made out of things that are visible" (11:3). Quoting Psalm 102:25, the writer describes the work Jesus did in the beginning: "You, Lord, laid the foundation of the earth in the beginning, and the heavens are the work of your hands" (Hebrews 1:10).

Various passages in which the phrase "in the beginning" is used describe the world as already finished at that time. For example, Isaiah prophesied that the Lord would put Cyrus on the throne of the Persian Empire. God would then prompt Cyrus to let the people of Judah return to their homeland. The Lord asked, "Who has performed and done this, calling the generations from the beginning? I, the LORD, the first, and with the last; I am he" (Isaiah 41:4). God has been calling forth generations "from the beginning." That tells us that from the beginning of the world, men and women were fully formed and able to serve as the Lord's agents to do his will.

In the same way, when Jesus and the writers of the New Testament spoke about the beginning, their arguments imply that people existed in their finished state as described in Genesis 1 and 2. For example, referring to Eve's temptation recorded in Genesis 3, Jesus told the religious leaders of his day: "You are of your father the devil, and your will is to do your father's desires. He was a murderer from the beginning, and does not stand in the truth, because there is no truth in him" (John 8:44). Satan's lies and the death he introduced into the world through those lies started shortly after Adam and Eve were created, which Jesus refered to as "the beginning."

For this to have happened, Adam and Eve had to have been created in their finished state. They had to have received God's command not to eat of the tree of the knowledge of good and evil, had to have possessed the linguistic ability necessary to converse with Satan, and had to have been able to make an informed choice between God's will and Satan's will.

Jesus corrected the Pharisees' mistaken ideas about marriage and divorce: "Have you not read that he who created them from the beginning made them male and female?" (Matthew 19:4). When God created Eve and brought her to Adam, the two were ready to begin living together in the state of marriage. Also, the marriage relationship was intended to be permanent "from the beginning." Jesus explained that Moses was forced to regulate divorce: "Because of your hardness of heart Moses allowed you to divorce your wives, but from the beginning it was not so" (Matthew 19:8).

Jesus condemned the Jews, who throughout their history persecuted the prophets: ". . . so that the blood of all the prophets, shed from the foundation of the world, may be charged against this generation, from the blood of Abel to the blood of Zechariah, who perished between the altar and the sanctuary" (Luke 11:50,51). Cain's murder of Abel took place not that long after mankind fell into sin, yet this happened at "the foundation of the world" recorded in Genesis 1 and 2.

Paul wrote, "For his invisible attributes, namely, his eternal power and divine nature, have been clearly perceived, *ever since the creation of the world*, in the things that have been made" (Romans 1:20). This statement implies two things: (1) that the world was created in its finished state and could display the glory of God from the outset; and (2) that people were in existence from the time of creation and had the ability to observe the creation and draw conclusions about God from it.

The writer of Hebrews understood the framework of our existence in terms of "perfection/fall into sin/God's promise of salvation." He explained that if Christ had not been able to offer a sacrifice that could cover the sins of all people, "he would have had to suffer repeatedly since the foundation of the world. But as it is, he has appeared once for all at the end of the ages to put away sin by the sacrifice of himself" (9:25,26). In other words, if Jesus had not been able to offer a one-time sacrifice that covered the sins of all people, he would have had to begin making sacrifices from the moment Adam and Eve sinned, which happened at "the foundation of the world."

God created a perfect world

God's assessment of his creation is clear: it was good. Six times God looked at what he had made and said that it was good. When the entire creation was finished, God concluded that it was "very good" (Genesis 1:31).

Cliché: The Bible says the world was "good," but that doesn't mean it was "perfect."

This cliche sounds innocent on the surface, a little concession to allow the possibility of evolution. But think of what this statement is asking you to confess.

You are being asked to define scarcity, struggle, competition, death, and extinction as mere "imperfections" in an otherwise good creation. What's more, if God called the creation good, then such im-

19

perfections must be good things. And as we will see in the final chapter, Jesus' work must be defined as ridding people of the guilt that comes from being active participants in the imperfect process that God himself created to enable us to evolve.

God saw creation and said it was good in the same sense that we praise his goodness. The psalmist praises God for his goodness to Israel. "Oh, taste and see that the LORD is good! Blessed is the man who takes refuge in him!" (Psalm 34:8). "For the LORD is good; his steadfast love endures forever, and his faithfulness to all generations" (Psalm 100:5). "The LORD is good to all, and his mercy is over all that he has made" (Psalm 145:9).

In these verses, Christians are glad to read the word *good* as absolute perfection. No Christian would want to say, "Oh, taste and see that the Lord is mostly good" or "For the Lord is fairly good, and is usually faithful" or "The Lord is merciful to the majority of his creatures."

It is impossible to conclude that "good" means anything other than perfect. If God is perfect, then what he does is perfect.

Suffering, scarcity, competition, and death came into the world because sin and evil came into the world. God did not include these things in his original creation.

When God said that he would re-create the world on the Last Day, he described some ways in which the world would be restored. After the flood, God made animals afraid of mankind (see Genesis 9:2), but that fear will be gone. In the new heavens and earth, animals will live in peace with each other and with mankind:

> "For behold, I create new heavens and a new earth, and the former things shall not be remembered or come into mind. . . . The wolf and the lamb shall graze together; the lion shall eat straw like the ox, and dust shall be the serpent's food. They shall not hurt or destroy in all my holy mountain," says the LORD." (Isaiah 65:17,25)

When God said he will create "a new heavens and a new earth" and that the former things had passed away, he was not saying that he would create an entirely new *kind* of world. Rather, he would restore the world to what it had been before sin and evil entered it. Jesus ascended into heaven "until the time *for restoring all the things* about which God spoke by the mouth of his holy prophets long ago" (Acts 3:21). When God restores all things in the new heaven and earth, "he will wipe away every tear from their eyes, and death shall be no more, neither shall there be mourning, nor crying, nor pain anymore, for the former things have passed away" (Revelation 21:4). This is God's definition of *good*. This is how it was "in the beginning."

Rebellion against God's will changed the universe

The world's history from beginning to end includes a change that took place in the original creation.

Scripture tells us that evil did not have its origin in the good and changeless God. Rather, evil entered his creation from the outside. Solomon observed, "This only have I found: God created mankind upright, but they have gone in search of many schemes" (Ecclesiastes 7:29 NIV84).

Satan rebelled against God. Then he introduced his sinful rebellion into God's perfect world by leading Adam and Eve to rebel against the one commandment God had given them. In the framework of Scripture, Satan, not God, is the originator of evil. He entered the world from the outside with deception and lies. He changed Adam and Eve from what God had created them to be like. As soon as they sinned, "the eyes of both were opened, and they knew that they were naked" (Genesis 3:7). Their former untainted appreciation of each other's beauty was now contaminated by elements of lust. So they felt the need to cover themselves.

As people created in the image of God, Adam and Eve had been able to enjoy God's company. But after they sinned, they were no longer at ease in his presence. When he came looking for them, they cowered in fear. They knew their will was at odds with his.

They tried hard to argue themselves out of their predicament. They still had the power of reason, but their logic was marred. Adam foolishly explained that he and his wife had hidden from God because they were naked. It was foolish because that was the way God created them.

Adam and Eve's perfect love for God and for each other changed into self-centered blame and accusation. Adam and Eve both tried to rid themselves of responsibility for their sin. Adam blamed Eve (the *woman* you gave me), and he blamed God himself (the woman *you* gave me). Eve passed the blame on to the serpent (Genesis 3:11-13).

Later, when God banned Adam and Eve from the Garden of Eden, he acknowledged that sin had changed Adam and Eve: "Then the LORD God said, 'Behold, the man has become like one of us in knowing good and evil'" (Genesis 3:22). It was one thing for Adam and Eve to understand evil as something that exists. It was quite another for them to understand evil in all its depth as God did. But unlike God, evil was now living in them and controlling them.

Many other changes followed. These changes were not always the *natural* result of the presence of sin. Rather, they were special acts of God imposed on the creation in its fallen state. Some of these changes are recorded in Genesis 3. Eve was told that childbirth would be difficult. The ground would not cooperate with Adam. Both were told they would die.

We should never underestimate the magnitude of the changes that took place in creation after the fall into sin. Spiritual changes included lust, guilt leading to fear of God, self-centered casting of blame, and the sorrows that accompanied the many physical changes God made. Eve's body must have changed in various ways causing pain in childbirth. Plant life must have undergone changes when thorns and thistles were introduced into Adam's field. Mankind's entire physiology changed with the introduction of the aging process and death.

In addition to the changes listed in Genesis 3, we should note other changes referred to later. When God allowed people to eat animals for food (Genesis 9:3), he must have changed human physiology. When he established the food chain, whose existence is referred to in Scripture (Psalm 104:20-22), God must have made changes to animal physiology as well. When God created a natural fear of mankind in animals (Genesis 9:2), he must have changed their perceptions and emotions. When God created the rainbow as a witness to his promise not to again destroy the earth with a flood (Genesis 9:13), he may have altered the laws of physics in some way, which would have affected everything else. His creation of multiple languages to force people to move outward and fill the earth (Genesis 11:6,8) must have meant massive changes in the minds of those who first spoke the new languages. Through this change he also changed human society as a whole—unity was replaced by division. The change in the human lifespan (Genesis 10:10-32; Psalm 90:10) would have included more large-scale changes. We even hear Peter tell about another large-scale change the universe underwent (2 Peter 3:7).

It is fruitless to speculate on how God did this. But the move from a perfect world to a world operating with sin would have required such large-scale changes. But if God created the world through the power of his Word, he can change it through the power of his Word as well.

God promised to restore the world to its original state

God immediately began to relieve the spiritual chaos introduced by Satan. In Genesis 3 God told Satan that one of the woman's offspring would destroy him: "He shall bruise your head, and you shall bruise his heel" (Genesis 3:15). In the context of Scripture, this can only refer to Jesus Christ.

Before they fell into sin, Adam and Eve were at peace with God, which implied that there was hostility between them and God's adversary, Satan. Now, after the fall into sin, the opposite was true; they were hostile to God and at peace with Satan. But God promised to restore hostility to where it had been before, where it belonged: "I will put enmity between you [Satan] and the woman, and between your offspring and her offspring" (Genesis 3:15).

From here to the end of the book of Revelation, Scripture's theme is how God fulfilled and is continuing to fulfill this promise. Christ came to restore us to God through the preaching of "repentance and forgiveness of sins" (Luke 24:47). Paul described Jesus' work in the context of Adam's fall: "For as by the one man's disobedience the many were made sinners, so by the one man's obedience the many will be made righteous" (Romans 5:19). Just as Adam's sin changed the world and introduced sin and death, so Christ's work changed the world and enables people to repent of their sins, find forgiveness, and live in righteousness before God.

What's more, the entire creation can now be restored because of Jesus: "For God was pleased to have all his fullness dwell in him, and through him to reconcile to himself all things, whether things on earth or things in heaven, by making peace through his blood, shed on the cross" (Colossians 1:19,20 NIV84). According to Scripture, the present heaven and earth will come to an end. The end of the earth in its present form will coincide with Jesus' second coming when he will judge all people.

Jesus used the two bookends—the beginning and the end—in his description of the difficulties to come on the church in the last days: "Those will be days of distress unequaled from the beginning, when God created the world, until now—and never to be equaled again" (Mark 13:19 NIV).

The lines are clearly drawn in Scripture. There is the beginning when God created a perfect world. There is the present, when God through his Son is working to recreate his family in Christ. And there will be a day when the universe in its present form will be destroyed and re-created.

We will examine the end of the world more closely in chapter 7. For now, note Peter's description of the end,

> The Lord is not slow to fulfill his promise as some count slowness, but is patient toward you, not wishing that any should perish, but that all should reach repentance. But the day of the Lord will come like a thief, and then the heavens will pass away with a roar, and the heavenly bodies will be burned up and dissolved, and the earth and the works that are done on it will be exposed. . . . But according to his promise we are

waiting for new heavens and a new earth in which righteousness dwells
(2 Peter 3:9,10,13).

This present universe will not go out with a whimper. The end will be a time
of sudden, violent destruction. Peter shows no feelings of sentimentality toward
this venerable old earth that has so nobly evolved over eons of time. Sin entered
a world that had been created perfect. God is calling all people to repent of the
evil they do. Someday "the works that are done in it will be exposed" (verse 10);
that is, they will be exposed as evil. The Lord wants people to live now as they
were created to live, namely, in "holiness and godliness" (verse 11). Someday the
Lord will restore his creation as a place "in which righteousness dwells" (verse 13).

The Universe From Beginning to End According to Evolution

The beginning according to evolution

In the 17th century, natural philosophers (today we call them scientists) began to study the world in earnest. They worked to collect and categorize rocks and minerals and to understand geologic formations. The solar system became an important object of study. During the early years of this period, most natural philosophers accepted the six 24-hour-day creation as described in Scripture. They carried out their research under the conviction that every discovery revealed another aspect of God's power and wisdom.

However, by the late 1600s, many natural philosophers were concluding that rock formations had formed very slowly. Some began to call into question Scripture's teaching of a relatively recent creation.

In the next century, other natural philosophers began discovering common features in the various species of animals. They began concluding that animals had a common ancestor and were not fixed in "kinds" as Genesis tells us. They suggested that animals changed their characteristics slowly over long periods of time.

The changes God made to the creation after the fall into sin came to be viewed as an integral part of creation from its inception. The idea that sudden changes to the earth's crust must have taken place in the flood had to be rejected.

But there is no need to belabor the point. No one disagrees that evolution teaches a radically different "beginning" than a straightforward reading of Genesis 1 and 2 teaches. In fact, if evolution is taken seriously, there is no true beginning in scriptural terms. "The beginning" in evolutionary terms is only the start of a long process that continues up to the present.

How theistic evolutionists approach the major issues

We will look at an example of how one author attempts to combine the overall structure of Scripture and that of evolution. Before we do that, let me offer a general observation about how theistic evolutionists deal with all the the major issues covered in this book. We'll also look at one of the most common clichés found in theistic evolutionary writings.

Theistic evolutionists do, in fact, explore the implications of evolution on the major teachings of Scripture. But the driving force in the literature is to protect evolution. This is a major shortcoming and a fault for which theistic evolutionists should be criticized. Even if a theistic evolutionist does not accept the conclusions of this book, that person has the responsibility to cover the whole topic, that is, to explore whether evolution adversely impacts the major truths of the Christian faith.

The reason for this lack of attention is not hard to find. Theistic evolutionists, *by definition*, have already accepted evolution and chosen the evolutionary framework of the history of the universe as their framework of reality. Once a person has concluded that evolution is true, the goal of any exploration of the framework of Scripture and the broader topics of Christianity can only be to discover how Scripture might be interpreted to support the ideology evolution requires.

Some theistic evolutionists seem content merely to say that God in some way played a role in the process of evolution. Others want Scripture to have more of a say. However, too often they become bogged down in questions about the interpretation of various passages. Of course, the interpretation of passages is very important, and in many cases, how they are interpreted has a direct bearing on the big picture. But many of these discussions have such a narrow focus that they divert attention away from the big issues. Readers end up not seeing the forest for the trees.

On a more subtle level, questions are phrased in such a way as to imply that evolution is beyond doubt true. But it cannot be otherwise; the authors are theistic *evolutionists*. Scripture is almost always on the defense. For example, "If Adam and Eve fell into sin and died as a result, must we conclude that animals started dying at that point?" "If fossil evidence shows that human beings (*Homo sapiens*) have been developing for tens of thousands of years, at what point did Adam and Eve as described in Genesis 1 and 2 come into existence?" "When and how might Adam, Eve, and their contemporaries have acquired the image of God?"

The attempt to classify the various approaches to the debate has the same effect. In his book *Mapping the Origins Debate*, Gerald Rau says that today "there are four major origins that need to be explained: the origin of the universe, of life, of species and of humans." Later in his book, he maps how various groups treat these origins, including traditional Christianity.[20] Rau wants to be seen as approaching the topic objectively. But the very act of lining up the positions as he does implies that they can, in fact, be lined up, compared, and evaluated on the same terms.

Another approach is to start with the question of how great a role God chose to play in evolution. For example, how much did God rely on direct miraculous action to create the world and how much did he rely on the potential he built into matter to organize itself? That particular question was under debate some

---

[20]Gerald Rau, *Mapping the Origins Debate* (Downers Grove: IVP Academic, 2012), p. 28. This book is helpful for understanding the current nature of the debate.

two hundred years ago with increased interest in the natural laws of the universe. Some wondered, "Would it be possible to convince ordinary, deeply religious people that God might build laws into his world that would allow His creation to unfold as He intended, but without His continued miraculous interference?"[21] This question, too, is based on the assumption that evolution is true.

Such questions can become smoke screens that obscure the more basic questions every Christian should be trying to answer in regard to evolution. In terms of this book, Christians should be thinking about what evolution introduces into the room of one's Christian faith.

Perhaps I can be proven wrong, but based on the slice of theistic evolutionary literature I have read, I would advise those who read this literature not to read too much into the "theistic" side of theistic evolution. The theistic side—at least if it is based on Scripture—is treated as a set of ancient religious ideas that are malleable enough to fit into the solid mold of the modern theory of evolution. Christians ought to be thinking about core teachings of Scripture—that God sent his Son to destroy the guilt of sin, to re-establish peace between God and the world, and to restore the universe to its original condition We should be asking: "Are those teachings really *that* malleable?"

Cliché: Listen carefully to Saint Augustine's advice.

Theistic evolutionists like to use a quotation from the early church father Augustine (A.D. 354–430). Augustine warns Christians against mistakenly using the Scriptures to disprove the conclusions of natural philosophers about things in nature, conclusions that should be obvious to anyone who studies it. Theistic evolutionists say that Christians today should take Augustine's words to heart when they dispute something as obvious as evolution. This is an important argument. It deserves our attention. Here's the quotation from Augustine:

Usually, even a non-Christian knows something about the

---

[21] Peter Bowler, *Monkey Trials and Gorilla Sermons: Evolution and Creation from Darwin to Intelligent Design* (Cambridge: Harvard, 2007), loc. 813, Kindle. See Ted Peters and Martinez Hewlett, *Can You Believe in God and Evolution?* (Nashville: Abingdon, 2008), p. 7 for a helpful chart to show the degree to which God is thought to play a role in creation. The Biologos position is typical: "The model for divinely guided evolution that we are proposing here thus requires no 'intrusions from the outside' for its account of God's creative process. We do not rule these out, of course, nor claim they are not possible. Rather, we suggest that 'once life arose, the process of evolution and natural selection permitted the development of biological diversity and complexity.' . . . Moreover, once evolution got under way, no special supernatural intervention was required," quoted in Karl Giberson and Francis Collins, *The Language of Science and Faith* (Downer's Grove: InterVarsity, 2011), p. 115.

earth, the heavens, and the other elements of this world, about the motion and orbit of the stars and even their size and relative positions, about the predictable eclipses of the sun and moon, the cycles of the years and the seasons, about the kinds of animals, shrubs, stones, and so forth, and this knowledge he holds to as being certain from reason and experience.

Now, it is a disgraceful and dangerous thing for an infidel to hear a Christian, presumably giving the meaning of Holy Scripture, talking non-sense on these topics; and we should take all means to prevent such an embarrassing situation, in which people show up vast ignorance in a Christian and laugh it to scorn. [22]

Augustine's concern is that some Christians were appearing foolish by using Scripture to disprove certain indisputable scientific observations. When they do this, "the writers of our Scripture are criticized and rejected as unlearned men" and the spread of the gospel is hindered.

Who can dispute this? We all see the stars moving in the heavens, and we can study their behavior. We observe the characteristics of plants and animals, and we can analyze those characteristics. Christians are foolish to question such observations and carelessly cite Scripture to prove them wrong

Nevertheless, Augustine realized that much of natural philosophy was a mixture of observation and speculation. In his literal commentary on Genesis, Augustine himself was speculating on how statements in Genesis 1 might be interpreted to shed light on what we observe in nature. He also knew that Scripture says nothing about most of the items in nature the philosophers were studying. But based on his own experience, Augustine had this advice for Christians on how to use Scripture to evaluate the findings of the natural philosophers:

When they [natural philosophers] are able, from reliable evidence, to prove some fact of physical science, we shall show that it is not contrary to our Scripture. But when they pro-

---

[22] Saint Augustine, *The Literal Meaning of Genesis,* Vol. 1, Ancient Christian Writers., Vol. 41, Translated and annotated by John Hammond Taylor, S.J. (New York: Paulist Press, 1982), Book One, Chapter 19, Paragraph 39.

duce from any of their books a theory contrary to Scripture, . . .either we shall have some ability to demonstrate that it is absolutely false, or at least we ourselves will consider it to be false.[23]

This statement follows closely on the statement theistic evolutionists like to quote. But no theistic evolutionary author that I have read quotes it.

Augustine continues. When Christians undertake to interpret Genesis as Augustine was doing in his commentary, they must always choose the interpretation that is clearly intended by the author. But if we cannot be sure,

> then at least we should choose an interpretation in keeping with the context of Scripture and in harmony with our faith. But if the meaning cannot be studied and judged by the rest of Scripture, at least we should choose only that which our faith requires. For it is one thing to fail to recognize the primary meaning of the writer, and another to depart from the norms of religious belief.[24]

In the final sentence of Book One of his literal commentary on Genesis, Augustine repeats his appeal to Scripture: If the Bible writer's intention is uncertain, then "one will find it useful to extract an interpretation in harmony with our faith."[25]

Theistic evolutionists use the first quotation from Augustine (quoted at the beginning of this cliché) to warn Christians against citing Scripture to contradict evolutionary theory. But Augustine is simply warning Christians against using Scripture to refute the teachings of science that are based on simple observation and require no speculation.

If the theory of evolution could be shown to be as true as, for example, the relative hardness of a rock or where a star can be located in the heavens at night, theistic evolutionists would be correct in using that quotation. Evolution, however, cannot be observed like a rock or a star. It is a matter of drawing conclusions about what we observe in nature. And that is what Augustine has in mind when he

---

[23]St. Augustine, *The Literal Meaning of Genesis,* Vol. 1, Book One, Chapter 21, Paragraph 41.

[24]St. Augustine, *The Literal Meaning of Genesis,* Vol. 1, Book One, Chapter 21, Paragraph 41.

[25]St. Augustine, *The Literal Meaning of Genesis,* Vol. 1, Book One, Chapter 21, Paragraph 41.

urges caution in deciding whether or not to accept the theories of the natural philosophers of his day.

Augustine is hardly giving a blank check to scientists to draw whatever conclusions they wish and demand that in every case Christians not use Scripture to disprove them. In his commentary on Genesis, Augustine himself is engaging in a fair amount of speculation about the origin of the world. In regard to his own speculative conclusions as well as those of the natural philosophers, he is confident that if the conclusion is true, it will not contradict the rest of Scripture or the accepted teaching of the Church. And if it does, says Augustine, Christians will either show it to be false or simply believe it to be false.

By letting Scripture itself guide our interpretation of Genesis, Augustine writes, we "cling to our Mediator, 'in whom are hidden all the treasures of wisdom and knowledge'" (Colossians 2:3). We might not always agree with Augustine's method of interpreting Scripture or with his own interpretation of Genesis 1 and 2. But Augustine's position on how to read Genesis is actually no different from the modern creationist position; that is, if a scientific conclusion contradicts the faith, it can be proven false, but even if a Christian cannot prove it false, it must still be rejected.[26]

Henri Blocher: an attempt to combine the two histories

In general, theistic evolutionists admit that the framework of Scripture and the framework of evolution cannot coexist peacefully. But they consider it to be relatively unimportant. They simply teach that uniformitarianism—the idea that all things evolved according to natural laws in a relatively *uniform* way over long periods of time—is correct.

But does uniformitarianism merely force us to adjust our understanding of a few chapters and scattered verses of Scripture, which talk about the actual act of creation? Might it not affect our understanding of God's nature? of how we understand ourselves as human beings? of how we define right and wrong? or even of the purpose for which God's Son came to earth? What happens if a person answers yes to those questions, but also wants to accept evolution? Henri Blocher is one such person, and he helps us see what happens when evolution is pitted against Scripture.

---

[26]See Tim Chaffey's article on this topic at https://answersingenesis.org/reviews/books/augustines-commentaries-on-genesis-one-and-modern-theology/. Accessed May, 2019.

Blocher is a French theologian with close ties to American Evangelicalism. He taught systematic theology at Wheaton College from 2003 to 2008 and has close ties to Westminster Theological Seminary.[27]

Blocher is serious about the framework of Scripture, which makes him somewhat of an exception in theistic evolutionary circles. He sees clearly the implications of evolution on the message of Scripture. He insists that we must uphold the basic framework of Scripture, namely, that the world was created perfect, that sin entered the world at a certain point, and that Christ has redeemed the world from sin and its consequences. He says, "The Bible teaches the order creation-fall-redemption and does not reverse it."[28]

Evolution uses the evils of suffering and death to accomplish its goals. Blocher takes this fact seriously. He has no place in his theology for the idea that evil is a natural part of the world or is a tool God used to create it. Blocher refreshingly points out that evil finds no place "within the system."[29] His position is that in some way there had to have been a historical fall—a time when evil came into God's creation from the outside. He writes, "Whatever the tensions, the non-historical interpretation of Genesis 3 is no option for a *consistent* Christian believer."[30] It must be an actual event in history.

In another place Blocher quotes philosopher Paul Ricoeur: "Evil becomes scandalous at the same time as it becomes historical."[31] In other words, evil is serious only if it entered the world at a particular point in the world's history. Otherwise, as Blocher explains: "If evil belongs to being, how can we protest against it? How can we repent of it?"[32] Blocher writes, "The prophetic denunciation of sin and call to repentance cannot be grounded in any other way. The issue of historicity here is not a peripheral matter for hair-splitting theologians: it is vital for the biblical message—it is the heart of the message."[33] He says that

---

[27] Pertinent books are Blocher's 1984 *In the Beginning: The Opening Chapters of Genesis* and his 1997 *Original Sin: Illuminating the Riddle*. I draw mostly from the article "The Theology of the Fall and the Origins of Evil," in *Darwin, Creation and the Fall: Theological Challenges*, ed. R. J. Berry and T. A. Noble (Nottingham: Apollos [InterVarsity], 2009), pp. 149-172. This is a concise presentation of his views, and it is more recent than the other publications.

[28] Henri Blocher, *In the Beginning: The Opening Chapters of Genesis* (Downers Grove: InterVarsity, 1984), p. 17.

[29] Henri Blocher, "The Theology of the Fall," in *Darwin, Creation and the Fall: Theological Challenges*, ed. R. J. Berry and T. A. Noble (Nottingham: Apollos [InterVarsity], 2009), p. 162.

[30] Henri Blocher, "The Theology of the Fall," p. 155 (emphasis author's).

[31] Henri Blocher, *In the Beginning*, p. 161, quoting P. Ricoeur, *The Symbolism of Evil*, trans. Emerson Buchanan (Boston: Beacon, 1974), p. 203.

[32] Henri Blocher, *In the Beginning*, p. 161.

[33] Henri Blocher, "The Theology of the Fall," p. 158.

"in the debate on the 'historicity of the content' of Genesis 3 *nothing less than the gospel is at stake.*"[34]

Blocher is quite hard on theistic evolutionists who reject the idea that the world became corrupt at a specific point in history. They must in some way "find a place for evil," which, he explains, "amounts to explaining away its evilness."[35] According to Blocher, they try

> to view the negative aspects of experience [evil and its results] as part and parcel of normal reality, as natural features of the universe (progress is achieved through struggle, life arises from death, power with its destructive effects is the affirmation of value). Evil is naturalized, made into an ingredient of being: a strategy wholly opposed to the unique message of Genesis.[36]

Yet Blocher also believes that evolution is true. He writes, "The agreement of thousands of researchers is reached neither by chance nor by conspiracy!"[37] This, of course, creates a problem with which Blocher must wrestle. How does he do that?

One solution is to separate the hard science of evolution from philosophical ideas that don't necessarily have to be associated with it. In one place Blocher writes, "The theory of evolution, when it is not expanded to philosophical dimensions, does not raise insuperable objections from the point of view of evangelical theology."[38]

We applaud Blocher's statements about the necessity of accepting Scripture's teaching of creation, the fall, and restoration. But can the theory of evolution actually be stripped of certain "philosophical dimensions" and made into a harmless set of natural laws, which can then be merged with the framework of Scripture? There seems to be an inconsistency between this idea and Blocher's convictions as described above. The details of Darwin's survival of the fittest— scarcity of resources, competition, and death—are not just philosophical ideas that can be shoved into a corner and kept safely out of sight. These are the very nuts and bolts of biological evolution.

Henri Blocher is a recognized scholar on the topic of creation and evolution. He goes as far as anyone can go in trying to keep evil out of God's original creation while still confessing that God used evolution to create the forms of life we

---

[34] Henri Blocher, *In the Beginning*, p. 170 (emphasis added).

[35] Henri Blocher, "The Theology of the Fall," p. 162.

[36] Henri Blocher, "The Theology of the Fall," p. 161.

[37] Henri Blocher, *In the Beginning*, p. 23.

[38] Henri Blocher, *Original Sin* (Downers Grove: InterVarsity, 1997), p. 39.

see around us. In the end, however, Blocher must resort to the same arguments used by other theistic evolutionists who do not share his concern for a historic entrance of evil into a perfect world.

Blocher provides an example of how the the world can be considered very good and still contain the suffering that is necessary for the evolution of plants and animals, which at heart is a violent and evil process. He adjusts the definition of evil. According to Blocher, animal death need not be considered evil, and the process of extinction is not necessarily a bad thing.[39] So God's creation can still be considered perfect in spite of animal death and extinction.

Another way Blocher alleviates the difficulties is by rejecting a straightforward reading of Genesis. Genesis, although historical, cannot be viewed as literal. Blocher explains that God's Word must be defined as both human and divine: "The biblical Word has two 'authors,' God and the inspired writer."[40] Interpreters of Scripture must leave room for the human element. What's more, the writers of Scripture may have spoken in literal terms, but they did not always mean for us to take their accounts as a record of something that actually happened. Applying this approach to Genesis 3, Blocher contends that "the issue is not whether we have a historical account of the Fall, but whether we have the account of a historical Fall."[41] In other words, Genesis need not be considered a literal account of *the* fall into sin but can simply refer to a time in the past when human beings became sinful.

Blocher must speculate on when this happened. With evolutionary explanations of mankind's development in mind and noting fossil evidence and DNA studies, Blocher suggests that "three timings seem possible for Adam, none of them free from difficulty."[42] Adam might have been a farmer living around 10,000 B.C. Or he might have been the source of a small original population about 40,000 B.C. Or he might have lived before 100,000 B.C. Blocher points out difficulties for each of these dates. (We will meet this kind of speculation again in the chapter on who we are according to theistic evolutionists.)

But Blocher acknowledges that the problem has not been solved. At the end of the article we have been using, "The Theology of the Fall," Blocher asks how the goodness of creation can be reconciled with the various forms of suffering—the

---

[39] Henri Blocher, "The Theology of the Fall." See his arguments on pp. 164-168. Blocher says that "Biblical perspectives on carnivory are hardly compatible with an 'evil' assessment of animal death" (pp. 166,167). I assume this includes God's laws of sacrifice and God's establishment of the food chain. But these systems came into being after the fall, as did God's introduction of human death, which is certainly part of the evil that exists in a fallen world.

[40] Henri Blocher, *In the Beginning*, p. 26.

[41] Henri Blocher, "The Theology of the Fall," p. 159.

[42] Henri Blocher, "The Theology of the Fall," p. 171.

evil—that must be present in creation if evolution is true. He can only answer that this is an "inscrutable mystery."[43] Blocher ends his article with the following rebuke of those who read the Genesis account in a straightforward way: "We should not be embarrassed to conclude with uncertainty: it is a mark of a mature faith, properly based on adequate evidence and serenely bearing the tensions of a pilgrim's progress by faith, not sight. Free from a neurotic need for certainty on every matter, we trust the trustworthy Creator and Redeemer."[44] With this bit of flowery rhetoric, God's injunction to live by faith and not by sight becomes permission to exempt evolution from the scrutiny of Scripture.

Cliché: We must read the Bible literally, but not literalistically

Many theistic evolutionists believe that Genesis 1-3 is ancient mythology. Since that is the case, they argue that they are interpreting Scripture "literally" when they deny that the events recorded in Genesis 1-3 are actual historical events. They argue that those who believe that Genesis teaches the history of God's creation of the world in six 24-hour days are reading Scripture in a "literalistic" or "ultraliteral" way.

Young-earth creationists, on the other hand, claim that they are interpreting Scripture literally and that theistic evolutionists are interpreting it incorrectly by reading the early chapters of Genesis as "mythology."

This debate centers on word meanings. So let's illustrate the distinction between 1) literalistic (or ultra literal), 2) literal, and 3) mythological.

We'll use one of the most well-known sports articles ever written. It was written in 1924 after Notre Dame defeated a good Army team. The author, Grantland Rice, began his memorable article like this:

> Outlined against a blue-gray October sky, the Four Horsemen rode again. In dramatic lore their names are Death, Destruction, Pestilence, and Famine. But those are aliases. Their real names are: Stuhldreher, Crowley, Miller and Layden. They formed the crest of the South Bend cyclone before which

---

[43] Richard Mortimer, "Blocher, Original Sin and Evolution," in *Darwin, Creation, and the Fall*, p. 182. He is quoting Henri Blocher, *Evil and the Cross* (Leicester: Apollos, 1994), p. 128.

[44] Henri Blocher, "The Theology of the Fall," p. 172.

another fighting Army team was swept over the precipice at the Polo Grounds this afternoon as 55,000 spectators peered down upon the bewildering panorama spread out upon the green plain below.

Let's interpret this passage in the three ways listed previously. Our first reader is literalistic, or ultra literalist. He interprets the article like this: "On October 18, 1924, four horsemen appeared. They were named Death, Destruction, Pestilence, and Famine, but they had other names by which they were better known. That day a cyclone from South Bend, Indiana, blew in, driving the four horsemen ahead of it. The horsemen pushed an army over a cliff located in a field on which the game of polo was usually played. This odd scene was witnessed by 55,000 onlookers who somehow found a good place to observe the spectacle below them."

This interpreter overlooks the clues for interpretation found in the article itself. He neglects the fact that this is an article about sports. He disregards how previous commentators have interpreted the article. He doesn't allow for the use of symbolical language. Yet because he is being serious about the author's words, he is convinced he is reading the article literally. But he is interpreting it in a wooden, literalistic manner.

A second reader approaches the report from the entirely opposite direction. He knows the report was written in the past. Therefore, he assumes he cannot be absolutely sure how the first readers would have understood it. He must evaluate the date of writing, given as April 1924, by comparing it to other documents written about that time whose dating is more certain. Likewise, he cannot be sure the byline indicates the article was actually written by the famous reporter, or if that writer's name was used to give the article an aura of authority. The symbolism used in the article might have been understood by the first readers, but he cannot be sure. Nor can he be certain if the writer really believed that he was writing about an actual historical event. It is clear that the report deals with a contest, likely a sporting contest, but it is uncertain what point the writer was trying to make. We might speculate that he had a higher purpose for the article. In the context of the post-World War I years, the author might have been praising the victory of the Allied forces over the evil Central powers. Or perhaps the author's exalted language was intended to praise bravery when it triumphs over unjustified aggression. The number at the end of the article could be the final attendance of a sporting event. But it could also play a more subtle role understood by the first readers—perhaps a symbolic reference to the number of those who lost their lives in a certain battle.

In this case the reader has adopted a set of presuppositions about old newspaper articles, and he has interpreted the report in the light of those presuppositions. He has given himself permission to read the report as mythology. He can only express his conclusions in a tentative way. But in his mind, he is reading the account literally.

A third reader approaches the article differently. From the location of the article on the sports page and not on the poetry page, he knows the author is describing an actual sporting event. Nothing in the report leads him to assume otherwise. He realizes that the report is a complex combination of symbols, poetry, and narrative. He easily moves between those different kinds of writing. He realizes that the four horsemen and their ominous names is based on the symbolism of the four horses of the apocalypse in Revelation 6. When the author calls them by their last names as we often do in contemporary culture, the reader quickly shifts gears and understands them to be the players' actual last names. The cyclone is a picture of the Notre Dame team as a whole. The four horsemen riding its "crest" is a shift in symbolism—from a whirlwind to a wave. The reader takes this shift in stride. The precipice invokes a picture of complete destruction, such as what happens when something is pushed over a cliff. The spectators were looking down because they were sitting on bleachers. The green plain was the football field, and the game was played at the famous New York ballpark called the Polo Grounds. He notes that his interpretation is consistent with how others in the past have interpreted the article.

This reader depends on his native ability to understand language. He is basing his interpretation on the normal way people write. He is sure that the first readers of the article shared his ability to handle language in the same way. He knows he has interpreted the article literally, and he has.

Some theistic evolutionists try to scare Christians against believing in a six 24-hour-day creation like this: "Bible readers must realize how complex a literary document the Bible really is. Otherwise you cannot understand the Bible. You will fall into literalism."

They use this as a springboard to instruct their readers how to approach the creation account: "When we call the creation account mythology and read the early chapters of Genesis in the light of scholarly research, especially in light of the many other ancient Near Eastern documents archaeologists have recently discovered, we are honoring the complex nature of language and culture. We are interpreting Scripture literally." What they fail to acknowledge is that their opponents (the true literal interpreters) also understand the complex nature of Scripture. They too recognize symbolism, figures of speech, different types of literature, etc.

But because they believe in evolution, theistic evolutionists must redefine what it means to read the Bible literally. Their belief in evolution forces them to categorize the entire account of creation in Genesis 1 and 2 as figurative language.

If you believe in a six 24-hour-day creation week and are accused of interpreting the Bible literalistically, you have the right politely to say: "No, as I interpret Scripture I am keeping in mind the nature of language and the many literary devices Scripture uses. I am reflecting how Jesus and the New Testament writers interpreted the Genesis account. I am merely rejecting the methods of interpreting Scripture you must use in order to find a place in Scripture for evolution."

Knowledgeable theistic evolutionists understand that position. If they are fair, they will not try to scare you by implying that your interpretation of Genesis is literalistic. They will give you credit for interpreting Genesis as it has been interpreted by Jesus and the writers of Scripture, and for centuries by the Christian church. They will only blame you for rejecting the conclusions of today's scientists and for being unwilling to explore new ways of approaching the Bible.

Elephants in the room

Scripture teaches that when God created the world "in the beginning," it was finished and it was perfect. Scripture teaches that evil entered God's creation from the outside. Scripture teaches that Jesus reconciled all things to God and will re-create the world when he returns.

In discussing evolution, Christians must always remember that evolution teaches a completely different framework for the beginning and end of the universe. The framework of perfection/fall/restoration is replaced with the idea that the world in the beginning was no different than the world is now. Since theistic evolutionists want to keep God in the picture as the world's Creator, they must teach that the evils associated with evolution, natural selection in particular, originated with God.

These are the first two elephants that theistic evolution allows into the room:

- **The basic framework of the world's history as taught in Scripture is wrong.**

- **The evil associated with evolution came from God.**

As you can see, these are pretty big elephants. With these elephants in the room, the message of Scripture starts to become incoherent.

Chapter 3

God's Love in the Midst of Suffering

According to Scripture

Cliché: What's important is *who* created the world, not *how* he created it.

The claim is this: The Bible tells us *who* created the world; modern science tells us *how* he did it. It sounds reasonable on the surface, but it is made without much thought.[45]

Distinguishing the *who* from the *how* is artificial. *Who* a person is refers to more than just his or her given name. People are also defined by their attitudes and actions. In other words, *how* someone does something tells us about *who* that person is.

For example, two of your high school buddies, John and Frank, both wanted to get rich. John worked hard, came up with some good ideas, started his own company, and in time built up a considerable fortune. Frank, on the other hand, came up with a plan to rob a bank, pulled it off, bought a ticket to Brazil, and is living off what he stole. Both men got what they wanted, but *how* John and Frank got their fortunes tells us much about *who* these people are.

How the world was created—whether in six 24-hour days or through evolution—goes a long way toward helping us know about the One *who* created it.

As we saw in the last chapter, if Genesis is read in a straightforward way, evil, suffering, and death entered God's creation from outside. But if evolution is true, then God gave evil, suffering, and death a place and a role in his creation. The purpose of this chapter is to explore God's love in view of the evil, suffering, and death we find in our world.

---

[45] See Daniel Harrell, *Nature's Witness: How Evolution Can Inspire Faith* (Nashville: Abingdon, 2008), p. 46, Kindle. Harrell accepts evolution, but he recognizes the problem. He says, "And that [way of speaking about how and who] works as long as you don't think about it too much. . . . But as soon as you start thinking about what an evolving creation truly reveals . . . you can't help but wonder about your faith and about the God to whom that faith points."

Scripture's teaching about the love of God [46]

God is love

Everything Scripture says about God's love is set in the context of a perfect world into which evil entered as a stranger from the outside. The original creation was an act of God's love. How God deals with a fallen world is an act of love. God's work of creating a new heavens and earth will be an act of love.

From beginning to end, Scripture praises God for his perfect and unfailing love. The psalmist wrote, "For the LORD is good; his steadfast love endures forever, and his faithfulness to all generations" (Psalm 100:5).

The apostle John described God like this:

> And we have seen and testify that the Father has sent his Son to be the Savior of the world. Whoever confesses that Jesus is the Son of God, God abides in him, and he in God. So we have come to know and to believe the love that God has for us. God is love, and whoever abides in love abides in God, and God abides in him. (1 John 4:14-16)

According to John, God is not just *loving*; he *is* love. God loves the people of the world so much that he sent his Son to save the world from sin and give everyone the right to spend eternity with him in heaven (John 3:16).

According to John, all true love starts with God in Christ: "This is love, not that we have loved God but that he loved us and sent his Son to be the propitiation for our sins" (1 John 4:10). If we love others, it is evidence that we live in God and he in us. Paul lists love as one of the qualities believers share as those in whom the Holy Spirit dwells: "But the fruit of the Spirit is *love*, joy, peace,

---

[46] In the theistic evolution discussion, some of God's qualities are more at issue than others. God's power is usually not an issue. Both sides agree that God had the power to create the world in whatever way he chose, even if that meant willingly allowing the world to evolve in a random way. God's wisdom is not an issue. No matter which method God used to create the world, everyone confesses that he devised his plan with infinite wisdom. God's knowledge of all things is usually not at issue. Usually, everyone agrees that God knows everything that happens in the world. Scripture's teaching that God is love, however, is *always* an issue in the discussion. This is because evil, suffering, and death implies that God's love is imperfect.

Darwinian evolution demands pure randomness. This impacts how a person views God's control of creation and God's knowledge of what the end result will be. In order to remain faithful to the random nature of current evolutionary theory, some theistic evolutionists claim that God by his own choice allows a *purely* random series of mutations and outcomes. Even *he* does not know what will happen. My impression is that this position does not satisfy many theistic evolutionists who want God to play a more active, hands-on role in evolution. They want him to be fully aware of how things are progressing, determining which mutations must take place, and making sure they do, etc. There is a tension here. Once God plays a role in evolution, randomness ceases, and so does evolution, at least as defined by Darwin.

patience, kindness, goodness, faithfulness, gentleness, self-control. . . ." (Galatians 5:22,23).

In love, God created everything "good"

If God is perfect love, then everything he does is perfect, including his creation of the world. The description of God's creative work in Genesis 1 and 2 points this out. After each day of creating activity (except the second when God separated the waters he had already created), God assessed his work. On the first day, God created light—"And God saw that the light was good" (Genesis 1:4). On the third day, God separated the seas from the dry land—"And God saw that it was good" (Genesis 1:10). On the third day, God also created vegetation—"And God saw that it was good" (Genesis 1:12). On the fourth day, God created the sun, moon, and stars—"And God saw that it was good" (Genesis 1:18). On the fifth day, God created birds and fish—"And God saw that it was good" (Genesis 1:21). On the sixth day, God created animals and mankind. After he created the animals we are told, "And God saw that it was good" (Genesis 1:25).

In Genesis 2, before God had created the woman, he said, "It is not good that the man should be alone" (Genesis 2:18). But at the end of the sixth day after God had created Eve and the creation of mankind had been completed, "God saw everything that he had made, and behold, it was very good. And there was evening and there was morning, the sixth day" (Genesis 1:31). The sequence of "good, good, good . . . " culminating in "very good" is impossible to miss, nor is its reference to the Creator.

In love, God created everything that needed to be created

Genesis 2:1,2 brought God's creating activity to an end: "Thus the heavens and the earth were *finished*, and all the host of them. And on the seventh day God *finished his work that he had done*, and he rested on the seventh day from all his work that he had done." The word "rest" is used here as it is used in a courtroom: "The defense rests." The defense lawyer has nothing more to say. God rested because he had nothing more to create.

There was no built-in food shortage, as must have been the case if evolution is God's tool of creation; there was enough food for all the living creatures. God told Adam and Eve:

> Behold, I have given you every plant yielding seed that is on the face of
> all the earth, and every tree with seed in its fruit. You shall have them
> for food. And to every beast of the earth and to every bird of the heav-

ens and to everything that creeps on the earth, everything that has the breath of life, I have given every green plant for food. (Genesis 1:29,30)

God declared his day of rest "holy"

To call something holy is to set it apart as worthy of special recognition. God said that the seventh day was to be set apart from the other days because on that day everything was finished. God set aside this day as a time to commemorate his perfect creating work, a work of perfect love. Adam and Eve could rest in his finished work. Later, the seventh-day rest came to include the rest we have in Christ, who has freed us from having to work for salvation: "So then, there remains a Sabbath rest for the people of God, for whoever has entered God's rest has also rested from his works as God did from his" (Hebrews 4:9,10).

In love, God blessed Adam and Eve to be a blessing to the rest of creation

God wanted his creation to enjoy his goodness and love. From the very beginning, Adam and Eve were to play a major role in this:

Then God said, "Let us make man in our image, after our likeness. And let them have dominion over the fish of the sea and over the birds of the heavens and over the livestock and over all the earth and over every creeping thing that creeps on the earth." (Genesis 1:26)

With a clear understanding of right and wrong and with a will that coincided with God's will, they were able to care for the creation wisely and with the same love and concern God had for it. They could have dominion over it—not with the heavy-handed fist of exploitation but with the goal of helping the creation develop in whatever way God intended.

In love, God gave living creatures the command to be fruitful and multiply

God created the fish, the birds, and the land animals according to their "kinds" (Genesis 1:21,24,25). He also created mankind. He told all these creatures to multiply and fill the earth (also see Genesis 8:17). The term "kinds" denotes classes of animals that God made, and the command to multiply and fill the earth implies that these classes of animals were the ones God intended to receive his blessing and obey his will. There was no need for extinction as a path for animals and mankind to develop.

When Genesis 1 and 2 come to a close, there is no indication of any lack that would make the original creation deficient in any way—no lack of resources, no lack of harmony, no lack of wise and loving supervision. It was perfect, a product of God's perfect love.

What Scripture says about God and evil

God and Satan are opposed to each other

In the last chapter, we noted that evolutionists teach that evil was part of the fabric of the world from its beginning.

Scripture, however, tells us that the Creator is not the cause of temptation or of the evil that results from it. And that includes death. James says,

> Let no one say when he is tempted, 'I am being tempted by God,' for God cannot be tempted with evil, and he himself tempts no one. But each person is tempted when he is lured and enticed by his own desire. Then desire when it has conceived gives birth to sin, and sin when it is fully grown brings forth death. (James 1:13-15)

According to Scripture, Satan is the source of sin and evil. He is the source of rebellion against God's will, of temptation, deceit, and opposition to the truth. He holds the power of death in the sense that he has the right to claim for hell those who die in their sins. He creates fear in the hearts of people who do not know Christ. He wants nothing more than to rob Christians of their faith and to lay claim to their souls.

God, on the other hand, abhors this evil. The psalmist wrote, "For you are not a God who delights in wickedness; evil may not dwell with you" (Psalm 5:4). God is an enemy to those who do evil: "The face of the LORD is against those who do evil, to cut off the memory of them from the earth" (Psalm 34:16). God's children have the same attitude: "The fear of the LORD is hatred of evil" (Proverbs 8:13). The fact that evil originated with Satan and that God opposes the works and will of Satan is part of the overall framework of reality as described in Scripture.

Satan's activity in the world

Satan was cast out of heaven because of his evil

Since God created Satan, logically the origin of evil must somehow be traced back to God. For centuries, philosophers have debated the matter on the basis of that logic. But Scripture rejects that logic and will not let us join the debate. Sin and evil did not originate with God. Nor was evil something he created to use in creating the world.

43

According to Scripture, evil began when one of the angels, Satan, rebelled against God. Peter says that Satan was created as a good angel who was not content with the role God had given him: "God did not spare angels when they sinned, but cast them into hell and committed them to chains of gloomy darkness to be kept until the judgment" (2 Peter 2:4). Jude also describes Satan's fall: "And the angels who did not stay within their own position of authority, but left their proper dwelling, he has kept in eternal chains under gloomy darkness until the judgment of the great day" (Jude 1:6).

Satan led Adam and Eve into sin

According to the Bible, Satan and his followers are part of the history of the world from beginning to end. Satan was present in Eden. In Genesis 3 we read that a snake tempted Eve and brought sin into the world. In Revelation the snake is identified as Satan. He is "that ancient serpent, who is the devil and Satan" (Revelation 20:2, compare 2 Corinthians 1:3).

We see him at work throughout the Old Testament. For example, he was prominent at the beginning of the book of Job, where he attempted to prove that Job's faith was not genuine (also see Zechariah 3:1,2). We see him standing against God's people when he incited David "to number Israel" (1 Chronicles 21:1).

Satan tried to end Jesus' ministry

The Son of God became a human being so he could destroy Satan and undo what Satan started in Eden:

> Since therefore the children share in flesh and blood, he himself likewise partook of the same things, that through death he might destroy the one who has the power of death, that is, the devil, and deliver all those who through fear of death were subject to lifelong slavery. (Hebrews 2:14,15)

Satan tried to lead Jesus into sin, which would have stopped his work as Savior: "Then Jesus was led up by the Spirit into the wilderness to be tempted by the devil" (Matthew 4:1). Jesus resisted Satan's temptations, which Adam and Eve had not done, and continued on in his work.

Jesus and his followers overcame Satan at every turn. They cast out demons who had made human beings their temporary home: "God anointed Jesus of Nazareth with the Holy Spirit and with power. He went about doing good and healing all who were oppressed by the devil, for God was with him" (Acts 10:38).

When Jesus sent out his disciples to preach the gospel, he said, "I saw Satan fall like lightning from heaven" (Luke 10:18). When people were loosed from their sins through the good news that God's kingdom in Christ was at hand, Satan could no longer stand before God and accuse these people of sin. (See Revelation 12:7-9 for a parallel to this.)

Jesus made life miserable for Satan and his followers. They knew there was an "appointed time" when God would judge them, and they wanted all the relief they could get before that happened: "'What do you want with us, Son of God?' they shouted. 'Have you come here to torment us before the time?'" (Matthew 8:29).

Satan certainly knew what Jesus said shortly before the end of his life. Jesus said, "Now is the judgment of this world; now will the ruler of this world be cast out. And I, when I am lifted up from the earth, will draw all people to myself" (John 12:31,32). In spite of Satan's knowledge, cunning, and power, he seemed unable to foresee the consequences of his actions. Otherwise he would not have worked to get Jesus killed.

Satan tries to stop the spread of the gospel

Satan is active wherever the gospel is preached. Peter gives a general description of Satan's work throughout the New Testament era:

> Be self-controlled and alert. Your enemy the devil prowls around like a roaring lion looking for someone to devour. Resist him, standing firm in the faith, because you know that your brothers throughout the world are undergoing the same kind of sufferings. (1 Peter 5:8,9 NIV84)

Satan has power to deceive: "But I am afraid that as the serpent deceived Eve by his cunning, your thoughts will be led astray from a sincere and pure devotion to Christ" (2 Corinthians 11:3).

Satan set up roadblocks to Paul's missionary work: "We wanted to come to you—I, Paul, again and again—but Satan hindered us" (1 Thessalonians 2:18).

In the last days, Satan will have his way in the hearts of many people: "The Spirit expressly says that in later times some will depart from the faith by devoting themselves to deceitful spirits and teachings of demons" (1 Timothy 4:1,2).

All of this shows that Satan and God are opposed to each other. Their methods and goals are the opposite. Good and evil, God and Satan, cannot be two forces working side by side in God's creating work.

The relation between God's love and the suffering we see in the world

An example of how theistic evolutionists treat the subject

Everyone acknowledges that this world is filled with evil and suffering. And Scripture does, in fact, teach that there is a relationship between God and this evil and suffering. Before we look at how Scripture describes that relationship, we'll look at an example of how theistic evolutionists describe it.

Theistic evolutionists attempt to prove that evil originated with God because God uses suffering and death to provide food for animals. Here is an example of theistic evolutionary logic: Psalm 104 gives glory to God. The psalmist used the six days of creation as his outline. When he came to the sixth day and the creation of animals, the psalmist wrote, "You make darkness, and it is night, when all the beasts of the forest creep about. The young lions roar for their prey, seeking their food from God" (Psalm 104:20,21). The psalmist was praising God for giving animals their food, but he praises God for providing food by means of the death of other animals who are killed and eaten. So, the argument goes, since the psalmist was talking about what God did on the sixth day, God must have *created* the animals to live on other animals, which means there has always been animal predation and the suffering that accompanies it.[47] Therefore Scripture is supposed to support natural selection.

But the reference to the food chain in Psalm 104 does not prove it was in place when God called his creation "very good." In order to discuss the relation between a loving God and suffering, a person must *first choose* between a creation that took place in six 24-hour days as described in Genesis 1 and 2 or a creation that took place through the process of evolution.

If we choose evolution and believe that creatures have been evolving uniformly over millions of years, then we might conclude from Psalm 104 that in the beginning God created a way to feed the animals that made use of suffering and death. In that case suffering and death must be "part of the system."

On the other hand, if we choose Scripture's account of creation, we believe that God created everything perfect, but that after Satan introduced evil into his creation, God changed the creation in various ways. In that case, we cannot argue that predation was part of God's original design. The psalmist has simply substituted how God originally provided for animals (by giving them plants to eat as Genesis 1:29 indicates) with how he provides for them now. If you were the psalmist, how else would you praise God for his providing for the animals in the present world? The psalmist was aware of the order of creation in Genesis 1, and he was praising God for creating the world as described in that chapter.

---

[47] For example, Richard Averbeck writes, "It is worthy of note that in Ps 104:20-21, which are the verses parallel to day 4 in Gen 1, the animals prowling for prey at night are part of the original created order. This hunting is part of God's gracious provision for his creatures as he is lauded in the psalm. If this is the case it is most likely a misreading of the end of the sixth day in Gen 1 to suggest that all species of animals and people were to eat only plants in the original created order." Richard Averbeck, "Chapter One: A Literary Day, Inter-Textual, and Contextual Reading of Genesis 1,2" in *Reading Genesis 1-2, An Evangelical Conversation,* ed. Daryl Charles (Peabody, MA: Hendrickson Publishers, 2013), loc. 866, Kindle.

He certainly knew verse 29 of that chapter where God gave animals plants to eat. Yet *not* providing a full explanation of God's original method of providing for animals and describing how that was changed after evil entered the world does not mean that he believed that in the beginning God created the food chain.

We might speculate a bit and describe the situation like this: God cursed the ground after Adam and Eve fell into sin (Genesis 3:17), and it became impossible for animals to find plants to live on. God also introduced death. God then established what we call the food chain, with all the suffering and death that structure implies. By creating this new structure, God provided for animals in a way he would not have used if his world had remained perfect. After the flood, God also allowed mankind to eat animals, likely for the same reason: "The fear of you and the dread of you shall be upon every beast of the earth and upon every bird of the heavens, upon everything that creeps on the ground and all the fish of the sea. Into your hand they are delivered. Every moving thing that lives shall be food for you. *And as I gave you the green plants, I give you everything*" (Genesis 9:2,3).

The sequence of events in Genesis 3 teaches us about God's relation to suffering

At the beginning of chapter 3, Satan led Adam and Eve into sin. They immediately changed. They began to feel shame over their nakedness and found something with which to cover themselves. They hid from God. They concocted a silly reason for hiding from him—they were naked. They began passing off the blame for their sin—to each other and to God.

God had warned them that if they sinned against his command, they would die. With this in mind, we realize that God immediately could have caused them to return to the ground.

Instead, God immediately began to show them his love. To be sure, his love came in different ways than it would have if they had not been corrupted by sin. When God found them in the garden, he questioned them about what they had done. From what follows, it is clear that he did not do that to make them squirm with fear (although that's what they did). God wanted to expose their sin so he could start to bless them.

When Adam and Eve started blaming each other, God could have responded, "Quit trying to pass the blame to others. Admit that you sinned." But he didn't. God immediately turned his attention to Satan. God was acknowledging that Satan was the source of evil in the world. God told Satan that one of Eve's offspring, a human being, would crush his head. That fatal blow would eliminate the burden of guilt Adam and Eve had brought on themselves, which had caused such fear in their hearts when they were confronted by God. The knowledge that God would send someone to crush Satan's head transported Adam and Eve back into God's family and enabled them to become Satan's enemies once again and be rid of the evil he had introduced into their lives. When Adam and Eve heard God telling this to Satan, they heard God expressing his love of them in no uncertain terms.

Once the promise was in place, God was at peace with Adam and Eve and they could be at peace with him. This was not a partial peace. There was no probationary period; they did not have to prove something to God—a change of attitude, perhaps—before God's peace went into effect. Peace between them and God was immediate, based on something God would do for them and for all their descendants. Now, through faith in his promise, they no longer had to hide from him in fear.

The sequence of events in the first 15 verses of Genesis 3 is crucial to understanding God's relation to suffering. Adam and Eve had become sinful. Their new sinful nature would continue to exert itself. God first restored peace between them and him. It was only *after* God restored peace between himself and mankind that he sent suffering into their lives. He did that in love.

This is just common experience. How we deal with someone we love can change even though our love remains as strong as it was before. For example, the way parents deal with a child changes if the child rebels. When the child was obedient and loving toward her parents, there was harmony between them. The parent could show love by giving their child expressions of love—gifts that made her happy. But if the child changes and becomes disobedient, her parents must rebuke and discipline their child whom they love, and discipline always involves a degree of suffering.

The theme of the last half of Genesis 3 is not punishment. Rather, it is God showing love to mankind in a different way. God's attitude toward Adam and Eve was not, "You sinned and need to be punished, so I'm going to bring suffering into your lives," but then as an afterthought: "But I feel sorry for you, so I will send you a Savior." It was just the opposite. Before there was any talk of suffering, God promised to reverse what Satan had done: "I am going to send you a Savior. He will inflict a fatal wound on Satan. He will reestablish peace between you and me. Live in that peace. When you fall into sin again—and you will fall—find your confidence in my promise of a Savior."

However, Adam's and Eve's new sinful nature would not simply disappear after they heard and believed God's promise. The temptations that had come from outside the creation through Satan would now come from within them and from the influence of the world around them. So God introduced suffering into their lives for the same reason a loving parent makes life difficult for a rebellious child—to keep that child from straying farther and becoming hardened in his or her rebellion.

The suffering described in Genesis 3 was not part of the original creation, nor should it be called a natural result of sin. It was something God himself introduced into the world after the fall into sin. We must never get the idea that once evil entered the world, Satan controls the evil things that happen but God is still in control of the good things. Nor must we think that if God uses suffering, he must somehow be in league with Satan and his evil. God and evil are still opposites. The suffering that is described in the rest of Genesis 3 came from a good and loving God and for a good and loving purpose, as extremely difficult as that often is for us to understand and accept.

God said to Eve, "I will surely multiply your pain in childbearing" (Genesis 3:16). She would also find her relationship with her husband strained.

God told Adam:

> Because you have listened to the voice of your wife and have eaten of the tree of which I commanded you, "You shall not eat of it," cursed is the ground because of you; in pain you shall eat of it all the days of your life; thorns and thistles it shall bring forth for you; and you shall eat the plants of the field. By the sweat of your face you shall eat bread. (Genesis 3:17-19)

By cursing the ground, God brought pain and hard toil into Adam's life and into the lives of all who struggle to make a living.

God then carried out the sentence he had promised for disobedience. Adam and Eve would "return to the ground, for out of it you were taken; for you are dust, and to dust you shall return" (Genesis 3:19).

Those who believe the promise see this as the fatherly chastening of our loving Creator. This becomes clear at the end of Genesis 3 where we read that God made clothing for Adam and Eve. Earlier they had tried to cover their shame and nakedness by themselves when they attempted to hide from God (Genesis 3:7). Now they were experiencing God himself hiding their nakedness and shame. It's as if God were saying to them, "Even though you sin daily, I will be with you in the days ahead. I myself will cover your sins and work in all things—yes, even in suffering—to keep you close to me."

God "sent [Adam] out from the Garden of Eden to work the ground from which he was taken" (Genesis 3:23). This sounds like another punishment. But it was a great blessing: ". . . lest he reach out his hand and take also of the tree of life and eat, and live forever" (Genesis 3:22). God did not want mankind to live forever in their sin-filled state. Death is a horrible evil, the separation of God's creatures from all the blessings God intends for us. Satan, who is dead to God, led Adam and Eve on the same path. Mankind would endure physical death, the separation of their bodies and spirits. But that would not end in eternal death. God's promise restored life. For those, like Adam and Eve, who believe in God's promise, it is the doorway to a restored and perfect life with him.

Paul explains the reason why God introduced these difficulties:

> I consider that our present sufferings are not worth comparing with the glory that will be revealed in us.
>
> The creation waits in eager expectation for the sons of God to be revealed. For the creation was subjected to frustration, not by its own choice, but by the will of the one who subjected it, in hope that the creation itself will be liberated from its bondage to decay and brought into the glorious freedom of the children of God. We know that the whole creation has been groaning as in the pains of childbirth right up to the present time.
>
> Not only so, but we ourselves, who have the firstfruits of the Spirit, groan inwardly as we wait eagerly for our adoption as sons, the redemption of our bodies. (Romans 8:18-23 NIV84)

God introduced suffering to make us yearn for the "redemption of our bodies." We yearn for the day when God will take us to himself, free us from the evil of this present world, and give us the perfection we once had in Eden. The rest of creation did not deserve its "bondage to decay" to which God subjected it. Yet it, too, looks forward to sharing in the glorious freedom that God's people will someday enjoy.

Although there is suffering in the world, God's love continues unabated

It bears repeating that Scripture never says God used suffering to create us. But Scripture gives us a clear and detailed description of how God uses suffering for the sake of his fallen people.

The world changed, but God's love did not. The same love that prompted God to create mankind in his image and give us a perfect world is now working unabated to restore what we lost.

Even in this world where suffering abounds, God's people praise God for everything he does. Abraham's servant thanked the Lord for giving Abraham's son a wife: "Blessed be the LORD, the God of my master Abraham, who has not forsaken his steadfast love and his faithfulness toward my master" (Genesis 24:27). Jacob confessed that he was "not worthy of the least of all the deeds of steadfast love and all the faithfulness" God had shown him (Genesis 32:10).

The psalmist confessed: "It is good to give thanks to the LORD, to sing praises to your name, O Most High; to declare your steadfast love in the morning, and your faithfulness by night" (Psalm 92:1,2). The psalmist wrote Psalm 136 to help people express their thanks to God

> who by understanding made the heavens,
> *for his steadfast love endures forever;*
> who spread out the earth above the waters,
> *for his steadfast love endures forever;*
> who made the great lights,
> *for his steadfast love endures forever;*
> the sun to rule over the day,
> *for his steadfast love endures forever;*
> the moon and stars to rule over the night,
> *for his steadfast love endures forever.* (Psalm 136:5-9)

The psalmist wrote, "I will give thanks to you, O LORD, among the peoples; I will sing praises to you among the nations. For your steadfast love is great above the heavens; your faithfulness reaches to the clouds. Be exalted, O God, above the heavens! Let your glory be over all the earth!" (Psalm 108:3-5).

The prophet Jonah was sent to preach to the people of the Assyrian city of Nineveh. Since the Assyrians were enemies of God's people, Jonah didn't want them to repent and be spared of God's judgment. In fact, he was afraid that God in love would do just that for the Assyrians. So he fled from Nineveh and explained his reasoning: "O LORD, is not this what I said when I was yet in my country? That is why I made haste to flee to Tarshish; for I knew that you are a gracious God and merciful, slow to anger and abounding in steadfast love, and relenting from disaster" (Jonah 4:2).

God loves all people, but only those whom he has called to faith can be confident of his love. "For you, O Lord, are good and forgiving, abounding in steadfast love to all who call upon you" (Psalm 86:5). Psalm 85 describes the blessings God would give his Old Testament people if they remained faithful to him:

> Surely his salvation is near to those who fear him, that glory may dwell in our land. Steadfast love and faithfulness meet; righteousness and peace kiss each other. Faithfulness springs up from the ground, and righteousness looks down from the sky. Yes, the LORD will give what is good, and our land will yield its increase. Righteousness will go before him and make his footsteps a way. (Psalm 85:9-13)

God's promise of love for his people will never fail: "'For the mountains may depart and the hills be removed, but my steadfast love shall not depart from you, and my covenant of peace shall not be removed,' says the LORD, who has compassion on you" (Isaiah 54:10). Paul wrote to those who are in Christ: "He who did not spare his own Son but gave him up for us all, how will he not also with him graciously give us all things?" (Romans 5:8).

In love, God provides for the world, even in its sinful state

God continues to give his creatures everything they need. This teaching is particularly hard for theistic evolutionists to reconcile with the process of evolution, which relies on scarcity of resources. The psalmist wrote, "The eyes of all look to you, and you give them their food in due season. You open your hand; you satisfy the desire of every living thing. The LORD is righteous in all his ways and kind in all his works" (Psalm 145:15-17). God sees the look of hunger in the eyes of *all*. He provides food *for all,* and he does it *at the proper time.* He shows love *to all* he has made. He knows and satisfies the desires of *every* living thing.

Jesus said the same in the Sermon on the Mount: "He causes his sun to rise on the evil and the good, and sends rain on the righteous and the unrighteous" (Matthew 5:45 NIV). The birds need not struggle for food because their "heavenly Father feeds them" (Matthew 6:26). God clothes the grass of the field, "which is here today and tomorrow is thrown into the fire" (Matthew 6:30 NIV84). Scripture is not unaware that plants and living creatures sometimes experience lack. Neither is God. David wrote: "'Because of the oppression of the weak and the groaning of the needy, I will now arise,' says the LORD. 'I will protect them from those who malign them'" (Psalm 12:5). Yet God's promises will always be fulfilled, whether now or in heaven.

In love, the Lord shapes the course of people's lives. Paul taught the people of Athens about God, whom even their own writers knew existed:

> And he made from one man every nation of mankind to live on all the face of the earth, having determined allotted periods and the boundaries of their dwelling place, that they should seek God, and perhaps feel their way toward him and find him. Yet he is actually not far from each one of us, for "In him we live and move and have our being." (Acts 17:26-28)

In another sermon Paul spoke of God's love like this: "He has shown kindness by giving you rain from heaven and crops in their seasons; he provides you with plenty of food and fills your hearts with joy" (Acts 14:17 NIV84).

God's people know that God shows his love even when he sends suffering

God's people know that suffering is never a sign that God does not love them: "My son, do not regard lightly the discipline of the Lord, nor be weary when reproved by him. For the Lord disciplines the one he loves, and chastises every son whom he receives" (Hebrews 12:5-7).

The psalmist confessed, "It is good for me that I was afflicted, that I might learn your statutes" (Psalm 119:71). Paul wrote, "We rejoice in our sufferings, knowing that suffering produces endurance, and endurance produces character, and character produces hope" (Romans 5:3,4). In fact, James opened his letter with this note of encouragement: "Consider it pure joy, my brothers, whenever you face trials of many kinds" (James 1:2 NIV84).

To the church in Ephesus, which was going through difficult times, Jesus said, "Those whom I love, I reprove and discipline, so be zealous and repent" (Revelation 3:19). God chastened his Old Testament people for the same purpose. Nevertheless, the believers among them could look forward to blessings restored: "'For a brief moment I deserted you, but with great compassion I will gather you. In overflowing anger for a moment I hid my face from you, but with everlasting love I will have compassion on you,' says the LORD, your Redeemer" (Isaiah 54:7,8).

Believers might suffer in order for God to display his power in their lives

One time when Jesus and his disciples saw a blind man, the disciples asked, "Rabbi, who sinned, this man or his parents, that he was born blind?" Jesus said that neither he nor his parents sinned, but this happened to him "that the works of God might be displayed in him" (John 9:1-3). Then Jesus healed the man. The world still benefits from the suffering this man endured in the years before he met Jesus, even though the man had no idea why God was making him suffer.

The reason for suffering is sometimes hidden

On another occasion some people told Jesus about a tragedy that had happened to some Jews living in Galilee. Why did such a thing happen? Jesus didn't give a reason. He answered:

> Do you think that these Galileans were worse sinners than all the other Galileans, because they suffered in this way? No, I tell you; but unless you repent, you will all likewise perish. Or those eighteen on whom the tower in Siloam fell and killed them: do you think that they were worse offenders than all the others who lived in Jerusalem? No, I tell you; but unless you repent, you will all likewise perish. (Luke 13:1-5)

Jesus didn't explain God's reasons for making these people suffer. He merely explained the lesson we should all take away from such events. This is a good point for us who wonder why God sends disasters into our world and are tempted to question his love and justice for doing so.

Scripture is clear that God is both loving and the one who sends hardships

There is no dodging the difficulties by saying that God only "allows" Satan to bring suffering into the world. God—who is love—is himself the cause of everything that happens (without being the source of the evil behind them).

God promised to raise up a ruler named Cyrus, who would serve as his tool to release the Israelites from captivity in Babylon. God assured Cyrus that he, Cyrus, would conquer the world, which, of course, meant untold suffering in the wake of his advance. But Cyrus was serving God, who had taken him by the hand and sent him forth on his conquest.

God said this about himself: "I form light and create darkness, I make well-being and create calamity, I am the LORD, who does all these things" (Isaiah 45:7). These are strong words, and many are troubled by them. But it is better to know that God is in control of everything that happens than to think that Satan has a piece of that control.

When Job saw his flocks destroyed and innocent servants and children perish, he never said, "This is Satan at work. God would never do such things to me." Rather, he confessed that God was in complete control of his life, in the good as well as in the bad. He said, "Naked I came from my mother's womb, and naked I will depart. The LORD gave and *the* LORD has taken away; may the name of the LORD be praised" (Job 1:21).[48]

Believers can expect to suffer persecution

Genesis 3 teaches us another lesson about the suffering that comes into the lives of God's people. God told Satan, "I will put enmity between you and the woman, and between your offspring and her offspring" (Genesis 3:15). Before they sinned, Adam and Eve had been at peace with God. But after they sinned, they experienced only hostility toward him. Now, through God's promised Savior, *hostility* would be restored to where it belonged, namely, between Satan and

---

[48] Job knew that God had brought suffering into his life. God said the same when he described Job's faithfulness: "He still holds fast his integrity, *although you incited me against him to destroy him* without reason" (Job 2:3). Satan also knew he was not the real cause of the suffering that came into Job's life. At best he was a tool that God was using: "Then Satan answered the LORD and said, 'Skin for skin! All that a man has he will give for his life. But stretch out *your hand* and touch his bone and his flesh, and he will curse you to your face.' And the LORD said to Satan, 'Behold, he is in your hand; only spare his life'" (Job 2:4-6).

those who believe the promise. And *peace* would be restored to where it belonged, namely, between God and those who believe.

From that point on, the world would be divided into two groups—those who follow Satan and rebel against God and those who return to God on the basis of his promise. Jesus reflected this division when he said to some who rejected him, "You are of your father the devil, and your will is to do your father's desires" (John 8:44).

This division brings untold suffering into the world. Genesis 4, the account of Cain murdering Abel, is not just the story of the first murder. Abel was a believer; Cain was not. The story is the record of an unbeliever persecuting a child of God. The writer of Hebrews explains: "By faith Abel offered to God a more acceptable sacrifice than Cain, through which he was commended as righteous, God commending him by accepting his gifts" (11:4). Cain's unbelieving jealously sprang up and brought the ultimate suffering into Abel's life.

God is just, and punishment brings suffering

God loves all people, and he wants all people to be saved. Mercy and forgiveness are at the heart of God's glory. But he is also just. And punishing sin is also part of his glory. Moses asked God to show him his glory. The Lord described his glory like this:

> The LORD, the LORD, the compassionate and gracious God, slow to anger, abounding in love and faithfulness, maintaining love to thousands, and forgiving wickedness, rebellion and sin. *Yet he does not leave the guilty unpunished;* he punishes the children and their children for the sin of the fathers to the third and fourth generation. (Exodus 34:6,7 NIV84)

Moses warned the Israelites:

> Know therefore that the LORD your God is God, the faithful God who keeps covenant and steadfast love with those who love him and keep his commandments, to a thousand generations, and *repays to their face those who hate him*, by destroying them. He will not be slack with one who hates him. He will repay him to his face. (Deuteronomy 7:9,10)

Warnings of God's judgment are found throughout Scripture. Peter called Noah "a herald of righteousness" (2 Peter 2:5), who called the people of his day to repent of their sins. They continued to sin, so God judged them with a flood that "swept them all away" (Matthew 24:39). The cities of Sodom and Gomorrah were condemned to destruction. God made them "an example of what is going to happen to the ungodly" (2 Peter 2:6).

God's people, Israel, rebelled against him from the start. God sent suffering into their lives, but with the intent of leading them to repent. The people of Israel complained that God was mistreating them. God told Ezekiel how to respond: "As I live, declares the Lord GOD, I have no pleasure in the death of the wicked, but that the wicked turn from his way and live; turn back, turn back from your evil ways, for why will you die, O house of Israel?" (Ezekiel 33:11).

Peter applied this principle to the entire world: "The heavens and earth that now exist are stored up for fire, being kept until the day of judgment and destruction of the ungodly. . . . The Lord is not slow to fulfill his promise as some count slowness, but is patient toward you, not wishing that any should perish, but that all should reach repentance" (2 Peter 3:7,9).

In the parable of the sheep and goats, Jesus foretold what he himself will say on the Last Day to those who reject him: "Then he will say to those on his left, 'Depart from me, you cursed, into the eternal fire prepared for the devil and his angels'" (Matthew 25:41). These are hard words, but Jesus is warning us.

Of course, the greatest act of God's judgment is also the greatest act of his love. God judged his Son in our place. Isaiah said, "He has borne our griefs and carried our sorrows. . . . He was wounded for our transgressions; he was crushed for our iniquities; upon him was the chastisement that brought us peace, and with his stripes we are healed" (Isaiah 53:4,5). Since our sins have already been punished in Christ, any and all suffering a Christian endures was already endured by Christ. Suffering is designed by God to bless us: "And we know that for those who love God all things work together for good, for those who are called according to his purpose" (Romans 8:28).

Suffering is not God's preferred method to bless us

After Adam and Eve rebelled against God and let sin into the world, God began using suffering to bless us. But Scripture indicates—to use a human way of looking at it—he does so reluctantly.

Jeremiah wrote Lamentations when God was bringing horrible suffering into the lives of the Jewish nation at the hands of the Babylonians. Jeremiah analyzed God's judgment on his people like this:

> For the Lord will not cast off forever, but, though he cause grief, he will have compassion according to the abundance of his steadfast love; for he does not afflict *from his heart* or grieve the children of men. To crush underfoot all the prisoners of the earth, to deny a man justice in the presence of the Most High, to subvert a man in his lawsuit, the Lord does not approve.

> Who has spoken and it came to pass, unless the Lord has commanded it? Is it not from the mouth of the Most High that good and bad come? Why should a living man complain, a man, about the punishment of his sins? Let us test and examine our ways, and return to the LORD! (Lamentations 3:31-40)

God does not bring affliction into the lives of his people "from his heart" ("willingly" NIV). Nor does he intend for his judgment to last forever. God sometimes causes suffering because sinners need to examine themselves, repent of their sins, and turn to him for mercy. He uses suffering to correct and counter what sin and Satan are trying to do in this world and in our lives.

The account of Job provides another example. God uses suffering to satisfy his claim about Job's steadfast love. Satan challenged Job's love for God. God brought suffering into Job's life to prove that Job *did* love him and would not stop loving him even if God took everything from him. Job rose to the occasion and said, "The LORD gave, and the LORD has taken away; blessed be the name of the LORD" (Job 1:21). A few verses later, we sense the Lord's reluctance (humanly speaking) over what he was doing to Job: "And the LORD said to Satan, 'Have you considered my servant Job, that there is none like him on the earth, a blameless and upright man, who fears God and turns away from evil? He still holds fast his integrity, *although you incited me against him to destroy him without reason*'" (Job 2:3).

Throughout their history, God used suffering to lead his people, Israel, to repent and turn back to him.

The goodness of God leads us to repentance

This short section may appear to be an afterthought. But it isn't. Talk about God working through suffering should never lead us to forget all the good things God gives us. Paul encouraged the Jewish people of his day to reflect on their history: "Or do you show contempt for the riches of his kindness, tolerance and patience, not realizing that God's kindness leads you toward repentance?" (Romans 2:4 NIV84). God had never forgotten his people, nor did he judge them with the speed and severity they—and we—deserve. God's patience should have led them to get down on their knees, repent of their sins, and live in a spirit of thanks to the Lord.

Paul is saying that God works on our hearts through acts of kindness, not just through the suffering he sends into our lives. All Christians confess that the suffering God sends into our lives are his tools to bless us. But we also confess that the undeserved blessings he sends into our lives are often more effective in making us get down on our knees, repent of our sins, and live in a spirit of thankfulness to God.

A strong focus on Scripture's teaching of the relationship between God and suffering is necessary for the next section on evolution and suffering. That is why it has received so much attention here.

Conclusion

Theologians construct "theodicies." A theodicy is the technical term for a system of thought that attempts to reconcile God with the suffering we see in the world. The only true theodicy, however, is found in Scripture. It depends on the framework of the history of the world from beginning to end as described in Scripture. God's creation was perfect; there was no suffering or death in it. Sin and evil entered God's creation from the outside. Since that time, the world has experienced suffering. But God sent his Son to destroy the guilt of sin and its power over us. On account of this, everything God does in the present world is prompted by his unconquerable love. The curse God placed on creation serves to point out the transitory nature of this present earth and make us yearn for the day when God will restore it. Scripture describes many reasons why God sends suffering into our lives. We must confess, however, that God's ways are most often hidden from us.

This is Scripture's "theodicy," and only on this foundation can we confess with Moses: "His work is perfect, for all his ways are justice. A God of faithfulness and without iniquity, just and upright is he" (Deuteronomy 32:4). All God's people can confess, "The LORD is upright; he is my rock, and there is no unrighteousness in him" (Psalm 92:15).

God's Love in the Midst of Suffering

According to Theistic Evolutionists

Theistic evolutionists certainly believe that God is loving, but they have abandoned the basic framework of Scripture and teach that evil was part of God's system from the beginning. This reverses one's way of understanding the relationship between God and suffering. It is a particularly difficult task to answer why a loving God would use a method of creating the world that relies on evil and suffering.

We'll first examine the problem. Then we will look at some ways theistic evolutionists try to justify God's use of evolution as his tool of creation.

Natural selection

At the heart of the evolution of plants, animals, and mankind is the process of natural selection. Natural selection is

> the process by which forms of life having traits that better enable them to adapt to specific environmental pressures, . . . changes in climate, or competition for food or mates, will tend to survive and reproduce in greater numbers than others of their kind, thus ensuring the perpetuation of those favorable traits in succeeding generations.[49]

The steps in the process of natural selection can be described like this:

- Gene mutations occur randomly in the DNA of living creatures.

- A favorable gene mutation may produce a favorable characteristic in a living being.

- The favorable characteristic allows that living being to compete more successfully for scarce resources and have a greater chance of survival.

- The descendants of this fortunate living being inherit this favorable characteristic. Gradually, those who lack it die off because of their inability to compete, and all members of that species eventually come to possess it.

- As more random mutations and the favorable characteristics they produce accumulate in a species, an entirely new species may emerge.

---

[49]http://dictionary.reference.com/browse/natural+selection

The horrors of natural selection

The process of natural selection is easily taught in the academic environment of a classroom. But in real life, it is a horribly pain-filled and cruel process, as all evolutionists agree. One author explains:

> But in spite of the differences [of the various approaches to evolution], they [those who accept evolution] are all in agreement concerning their assumptions that death, disease, birth defects, struggle, suffering, inordinate pain, carnivorous violence, bloodshed, and destructive ecological disasters of every kind, were all prevalent on earth from its earliest beginnings.[50]

If theistic evolution is true and for natural selection to work, God had to have created each of the following:

- Birth defects

    Natural selection relies on a massive number of birth defects. The concept of "favorable gene mutations" seems rather harmless on the surface. But for every favorable mutation there are countless more unfavorable mutations, most of which result in death. Others result in what we today call birth defects—lack of limbs, lack of ability to perform certain functions, skin discoloration, etc. Such things cause physical suffering and may lead those affected to be ostracized from their society.

- Scarcity and struggle

    Natural selection depends on a lack of food and other resources. If there is enough food to go around, every creature could live and produce offspring. Only in the context of the struggle for survival do favorable characteristics provide an advantage and assure that those with the advantage will survive and produce offspring.

- Inordinate pain and suffering

    The mechanism of natural selection causes inordinate pain and suffering. We are sorry when we see a human being or an animal suffer from a painful disease. But we can't even imagine the pain and suf-

---

[50]Greg Haslam, "The Fall and Death," in *Should Christians Embrace Evolution?*, ed. Norman C. Nevin, p. 58.

fering endured by trillions of living creatures over billions of years if evolution is true.

- Carnivorous violence and bloodshed

  The way to a species' development is pure competition, a road paved with violence and bloodshed. The mechanism of natural selection pits animal against animal and human being against human being.

- Pure self-centeredness

  The struggle to survive includes concern for oneself alone and a callous attitude toward the suffering and death of others. It condones taking limited resources for oneself and consigning others to want, hunger, and starvation. The methods for gaining limited resources include deceit, hoarding, theft, physical harm to others, and segregation from the less fortunate.

- Death

  Evolution by natural selection relies on the survival of the fittest and the death of the less fit. It relies on a continual parade of species that rise only to become extinct. An estimated 98% of the world's species came into being and disappeared over the millennia.[51]

- Creation was never finished

  Evolution is an ongoing process. There is no evidence for a time when evolution reached its goal and when the creation was finally finished.

We must emphasize this point: According to theistic evolution, *God himself* created all these elements to use in creating plant life, animals, and mankind. When God told Adam and Eve to "be fruitful and multiply," evolution has God adding the warning: "But this blessing will come your way only through hunger, competition, and the need to kill off the less fortunate."

How theistic evolutionists try to deal with these problems

It is easy for *secular* evolutionists to avoid the problem of reconciling God's love with the horrors of biological evolution. For them, God is not in the picture. But for Christians who want to accept evolution, God is always in the picture.

---

[51] Henri Blocher, *The Theology of the Fall*, p.154.

There is no avoiding the conclusion that God created and used all these elements—these evil elements—as his tools of creation. God, who is completely loving, chose a brutal, pain-filled process to create animals and mankind.

Theistic evolutionists have suggested a number of solutions. (The very fact that there are multiple solutions indicates that there is not an obvious choice.) Henri Blocher explains, "To deal with evil thus approached, many thinkers offer some sort of a theodicy, developed along three main lines, with various combinations."[52] They are:

> 1. *The constraints of the case.* This was the "only way" God could have chosen to create living creatures. Only if creatures had the ability to make choices along the way could they remain free. The clearest application is to mankind: "God had to take the risk of human beings choosing badly in order to make possible a free response of loving obedience."

> 2. *On balance.* This solution emphasizes the good the evolutionary process has achieved. The good outweighs all the evils associated with creation by evolution.

> 3. *God so human.* The picture of God as almighty is discarded; God becomes a co-sufferer with his creatures. The result is that when people watch God suffer along with his creation, they are inspired to sympathize with and respond to the sufferings of others. In this view, God "can also be conceived as a finite partner in the evolving world process."

The "only way" and "on balance" solutions

Blocher's first two solutions are often found side by side. The most often used argument is that by using the process of evolution, God created people who freely serve him with no hint of being coerced. That freedom is worth more than all the evils associated with the process. Quotations from various authors will help us understand the "only way" and "on balance" arguments.

Christopher Southgate

Christopher Southgate is a biochemist who lectures on theology and religion at the University of Exeter, England. His book *The Groaning of Creation: God, Evolution, and the Problem of Evil* is often quoted in theistic evolutionary literature.

---

[52]Content and quotations in this and the next three paragraphs are from Henri Blocher, *The Theology of the Fall*, pp. 154,155.

Like all theistic evolutionists, Southgate considers it impossible to analyze what he sees around him in terms of the events of Genesis 1-3. Viewing the evils of evolution as the only way God could have created a good world "must be the starting point for any evolutionary theodicy that does not allow itself to be lured down the blind alleys—such as a spurious appeal to fallenness."[53] The "postulate of a 'cosmic fall' to account for suffering" will not do for two reasons:

1. There is no scientific evidence that the biological world was ever free of predation and violence. Evidence of predation and of the extinction of species goes as far as the fossil record can take it.

2. The suffering of creatures is *instrumental*. It serves God's purposes, if those purposes are to realize more and more sophisticated and better adapted ways of being in the world. [54]

By combining Paul's statement in Romans 8:22 that "the whole creation has been groaning ... until now" with the statement in Genesis 1:31 that the finished creation was "very good," Southgate's goal in his book *The Groaning of Creation* is "to show that God's creation can be seen as *both* good *and groaning*."[55]

Southgate explores the various ways others have justified God for using evolution. Central to the various approaches is the contention that the method of evolution, with all its suffering, can only be judged after viewing the outcome (Blocher's "on balance" solution). Southgate says that evolutionists must be convinced that "there is a necessary correlation between the values to which the evolutionary process gives rise and the disvalues of suffering and extinction."[56] God's way is always the best way: "A good and loving God would have created the best of all possible universes in terms of the balance between its potential for realizing creaturely values and the concomitant pain."[57]

The valuable results of the process of evolution can *only* come from the suffering that is built into it (Blocher's "constraints of the case," solution). Southgate asks, "Why did God not create a world free from all this suffering and struggle? ... We cannot know the answer to this question." [58] But one thing is certain:

---

[53]Christopher Southgate, *The Groaning of Creation: God, Evolution, and the Problem of Evil* (Louisville: John Knox Press, 2008), p. 47.

[54]Christopher Southgate, *The Groaning of Creation*, p. 5 (emphasis author's). Southgate defines God's purpose as being "to realize more and more sophisticated and better adapted ways of being in the world."

[55]Christopher Southgate, *The Groaning of Creation*, p. 2 (emphasis author's).

[56]Christopher Southgate, *The Groaning of Creation*, p. 47.

[57]Christopher Southgate, *The Groaning of Creation*, p. 48.

[58]Christopher Southgate, *The Groaning of Creation*, p. 47.

We must begin with the assumption, "that the formation of the sorts of life forms represented in the biosphere *required* an evolutionary process."[59]

He explains:

> I hold that the sort of universe we have, in which complexity emerges in a process governed by thermodynamic necessity and Darwinian natural selection, and therefore by death, pain, predation, and self-assertion, is the only sort of universe that could give rise to the range, beauty, complexity, and diversity of creatures the Earth has produced.[60]

Central to that goodness is human freedom: "The only way to arrive at certain good features of creation, including freely choosing self-conscious creatures, [is] via a route involving creaturely suffering."[61] If God simply spoke his Word and created perfect beings, living creatures would be nothing more than robots acting as they were programmed to act.

Southgate takes that one step further. He observes that human beings have evolved with a penchant for doing evil things, and he asks, "How then do evil powers have such a hold on the human will? Because of the consistency with which God upholds and treasures the evolved freedom of that will. The same processes that gave rise to that freedom are the ones that endowed humans with their capacities for its misuse."[62] In other words, God will not hinder our evil will because if he did, he would also be hindering our ability to choose freely.

Southgate wants to enrich the discussion by retaining Scripture's emphasis on Jesus' work. "It is possible to postulate that the creation has unfolded as God intended it to unfold, and yet is still in need of final healing and consummation."[63] That is, evolution can take creation only so far. The task of healing creation—ridding it of the tools God had to use to create it—is Jesus' work. And this is also the work of God's people as they work along with God to overcome the reasons why the creation is groaning.

Christopher Southgate expresses well the theistic evolutionist's conundrum. When he explained the goal of his book, he admitted, "I seek to show that the evolving creation is an ambiguous place with an ambiguous history, and that God may be both praised and questioned when God's creation is contemplated honestly."[64]

---

[59]Christopher Southgate, *The Groaning of Creation,* p. 47 (emphasis author's).

[60]Christopher Southgate, *The Groaning of Creation,* p. 29.

[61]Christopher Southgate, *The Groaning of Creation,* p. 31.

[62]Christopher Southgate, *The Groaning of Creation,* p. 39.

[63]Christopher Southgate, *The Groaning of Creation,* p. 31.

[64]Christopher Southgate, *The Groaning of Creation,* p. ix.

Statements of other theistic evolutionists

John Walton wrote:

> God in his wisdom has done things in the way that he has. We cannot
> stand in judgment of that, and we cannot expect to understand it all. . . .
> Our question then cannot be whether one model of explanation for the
> cosmos and its origins is reconcilable with the nature of God. We don't
> have enough information to make that assessment. We can only ask
> what Scripture requires us to defend.[65]

Evolution cannot be contested. And we can't reconcile the process with the
nature of God. We must be content with defending basic truths Scripture requires
us to defend. In the end, however, this approach gives the process of evolution
the right to determine which truths Scripture requires Christians to defend.

The title of Daniel Harrell's book *Nature's Witness: How Evolution Can Inspire
Faith* illustrates the power of evolutionary teaching when it becomes part of
the Christian faith. Harrell writes, "Ironically, therefore, death must be another
part of God's good creation. . . . To accept death as essential to biological life is
easier if you view natural selection as a positive process whereby the negativity
of death is redeemed for the sake of new life."[66]

John Polkinghorne and Nicholas Beale offer their solution: "We know God
loves us, and we know there is evil in the world. God must have good enough
reasons for allowing the evil to exist."[67]

These arguments usually end with the idea we noted in discussing Christopher Southgate, that God could create free human beings only through the
process of evolution. Daniel Harrell uses this argument to prove God's love: "As
a loving God, he could not have forced creation into what he wanted it to be
and called it love."[68]

Keith Ward writes, "But those laws, and that element of randomness, may be
necessary to lay the foundation for the moral freedom that will later characterize
intelligent life."[69]

---

[65] John Walton, *The Lost World of Genesis One: Ancient Cosmology and the Origins Debate*
(Downer's Grove: InterVarsity Press, 2009), p. 133.

[66] Daniel Harrell, *Nature's Witness: How Evolution Can Inspire Faith,* p. 108.

[67] John Polkinghorne and Nicholas Beale, *Questions of Truth: Fifty-one Responses to Questions About God, Science, and Belief* (Louisville, KY: Westminster John Knox Press, 2009), p.
63, Kindle.

[68] Daniel Harrell, *Nature's Witness: How Evolution Can Inspire Faith,* p. 79.

[69] Keith Ward, *The Big Questions in Science and Religion* (West Conshohocken, PA: Templeton Press, 2008), p. 48.

Laurie Braaten writes, "The general Christian approach, then, to justifying both moral evil and natural evil is a freedom defense—to be free, man and animal must be open to pain, suffering, and even death." [70]

Gregory Coostona agrees: "Moral evil represents the price for human freedom. . . . For there to be the possibility of good, ethical behavior—especially where we can love God and other human beings—there has to be freedom. This freedom allows for both good and evil." [71]

Denis Lamoureux takes it a step further. Evolution, he believes, leads to spiritual life:

> Christian evolutionists contend that an evolving universe is the perfect environment for humans to develop a true and loving relationship with the Creator. Indeed, this is a very good soul-developing world. . . . Indeterminate and chaotic processes provide *a distancing from God* and a non-coercive environment for humans to develop spiritually" [72]

Denis Alexander puts it in an interesting, somewhat tentative way: "*For some reason*, God's future redeemed family can be established only through the cross, through suffering, and living through his vale of 'soul-making.' There is a greater good that can only be achieved this way." [73] In the same vein, he writes:

> So *could it be* that the biological package deal we have, or something very like it, really *is* the only way in which truly free humans can be formed and fashioned in such a way that they can respond freely to God's love and know him forever? *We will never know the answer to that question,* not in this life anyway. *But even the possibility of an affirmative answer* provides a very powerful theodicy. [74]

His modesty is refreshing. But he arrives at his conclusion only after rejecting Scripture's own *non-tentative* framework in which evil is not part of God's creation but entered the world from the outside.

John Polkinghorne expresses the matter in theologically liberal terms:

[70] Laurie J. Braaten, "May the Glory of the Lord Endure Forever! Biblical Reflections on Creation Care," in *Perspectives on an Evolving Creation,* ed. Keith Miller (Grand Rapids: Eerdmans, 2003), p. 446.

[71] Gregory Cootsona, *Creation and Last Things* (Louisville: Geneva Press, 2002), pp. 64,65.

[72] Denis Lamoureux, *Evolutionary Creation* (Eugene, Oregon: Wipf & Stock, 2008), pp. 99-101 (emphasis added).

[73] Denis Alexander, *Creation or Evolution: Do We Have to Choose?* (Grand Rapids: Monarch Books, 2008), p. 290 (emphasis added).

[74] Denis Alexander, *Creation or Evolution,* p. 292 (emphasis added, except for "is").

The gift of love is always the gift of some due form of independence granted to the beloved. . . . The history of the universe is not the performance of a fixed score, written by God in eternity and inexorably performed by creations, but it is a grand improvisation in which the creator and creature cooperate in the unfolding development of the grand fugue of creation.[75]

Taking his argument to its logical conclusion, Polkinghorne uses cancer as an illustration of God's use of suffering:

The presence of cancer in the world is undoubtedly an anguishing fact, but it is not simply gratuitous, something that a Creator who was a bit more competent or a bit less callous could easily have eliminated. It is the shadow side of a world in which creatures can make themselves.[76]

He claims, "God hides things even from himself so creatures can develop freely."[77] Not all theistic evolutionists would take it this far, but it *is* the logical end to the argument.

Sometimes the argumentation turns to nice-sounding, impressionistic reverie. Keith Miller tells how contemplating evolution inspires him to worship the Lord:

Seeing the history of life unfolding with each new discovery is exciting to me. How incredible to be able to look back to the eons of time and see the panorama of God's evolving creation! God has given us the ability to see into the past and watch his creative work unfold. To do so is for me a very worshipful experience, and it has greatly broadened my perception of God's power and unfathomable wisdom. God has chosen to accomplish his creative will through a process that has been ongoing for billions of years. Clearly God cares for the path as well as the destination.[78]

Finally, Daniel Harrell speculates: "Creation, for all of its beauty and order, fought tooth and claw. There's no rhyme or reason. Maybe this is the miracle: that creation succeeded despite the haywire [nature] of life."[79]

---

[75]John Polkinghorne and Nicholas Beale, *Questions of Truth*, p. 15.

[76]John Polkinghorne and Nicholas Beale, *Questions of Truth*, p. 16.

[77]John Polkinghorne and Nicholas Beale, *Questions of Truth*, p. 32.

[78]Keith Miller, "Worshipping the Creator of the History of Life," in *Perspectives on an Evolving Creation*, ed. Keith Miller, (Grand Rapids: William B. Eerdmans, 2003), p. 205.

[79]Daniel Harrell, *Nature's Witness*, p. 49.

Is the creation really good?

Ways of defining good

The obvious question remains: If evolution with its attendant horrors of natural selection is true, then how can the Creator be a God of love and his creation be called good (Genesis 1:31)? Theistic evolutionists view God's verdict of "good" in different ways.

Daniel Harrell poses the question: "If the world was created by a good God as good, then you can't help but wonder whether *good* means something quite different from what the word *good* says."[80]

David Snoke, an old-earth creationist who believes that the creation is finished, says that since *God* used the process of evolution, the outcome of the process *must* be good. He writes, "A young-earth friend of mine asks whether I can really live with the idea that animals got painful parasites and died, long before human beings ever appeared. . . . We must simply trust [God] when he tells us it is all 'very good.'"[81]

Denis Lamoureux explains it in the same way: "The only one who defined the concept of 'good' is the Author of Good."[82] He explains, "But Scripture indicates that predation is part of God's ordained and sustained plan. . . . In this way, the suffering and death associated with evolution can be viewed in a new light, and even be seen as a good aspect of the Lord's method of creation."[83]

John Munday explains our aversion to animal suffering and death in similar terms: "Do we find it acceptable that his creating is responsible for millions of years of animal pain? The choice is before us whether or not to submit to him [God] as Creator and Merciful Judge, as urged in Romans 9."[84]

Malcolm Jeeves and R. J. Berry come to a similar conclusion in regard to the waste of life required by evolution: "At one level we cannot understand 'natural wastage'; at another level, we can only acknowledge that God's ways are not ours, and that we must allow him to decree the best way to produce the end result he desires, whether or not it is wasteful in our eyes." [85]

---

[80] Daniel Harrell, *Nature's Witness,* p. 47.

[81] David Snoke, *A Biblical Case for an Old Earth* (Grand Rapids: Baker, 2006), p. 94.

[82] Denis Lamoureux, *Evolutionary Creation,* p. 304.

[83] Denis Lamoureux, *Evolutionary Creation,* p. 296. Here Lamoureaux uses the argument referred to earlier: Since the psalmist praises God's provision for animals using the food chain, he must have created it in the beginning.

[84] John Munday, "Animal Pain: Beyond the Threshold?" in *Perspectives on an Evolving Creation,* ed. Keith Miller, p. 468.

[85] Malcolm Jeeves and R. J. Berry, *Science, Life, and Christian Belief* (Grand Rapids: Baker,

Some say that "good" refers to God's verdict on the process rather than his verdict on the final result. Or at least they weave that idea into the argument that evolution can be considered good. Lamoureax says that the process of evolution is good because it enables us to develop spiritually: "As difficult as it may be at first for Christians to appreciate, suffering and death are part of the Creator's glorifying activity in making a world that is perfectly suited for us to develop a genuine loving relationship with Him. Indeed, the evolved creation is very good."[86]

Daniel Harrell ends his book with a prayer asking God to help him combine evolution and his Christian faith. He sees the problem:

> Yet even as I pray all of these things, my mind feels like I'm forcing a fit. Science reveals a world where randomness seems the norm, death is constant, and the future is open-ended. How do I reconcile this? How do I make sense of what makes no sense? If all truth is your truth, how does what I believe come together with what nature reveals? How do I deal with this dissonance? [87]

He notes ways he could deal with the problem: "I could lower my expectations," and "It could be that my faith is in vain."[88] He rejects both. Only one option remains. He ends his prayer with the firm resolve: "I will deal with the dissonance by standing firm in my faith."[89] He concludes, "It really doesn't work to say that diseases and disasters are outcomes of a fallen creation. They're the outcomes of a competent yet free creation, a creation that operates the way God made it."[90]

Finally, some understand the word *good* as God's assessment of what the creation will be someday after it is finished (which is a silent admission that the present creation is *not* good).

Larry Witham, a journalist who studied the present debate, records the comments of a Presbyterian minister, James Miller, who told the conference he was speaking at: "If I hear another sermon in which God is spoken of as Creator in the past tense, I could scream. . . . Who says the universe is finished?" [91]

1998), p. 128.

[86] Denis Lamoureux, *Evolutionary Creation*, p. 305.

[87] Daniel Harrell, *Nature's Witness,* p. 101.

[88] Daniel Harrell, *Nature's Witness,* pp. 101,102.

[89] Daniel Harrell, *Nature's Witness,* p. 102.

[90] Daniel Harrell, *Nature's Witness,* p. 105.

[91] Larry Witham, *Where Darwin Meets the Bible: Creationists and Evolutionists in America* (Oxford: Oxford University Press, 2002), p. 191.

Southgate notes, "A strong emphasis within contemporary Christian theology is on creation as a continuous process, rather than something completed at the beginning of time." He agrees with those who find God's verdict of "very good" as something still to be realized in the future.[92]

All these authors are simply redefining good in the context of the process of natural selection. But *good* cannot simply be redefined to include evils Scripture in other places defines as not good. God's verdict on creation had nothing to do with the process but was his assessment of the things he had made. Nor was God predicting something that would take place in the future. He was speaking about what he had just completed.

The idea that God is suffering along with human beings

Henri Blocher lists a third way that some theistic evolutionists justify the horrors of natural selection. They claim that God is suffering along with his creation. This solution seems to originate in liberal theology.

Catholic theologian Denis Edwards will serve as a spokesman for this position. "Those, like myself, who take this position [that God is suffering along with creation], will want to hold together the data from revelation, that God is radically compassionate, with the data from evolutionary science, that evolution has serious costs. They will seek a theology of God that can affirm the divine compassion for the world and at the same time face honestly the negative side of evolution."[93]

To do this, Edwards must offer a new definition of God's almighty power. Divine omnipotence, he writes, "is really the divine capacity for love beyond all human comprehension. This means that God's omnipotence can be understood as God's capacity to enter into love with all its costs."[94] He explains:

> All of this means that God may not be free to overrule natural processes. . . . If this is the case, then God is not free or able to simply abolish all suffering. . . . Such a God will be understood as a God who freely accepts the limits of the process of emergence, a God who created through the losses and gains of evolutionary history . . . a God who suffers with and delights in the unfolding of creation.[95]

---

[92] Christopher Southgate, *The Groaning of Creation*, pp. 15,16.

[93] Denis Edwards, *The God of Evolution* (New York: Paulist Press, 1999), loc. 394, Kindle.

[94] Denis Edwards, *The God of Evolution*, loc. 412.

[95] Denis Edwards, *The God of Evolution*, loc. 447.

The practical result is this: If Christians are tempted to complain about the suffering they and the rest of creation undergo in the process of evolution, they must realize that God is suffering right along with them. And as God suffers along with his creation, he inspires us to sympathize with and respond to the sufferings of others.

It should not be difficult to recognize this argument as pure philosophical speculation. In Henri Blocher's view, this position makes God "a finite partner in the evolving world process."[96] According to Scripture, God suffered, but not because he couldn't fully control the evil involved in creating through evolution. Rather, with almighty power he suffered and died to overcome the guilt of sin and paved the way for creation's restoration. This is why *Good* Friday is good.

Cliché: God deserves more glory for using evolution.

Theistic evolutionists argue that God's use of the amazing process of evolution gives him more glory than if he simply spoke and brought everything into existence.

An evolutionist describes the amazing nature of human life—the unbelievable makeup of DNA, the formation of life in the womb, the human brain—and thinks, "God developed all this through a series of seemingly random mutations over millions of years. What a powerful God he must be! What glory he deserves!" One author suggests, "If God were to create like a magician with total control of things, then the result would be an impoverished world, lacking the drama, diversity, adventure, and beauty that evolution has produced."[97] In line with this, Christians who accept a perfect six-day creation are accused of limiting their understanding of God to what their small minds can accept.

Beware of this argument. It is nothing more than an appeal to emotions. How can a human being judge what is harder to do: bring creation into being with a series of commands given over a short period of time or by using random mutations and natural selection over billions of years? How can anyone claim that a creation completed in six days through the power of God's command is impoverished in comparison with one produced through the suffering of natural selection?

---

[96] Henri Blocher, *The Theology of the Fall*, p. 155.

[97] Denis Edwards, *The God of Evolution,* loc. 552. He is quoting John Haught.

Christians can just as easily argue that God deserves far more glory for creating living beings in a short time through his Word rather than using the untold suffering and death demanded by the process of evolution.

Nevertheless, all that matters is what God reveals in his Word. If the Bible says that God created the world in six days using the power of his Word, that is God's definition of his greatness and glory.

What is lost when God's love and goodness are defined by evolution

The meaning of God's love is lost

If God used billions of years of scarcity, bloody competition, suffering, death, and extinction to create the world and its inhabitants, it becomes harder and harder for Christians to believe that God and his love for us are perfect. Evil becomes a tool of creation. If that is true, then God and evil are closely associated.

What Scripture says about suffering is lost

In order to accept the theory of evolution, Christians will have to redo what Scripture says about the origin of suffering and how God often uses it for the good of his people. They will have to confess that God created the world using suffering, and death. They will have to deny that God created the world *good* as that term is naturally understood.

Scripture's meaning of freedom is lost.

Theistic evolutionists realize that evolution is a challenge to God's love. They know that Scripture's history of the universe—perfection, fall, and restoration—leads to a completely different understanding of suffering than in evolution's history. As we have seen, in order to justify God's use of suffering to create the world, they teach that evolution is the only way human beings could have developed the freedom to think and act. Human beings had to live in an environment in which they had to make choices with the complete freedom to decide which course of action to take. If God had created human beings in any other way, we would be robots. And the last thing God wants is to be served by robots who have no other choice but to do what he wants them to do.

We will return to this discussion when we talk about the work of Jesus Christ. But because it is so important, we will offer some initial thoughts.

This rhetoric ought to be examined carefully. Christians who are considering evolution must choose between two ways of understanding freedom: (1) God created Adam and Eve with the freedom to love and serve him. When they sinned, they lost that freedom for themselves and for their descendants. God, in Christ, restores that freedom to us. (2) Mankind gradually became free through the choices afforded by the process of evolution. Through the process of making choices between good and evil, mankind evolved to be the kind of being who is able to develop a relationship with God and to serve him willingly.

Consider option two. How can the ability to make the kind of choices required by evolution make a person free? The evolution of living creatures is built on the survival of the fittest, which includes competition for scarce resources and the right to harm or kill others. For billions of years living beings were forced by God to commit savage acts so their species would survive. In modern genetic terms, this means that God forced us to be selfishly concerned about the survival of our own genes at the expense of the gene pool of others.

Are we free when we are forced to fight for our own survival? Are we free when even our acts of kindness cannot rise above self-interest? If this is freedom, it's like the freedom given birds put in a cage for a cockfight; they can choose to fight any way they want. But they are still caged, and they still must fight.

Contrast this with option one. When God created Adam and Eve, they were hardly robots. This is shown by their tragic choice to yield to Satan's temptation. As creatures made in God's image, Adam and Eve had freedom like God has—the freedom to love unfettered by self-concern and selfishness. They could serve God without fear. They could care for his creation motivated only by love. There was no need to protect their gene pool because God had made them perfect from the beginning. There was no need to compete because God had given them and the rest of creation everything they needed.

As for choices, their lives were filled with them. They were to care for God's creation, which meant making choices every day. God told Adam to choose what name to give the animals, and "whatever the man called every living creature, that was its name" (Genesis 2:19). What's more, God had richly qualified Adam and Eve to make wise choices. There was no need for God to constrain, correct, or second-guess their decisions.

Adam and Eve were called to make the ongoing choice to keep or not to keep the command God gave them. And the very fact that they chose not to keep it shows that God was not coercing them to obey him.

When believers go to heaven, will they complain that they have lost their freedom because they have no option except to praise God? For all eternity we will thank God for his mercy in Christ. We will do so willingly with all our heart, glad that Satan has been destroyed and can never again lead us into sin.

St. Paul puts the matter of freedom and slavery into perspective. He encourages us, "But thanks be to God that, though you used to be slaves to sin, you wholeheartedly obeyed the form of teaching to which you were entrusted. You have been set free from sin and have become slaves to righteousness" (Romans 6:17,18 NIV84). In Christ we are slaves to righteousness, which is far different from being righteous robots.

Elephants in the room

To believe in evolution, a person must believe the following: First, the good and loving God used billions of years of scarcity, competition, and death to create plants, animals, and mankind. Second, God could not create people to freely serve him unless they had first been forced to make decisions in the brutal evolutionary school of survival.

Keeping the elephants all in view at the same time is important. In the last chapter we identified these:

- **The basic framework of the world's history as taught in Scripture is wrong.**
- **The evil associated with creation by evolution came from God.**

To those, we add two more:

- **God, whom Scripture says is love, used the evils of natural selection over billions of years to create living beings.**
- **The process of evolution—which locks mankind into a system of self-interest, competition, and death—leads to freedom.**

We close on a positive note. Paul wrote to the Ephesians:

> For this reason I bow my knees before the Father, from whom every family in heaven and on earth is named, that according to the riches of his glory he may grant you to be strengthened with power through his Spirit in your inner being, so that Christ may dwell in your hearts through faith—that you, being rooted and grounded in love, may have strength to comprehend with all the saints what is the breadth and length and height and depth, *and to know the love of Christ that surpasses knowledge,* that you may be filled with all the fullness of God. (Ephesians 3:14-19)

Chapter 4

Who We Are According to Scripture

Jesus and the New Testament writers teach us who we are

Before we begin looking at the origin of mankind in Genesis 1 and 2, we'll lay the foundation by examining how Jesus and the Old and New Testament writers interpreted the account of mankind's creation.

The writer of 1 Chronicles traces the history of the Israelites through Abraham back to Adam (1 Chronicles 1:1). Luke does the same (Luke 3:38). There is no indication that either author saw a major break in the genealogy, a point at which names that had been mythological became names of historical people.

Jesus and the New Testament writers understood the account of creation in Genesis to be a literal record of people and events. Some Pharisees once tested Jesus to see how he would handle Moses' allowing the Israelites to divorce their wives. They asked, "Is it lawful to divorce one's wife for any cause?" Jesus took them back to Moses' record of mankind's creation in Genesis 2: "Have you not read that he who created them from the beginning made them male and female, and said, 'Therefore a man shall leave his father and his mother and hold fast to his wife, and the two shall become one flesh?'" (Mathew 19:3-5).

When the apostle Paul addressed the Gentile crowd in Athens, he took them back to the beginning and the creation of Adam and Eve: "And he made from one man every nation of mankind to live on all the face of the earth" (Acts 17:26). Paul could say that only if he interpreted the Genesis account in a straightforward way.

Paul put Jesus and Adam in a parallel relationship. In Romans 5 Paul spoke of Adam's sin: "Therefore, just as sin came into the world through one man, and death through sin, and so death spread to all men because all sinned." (verse 12). Paul then referred to God's command not to eat of the Tree of the Knowledge of Good and Evil: "Death reigned from Adam to Moses, even over those whose sinning was not like the transgression of Adam" (verse 14). In verses 15-17 Paul refers to Adam in the singular: "Many died through one man's trespass," and "if, because of one man's trespass, death reigned through that one man. . . ." And he refers to Adam's sin as a specific act at a point in history: "The judgment following one trespass brought condemnation" (verse 16).

The same pattern continues in verses 18 and 19. The one sin of the one man is contrasted with the one act of righteousness performed by another individual person: "one trespass led to condemnation for all men," and "By the one man's obedience the many will be made righteous." This comparison between Adam and Christ could only have been written by someone who read Genesis as an historical narrative. What one man actually did continues to affect all people, namely, with sin and death.

When we read this and the verses above in the context of Acts 17:26, "And he made from one man every nation of mankind," it is clear that Paul is not saying that Adam was merely a bad moral influence on the people living around him. He was the literal father of all human beings and the one from whom all, by birth, became sinners.

Paul made the same point in 1 Corinthians 15:21,22: "For as by a man came death, by a man has come also the resurrection of the dead. For as in Adam all die, so also in Christ shall all be made alive." In 15:45 Paul contrasted what we are as descendants of Adam with what we will become when Christ refashions us so we can live with him in heaven: "Thus it is written, 'The first man Adam became a living being'; the last Adam became a life-giving spirit.'" Paul continues with a series of contrasts in which Adam and Christ are paralleled:

> But it is not the spiritual that is first but the natural, and then the spir-
> itual. The first man was from the earth, a man of dust; the second man
> is from heaven. As was the man of dust, so also are those who are of the
> dust, and as is the man of heaven, so also are those who are of heaven.
> Just as we have borne the image of the man of dust, we shall also bear the
> image of the man of heaven. (1 Corinthians 15:46-49)

We are descended from the man of dust, Adam (a clear reference to the creation of Adam's physical body). Through rebirth and restoration in Christ, "the man of heaven," we will enjoy the full blessings of God's image.

Paul taught that God created men and women with complementary roles. He based his argument on the events of Genesis chapters 2 and 3: "Neither was man created for woman, but woman for man" (1 Corinthians 11:9), and "For Adam was formed first, then Eve; and Adam was not deceived, but the woman was deceived and became a transgressor" (1 Timothy 2:13,14). Here, too, it would be hard to imagine Paul expecting people to accept this teaching unless he knew it was based on what actually happened.

The three sections of Genesis 1

Three kinds of life: plants, animals, and mankind

Genesis 1 is divided into three sections, separated by a special Hebrew word. Genesis 1 uses two words for God's act of creation: ASAH and BARA. ASAH is more general. It is usually translated "to make." ASAH is used throughout Genesis 1: God *made* the expanse (verse 7), he *made* the two great lights (verse 16), and he *made* the beasts of the earth (verse 25). God also said, "Let us *make* man in our image" (verse 26).

The other word, BARA, also means to make something. But BARA stands out in the Old Testament as special in comparison to the more general word ASAH. Whenever BARA is used, God is the one doing the making and he is often making something new. The current standard Hebrew dictionary calls BARA "a theological term." To distinguish the two words, translators of Genesis 1 often use "make" for ASAH and "create" for BARA.

Here are a few Old Testament passages that use BARA. They will give us a feel for how it is used in the Old Testament. God would show his favor to Israel with marvelous deeds never experienced by another nation: "Behold, I am making a covenant. Before all your people I will do marvels, such as have not been created [BARA] in all the earth or in any nation" (Exodus 34:10). When certain Israelites rebelled against Moses, God would make it clear to everyone that they had rebelled against God. Moses told the people: "But if the LORD creates [BARA] something new, and the ground opens its mouth and swallows them up with all that belongs to them, then you shall know that these men have despised the LORD" (Numbers 16:30). When David repented of his sins of adultery and murder (2 Samuel 11), he asked God to create (BARA) a new spirit in him (Psalm 51:12).

BARA is used only three times in the creation account. It is first used in Genesis 1:1: "In the beginning God *created* the heavens and the earth." It is used a second time in Genesis 1:21: "So God *created* the great creatures of the sea and every living and moving thing with which the water teems, according to their kinds, and every winged bird according to its kind." It is used a third time in Genesis 1:27 when God created mankind: "So God *created* man in his own image, in the image of God he created him; male and female he created them." These three uses of BARA divide Genesis 1 into three sections, each time signaling God's creation of something new. This division is important for understanding mankind in relation to the rest of creation and for understanding who we are.

Section One: Genesis 1:1-19

The first section of Genesis 1 describes the creation of things that *were not* "living creatures." This section of Genesis 1 describes how God prepared the world for the living creatures he would create in sections 2 and 3. Among the things God created in this period is plant life. We learn that plant life was created as the food supply for the living creatures God would create later (Genesis 1:29; 9:3).

Plants *seem* to be living creatures. They germinate and grow; they bud and flower; they reproduce according to their "kinds." In the evolutionary tree of life, plant life is included along with animals and mankind. But in Scripture, the plants God created on the third day are not referred to as "living creatures." We might think of them as being alive, but they are not alive in the way animals and mankind are alive. They do not possess a living spirit.

It may be difficult for us to separate the death and decay that happens to plant life from the death and decay of animals and mankind. The Bible, however, makes such a distinction. It does not speak about plants "dying." They simply wither or dry up. The psalmist writes, "Fret not yourself because of evildoers; be not envious of wrongdoers! For they will soon fade like the grass and wither like the green herb" (Psalm 37:1,2). Isaiah talks about plants in the same way: "The grass withers, the flower fades, but the word of our God will stand forever" (Isaiah 40:8).

In one place Jesus seems to say that plants are living creatures. In the Sermon on the Mount, he says, "But if God so clothes the grass of the field, *which today is alive* and tomorrow is thrown into the oven, will he not much more clothe you, O you of little faith?" (Matthew 6:30 ESV). But the ESV translation "which today is alive" is an interpretation, likely based on how we speak about plants today. The original Greek simply says, "If God so clothes the grass of the field, which *exists* today and tomorrow is thrown into the oven . . ."

The only exception to this way of speaking about plant life is Job 14:8, where Job speaks of a stump "dying" in the ground. But Job may simply be describing the "death" of a tree as we usually do.

Section Two: Genesis 1:20-25

The second time BARA occurs in Genesis 1 is in verse 20. God proceeds to create sea creatures, birds, and land animals. For the first time, God created "living creatures."

In an attempt to prove a common ancestry between mankind and animals, evolutionists focus on the similarities between the animals and mankind. As a reaction, those who believe in a six 24-hour-day creation counter (and rightly so) by listing everything that makes mankind and animals different. There *are* many differences between mankind and animals. But there is also a basic similarity: fish, birds, animals, and mankind are all "living creatures."

The attempt to contrast mankind and animals often begins with the argument that Scripture uses "living creatures" in reference to animals and "soul" in reference to mankind. This distinction stems from the King James Version (KJV). The KJV translates Genesis 1:24, which describes the creation of land animals: "Let the earth bring forth the *living creature* after his kind." It then translates chapter 2:7, which describes the creation of Adam: The Lord "formed man of the dust of the ground, and breathed into his nostrils the breath of life; and man became a *living soul.*" So, it is argued, human beings have souls and animals don't.

However, the KJV translation created a distinction that isn't found in the original. The Hebrew words Moses used to record the creation of fish, birds, and land animals are the same as those he used to record the creation of Adam. He used the words NEPHESH CHAYA, "living being," in both Genesis 1:24 and in 2:7. (Most modern translations use the same translation in both verses.)

Mankind and animals share this similarity: we are both "living beings." Scripture sometimes speaks about the spirit of animals and the spirit of mankind in the same breath.[98] Solomon points out the limits of human observation and understanding: "Who knows whether the spirit of man goes upward and the spirit of the beast goes down into the earth?" (Ecclesiastes 3:21).

Psalm 104, which is organized around the days of creation, speaks about the spirit of all living creatures, including mankind's, as dependent on God. The psalmist says that God gives a spirit to all living creatures and, in turn, he takes it away:

> These all look to you, to give them their food in due season. When you give it to them, they gather it up; when you open your hand, they are filled with good things. When you hide your face, they are dismayed; *when you take away their breath* [literally "spirit"], they die and return to their dust. *When you send forth your Spirit* [the same word as above,

---

[98] Hebrew uses two words in reference to the spirit of living creatures: NEPHESH and RUACH. These words can be used interchangeably, yet they have a different shade of meaning. Heinrich Vogel writes, "In some respects, the terms *ruach* and *nephesh* are interchangeable. Both refer to the spiritual part of man. Yet there is a clearly discernible difference in their use. *Nephesh*, or 'soul,' seems to be the essence of this spiritual part of man, whereas *ruach* or 'spirit' seems to be its active force or its activity." Heinrich Vogel, "The Old Testament Concept of the Soul," in *Our Great Heritage, Vol. 2,* ed. Lyle Lange (Milwaukee: Northwestern Publishing House, 1991), p. 200 (emphasis author's).

> "breath" or "spirit"[99]], they are created, and you renew the face of the ground. (Psalm 104:27-30)

The words "these all" and "their breath" in Psalm 104 refer to the breath or spirit of both animals and mankind (see verses 21-23).[100]

Section Three: Genesis 1:26–2:25

God's creation was a unified and orderly system. Its variety and beauty put the glory of the Creator on display: "O LORD, how manifold are your works! In wisdom have you made them all" (Psalm 104:24).

God had created plants in categories called "kinds." As noted above, plants are living, but they are not living creatures. They were given to the living creatures, to animals and mankind, as food (Genesis 1:29). Their variety and beauty, as was evident in the beauty of the Tree of the Knowledge of Good and Evil (3:6), was a reason to glorify the Creator. On the fifth day God created fish and birds, and on the sixth day he created land animals. They are living creatures, and the spirit that gave them life came from God. They too were given order, created according to "kinds."

The creation of mankind was God's final act of creating an orderly and beautiful creation. BARA is used a third time in Genesis 1:27, signaling a third major division in God's creating activity. In this section of Genesis, God created only one thing: mankind. "Then God said, 'Let us make man [Hebrew: ADAM] in our image, after our likeness.' . . . So God created ADAM [that is, Adam and Eve] in his own image, in the image of God he created him; male and female he created them" (Genesis 1:26,27). After God created ADAM, the creation was finished: "God saw everything that he had made, and behold, it was very good" (Genesis 1:31).

Note that the English word *mankind* can be misleading.[101] It could imply that ADAM was among the "kinds" of living creatures that God created on the sixth day. This can create an inaccurate (even evolutionary) association between the animals and ADAM. The creation of ADAM on the sixth day is separated from the creation of the land animals by the word BARA. The word *humans* or *human*

---

[99]Most translations capitalize the word and make it a reference to the Holy Spirit. Whether we translate "spirit" or "Spirit," the point is the same. God's Spirit is the one who gives and takes away the spirit of all living things.

[100]What similarities might exist between us and animals because of our common possession of a spirit? See Appendix 2 for additional thoughts on what Scripture says about this.

[101]The NIV 1984 used "man" to translate the Hebrew word ADAM, but the newer NIV 2011 uses "mankind."

beings better captures the meaning of ADAM, but mankind is the normal English word, so we continue to use it here.

Scripture's description of the creation of mankind

Mankind is a living creature along with the fish, birds, and animals. But we are very different from the other living creatures. We can organize these differences using the four main aspects of our creation. (1) the creation of mankind's body, (2) the creation of the human spirit, (3) mankind's creation in the image and likeness of God, and (4) God's command that mankind rule over the creation and subdue it.

1. The creation of Adam's body

Genesis 2 gives the details of how God created mankind on the sixth day.[102] In creating Adam, God did two things in quick succession. First, he made a complete human body from the dust of the earth. Second, he made this body into a living creature by giving it life.

We sometimes picture this body as a clay statue of a person—like a youngster might make in a grade school art class. But at this point Adam's body was complete, with all its bodily systems intact, with a fully formed brain, indeed, with all its cells in place—except that it was not living.

Nor was Adam's flesh like the flesh of fish, birds, and land animals. It was different. Scripture doesn't give us any details about how it was different, only that it was. And the flesh of the four major groups of living creatures differed from that of the others. Paul uses this fact in 1 Corinthians 15:39 to answer the objection of those who question the resurrection of the body by arguing that weak and corrupt bodies cannot live in the glory of God.

Paul answers that objection with examples of God's power. God can create objects with different forms (15:36-38) and with different levels of glory (15:40,41). Since this is so, God has the ability to change the characteristics of

---

[102]Theistic evolutionists often say that Genesis 2 is a second creation account. They say something like, "Modern biblical scholarship has shown that Genesis 2 is a second and in many ways a conflicting account of the creation of the world." This, of course, calls into question the truth of both Genesis 1 and Genesis 2. That claim about Genesis 2, however, is neither modern nor is it accepted by all modern biblical scholars. The traditional way of reading Genesis 2 as a detailed description of the creation of man on the sixth day is accepted by many modern Bible scholars, some of whom do not accept a straightforward reading of Genesis 1 and 2. Among them are C. John Collins who argues for theistic evolution (*Did Adam and Eve Really Exist?, Who They Were and Why You Should Care* [Wheaton: Crossway, 2011], pp. 52,53) and longtime Oxford professor and advocate of historical criticism John Barton (*Reading the Old Testament*, pp. 49,50). Both are major voices in the scholarly world.

our earthly, physical bodies (our flesh) so we are no longer limited by corruption and mortality. Paul refers to the four kinds of living creatures God created and argues, "For not all flesh is the same, but there is one kind for humans, another for animals, another for birds, and another for fish" (1 Corinthians 15:39). Paul does not go into detail about the differences. But the context makes it clear that Paul is not just talking about the appearance of these bodies but also about their very nature. If God was able to create different kinds of bodies, he can re-create a weak human body into something fit for heaven. This point is pertinent to the creation/evolution debate. If living creatures all have the same origin, they all have the same kind of flesh. Paul tells us that they don't.

Later, God brought the animals to Adam so he would name them. The fact that the animals were male and female led Adam to realize he had no female counterpart. God then took a rib from Adam's body and created Eve:

> So the LORD God caused a deep sleep to fall upon the man, and while he slept took one of his ribs and closed up its place with flesh. And the rib that the LORD God had taken from the man he made into a woman and brought her to the man. Then the man said, "This at last is bone of my bones and flesh of my flesh; she shall be called Woman, because she was taken out of Man." (Genesis 2:21-23)

Adam recognized that now he had a counterpart in Eve. When God brought Adam and Eve together, "The man called his wife's name Eve, because she was the mother of all the living" (Genesis 3:20). The bodies that all human beings possess have come from the first two human beings God created, not as part of an evolutionary tree of life.

2. The creation of Adam's spirit (or soul)

"Soul" is the name we give to the human "spirit"

When God was finished creating Adam's form from the dust of the earth, he breathed into his nostrils his own divine breath, and the form came to life. Man became a "living creature."

When we looked at God's creation of the animals, we noted that both animals and mankind are referred to as "living creatures." In this respect, mankind and animals have something in common. We both have physical bodies that are joined with a spirit.

In pointing out that the word *soul* is not found in Genesis 2, there was no intention to deny that the human spirit is different in many ways from the spirit of animals. The English word *soul* has come to reflect those differences, and as such, it is valuable. But it is more accurate to say that only human beings have a spirit with all the qualities human beings possess.

This point is important in the theistic evolution discussion. Theistic evolution requires a scenario for how and when God gave animal hominins a soul, thus making them human beings. But if evolution were true, changing animals to human beings would entail a much more radical and complicated process. It would not simply be a matter of adding a soul to a hominin. It would mean swapping out the hominins' animal spirit with a human spirit. It would mean God putting to death their animal spirit and then recreating them by breathing into them his own divine spirit, as he did when he created Adam. For that matter, it would also mean re-creating the hominins with a new kind of flesh, that is, replacing their animal flesh with human flesh.

Old Testament believers identified themselves as living beings

When God breathed into Adam, Adam became a NEPHESH CHAYA, namely, a *living being*. When we speak about ourselves, we usually don't convey the idea that we are "lives" or "living beings." But the Hebrew people spoke with an awareness of the life God had given them. When they spoke about themselves, they almost always used one of two words for spirit, NEPHESH (life) or RUACH (spirit).[103] For example, Jacob's household numbered 70 when he went down to Egypt. We would say there were 70 "people," or 70 "persons." The Hebrews, however, said there were 70 "lives" [NEPHESH] who went down to Egypt (Genesis 46:27). Jesus reflected this practice when he was in the Garden of Gethsemane. He told his disciples, "My PSUCHE [the Greek equivalent of NEPHESH] is very sorrowful, even to death" (Mark 14:34). We would be content simply to say, "I am sorrowful."

We might say, "It is wrong to take a person's life." When we say that, we usually mean nothing more than that it is wrong to murder someone. But the Hebrews would have used that expression in a more literal sense: It is wrong to take away from a person the life, the NEPHESH, that God had given him or her.

The following sample of passages where NEPHESH is used will give us a feel for this. As you read these passages, note how difficult it can be to translate the Hebrew words into English. We'll use the NIV11 instead of the ESV. The NIV aims for good English usage and is somewhat less literal than the ESV. It will serve our purpose in contrasting the Hebrew way of speaking with ours. I'll put the Hebrew word in brackets after the word used in the translation.

---

[103] The Old Testament uses only two words to refer to the life that God gave Adam, NEPHESH (life) and RUACH (spirit). The Greek New Testament has two corresponding words: PSUCHE is the equivalent of NEPHESH, and PNEUMA is the equivalent of RUACH.

Moses gave a regulation to the Israelites: "When anyone [a NEPHESH] brings a grain offering as an offering to the LORD. . . ." (Leviticus 2:1 NIV). And Moses repeatedly warned the Israelites against neglecting God's instructions: "Anyone [a NEPHESH] who touches something unclean . . . [that NEPHESH] must be cut off from their people" (Leviticus 7:21 NIV).

In Psalm 107, David praised God for his loving care: "For he satisfies the thirsty [the thirsty NEPHESH] and fills the hungry [the hungry NEPHESH] with good things" (verse 9 NIV). Through Jeremiah, God promised: "I will refresh the weary [the weary NEPHESH] and satisfy the faint [every faint NEPHESH]" (Jeremiah 31:25 NIV).

Rahab made a deal with the Hebrew spies that if she helped them escape when they took the city of Jericho, they would "save us [our NEPHESH, plural] from death" (Joshua 2:13 NIV). Mordecai urged Esther to appeal to the king on behalf of the Jews and warned her, "Do not think [think in your NEPHESH] that because you are in the king's house you alone of all the Jews will escape" (Esther 4:13 NIV).

When the priest Eli accused Hannah of drunkenness, she explained that she was only praying to the Lord: "I was pouring out my soul [NEPHESH] to the LORD" (1 Samuel 1:15 NIV). When Elijah was asked to help a woman whose child had died, he prayed, "LORD my God, let this boy's life [NEPHESH] return to him!" (1 Kings 17:21 NIV).

In distress, David cried to the Lord, "Many are saying of me [my NEPHESH], 'God will not deliver him'" (Psalm 3:2 NIV). In another psalm David praised the Lord, "I [my NEPHESH] will glory in the LORD; let the afflicted hear and rejoice" (Psalm 34:2 NIV).

The Old Testament uses NEPHESH hundreds of times like this. Each time, the Hebrew person would hear a reference to the life God breathed into mankind in Genesis 2:7. Good English almost always requires translators to paraphrase NEPHESH. Nevertheless, when they do, or even use the word *soul* (which leads many to think of a religious idea), they rob the word of its force. NEPHESH refers to life itself, the thing that enables our bodies to move, to think, to experience emotions, and to do everything else we as human beings do.

Human beings were created with both a body and a spirit

Human beings are body and spirit. This is clearly taught throughout Scripture. God did not give life just to Adam and Eve. He continues to impart life. "Thus says God, the LORD, who created the heavens and stretched them out, who spread out the earth and what comes from it, who gives breath to the people on it and spirit [RUACH] to those who walk in it. . . ." (Isaiah 42:5). And the opposite is true. The psalmist wrote, "When you take away their breath [their RUACH], they die and return to their dust" (Psalm 104:29).

The account of the death of Rachel, Jacob's wife, reflects the fact that the force of life lives in a person's body. Rachel's death is expressed like this: "And as her soul [NEPHESH] was departing (for she was dying). . . ." (Genesis 35:18). Or as another example, when an Amalekite claimed to have killed Saul, mistakenly thinking David would reward him for it, he recounted the event like this: "Then he [Saul] said to me, 'Stand here by me and kill me! I'm in the throes of death, but I'm still alive'" (2 Samuel 1:9 NIV11). The NIV paraphrases here. The original literally says, "For all my soul [my NEPHESH] is still in me" (Young's Literal Translation). Saul would be dead only when his spirit completely left his body.

Solomon describes our end like this: "The dust returns to the earth as it was, and the spirit returns to God who gave it" (Ecclesiastes 12:7). The New Testament speaks in the same way. We hear about Jesus raising the dead. The physical body was still there—in a tomb, on a bier, in a bed—but the spirit was gone. At the death of the daughter of Jairus, the people laughed when Jesus told them the girl was not dead but sleeping (Luke 8:52). They knew her spirit had departed. But Jesus knew he would restore her spirit, and so it was no different than if she were sleeping.

When Jesus himself died, he cried out, "Father, into your hands I commit my spirit!" (Luke 23:46). Jesus' body would soon lie in a tomb, but his spirit would be with his Father.

Jesus clearly distinguished between the body and the soul in this warning: "Do not fear those who kill the body but cannot kill the soul [PSUCHE, the Greek equivalent of NEPHESH]. Rather fear him who can destroy both soul [PSUCHE] and body in hell" (Matthew 10:28).[104]

The human spirit is immortal

God intended Adam and Eve to live forever—body and spirit joined together in a single person. God told them that they would die, but only if they ate from the Tree of the Knowledge of Good and Evil. After Adam and Eve sinned, the Tree of Life that God created in the garden ironically could be a source of harm to them. "And the LORD God said, 'The man has now become like one of us, knowing good and evil. He must not be allowed to reach out his hand and take also from the tree of life and eat, and live forever.' So the LORD God banished

---

[104]Note that here "life" and "soul" are both translations of the same Greek word PSUCHE. But translating PSUCHE consistently as "life" (as the RSV does) makes perfectly good sense and doesn't force the reader to make a distinction that isn't there in the original.

him from the Garden of Eden" (Genesis 3:22,23) to assure that they would not live on earth forever in their sinful state.

A person is alive when that person's body and spirit are joined. God breathed into Adam his own breath, and he became a living being. Death is the opposite. It's when the body and spirit separate. In Ecclesiastes 12:7, Solomon tells us that the spirit God breathed into Adam is not lost. It returns to God: "The dust returns to the earth as it was, and the spirit returns to God who gave it."

But when our spirit returns to God, is it simply "reabsorbed" into God? Or does the spirit God gave us continue to be *our own* spirit, awaiting the resurrection, just as *our own* body will lie in our grave also awaiting the resurrection?

The New Testament says more about the eternal nature of the soul than the Old Testament says. But as we work through these passages, bear in mind that Jesus was essentially talking to Old Testament believers. His audience had grown up under the Jewish rabbis. There is never any indication in the gospels that Jesus surprised the people by something he said in which he spoke about the soul as being eternal.

The religious sect called the Sadducees denied the resurrection of the dead. Jesus rebuked them and explained: "But in the account of the bush, even Moses showed that the dead rise, for he calls the Lord 'the God of Abraham, and the God of Isaac, and the God of Jacob.' He is not the God of the dead, but of the living, for to him all are alive" (Luke 20:37,38 NIV84). Jesus spoke of Abraham, Isaac, and Jacob as individuals, who at that very moment were known to God, not just dead bodies whose spirits no longer existed.

Jesus warned the people of his day: "I tell you, my friends, do not fear those who kill the body, and after that have nothing more that they can do. But I will warn you whom to fear: fear him who, after he has killed, has authority to cast into hell. Yes, I tell you, fear him!" (Luke 12:4,5). Jesus was referring to God, who has the power to consign a person's body and spirit to hell. A problem greater than the death of the body was to have one's spirit consigned to hell for eternity.

Jesus told a parable about a rich man and a poor man. The entire account is based on the immortality of the soul. He described the end of their lives like this: "The poor man died and was carried by the angels to Abraham's side. The rich man also died and was buried, and in Hades, being in torment, he lifted up his eyes and saw Abraham far off and Lazarus at his side" (Luke 16:22). Jesus then related the exchange between Abraham and the rich man. The rich man asked Abraham to send Lazarus back to earth to warn his brothers about what would happen to them if they didn't repent. True, in some of the details of the story Jesus spoke as if the bodily resurrection had already taken place. But Abraham, Lazarus, and the rich man, whose bodies were still in their graves, were present in heaven even before the Last Day because the rich man's brothers were still living in their time on earth. Everything Jesus said presupposed the immortality of the soul.

When Jesus was transfigured before his disciples, Moses and Elijah appeared and spoke with him. Moses' body was in a grave known only to God. But he was very much alive and aware of what was about to happen: "And behold, two men were talking with him, Moses and Elijah, who appeared in glory and spoke of his departure, which he was about to accomplish at Jerusalem" (Luke 9:30,31).

When he was on the cross, Jesus said to the criminal who had just confessed his faith in the kingdom of God: "Truly, I say to you, today you will be with me in Paradise" (Luke 23:43). That day, the man's body was in a grave. But he was personally with Jesus in heaven.

Other New Testament statements about mankind's spirit

In the early days of the Christian church, the deacon Stephen was stoned to death. Stephen saw Jesus in heaven, and as he was dying he asked Jesus to receive his spirit:

> But he, full of the Holy Spirit, gazed into heaven and saw the glory of God, and Jesus standing at the right hand of God. And he said, "Behold, I see the heavens opened, and the Son of Man standing at the right hand of God." . . . And as they were stoning Stephen, he called out, "Lord Jesus, receive my spirit." (Acts 7:55,56,59)[105]

Even though his body would soon lie in an earthly grave, Stephen knew he would soon be living in God's presence.

Both Paul and Peter knew they were immortal spirits who would continue to live on after they died. Paul told the Philippian congregation: "I am hard pressed between the two. My desire is to depart and be with Christ, for that is far better. But to remain in the flesh is more necessary on your account" (Philippians 1:23,24). Paul was body and spirit. But in this passage from Philippians, "I" is Paul's spirit, which would either remain *in* his earthly body or *leave* it and be with the Lord. Whether *in* the body or *separate* from it, Paul would remain the individual who lived and worked on earth at a particular point in time.

In even stronger terms, Peter compared his body to a temporary dwelling place, calling it "my tabernacle [his tent]" (2 Peter 1:13 KJV). Soon he would "put aside" the tent of his body and be with the Lord. He urged his readers to remember "after my departure" the things he had told them (2 Peter 1:13-15). Paul spoke about his death in the same way, as "my departure" (2 Timothy 4:6).

---

[105]Here Stephen uses the Greek word PNEUMA, "spirit," the equivalent of the Hebrew word RUACH.

Peter spoke about "the spirits in prison who disobeyed long ago when God waited patiently in the days of Noah" (1 Peter 3:19,20 NIV84). These were specific individuals who acted in a particular way at a certain point in history. They had been living in hell ever since they were killed and their bodies were destroyed in the flood.

Paul uses a very interesting way of speaking about what will happen when Jesus returns. In Colossians 3:4, Paul says, "When Christ who is your life appears, *then you also will appear with him* in glory." And he repeats that expression in 1 Thessalonians 4:14: "We believe that Jesus died and rose again, even so, through Jesus, *God will bring with* him those who have fallen asleep." When believers die, they continue to live in heaven with Jesus. If we die before Jesus comes, we ourselves will appear "with him" when he returns on the Last Day.

Paul could take it for granted that even unbelievers recognized that they are body and spirit. When he talked to people in Athens who worshiped idols, he told them that they were made alive—created body and spirit—by the one true God who "gives to all mankind life and breath and everything" (Acts 17:25).

3. Mankind was created in the image of God

Scripture tells us that God *created* mankind in his own image: "Let us make man in our image, after our likeness." This statement is immediately followed by the role God wanted mankind to play in his creation: "And let them have dominion over the fish of the sea and over the birds of the heavens and over the livestock and over all the earth and over every creeping thing that creeps on the earth" (Genesis 1:26). The close connection between these two statements likely links them. As creatures made in God's image, human beings were equipped to be God's fellow workers in caring for his creation.

But how did Adam and Eve's creation in the image of God enable them to serve God and rule over his creation? At this point we are tempted to make a list of qualities and characteristic that comprise the image of God. But we search Scripture in vain for such a list. Nor does Scripture even give us information that we could use to construct such a list.

Two passages of Scripture make points about mankind based on the fact that we were created in God's image. But neither tells us what makes up the image of God. After God gave mankind permission to kill animals for food, he warned them against concluding that they could take human life as well. God said, "Whoever sheds the blood of man, by man shall his blood be shed, for God made man in his own image" (Genesis 9:6). Human beings alone were created in God's image. Human beings are not to be considered animals.

James used our creation in God's image to issue a warning. He said that we know it is wrong to curse God, but we are perfectly willing to curse a fellow human being. James points out the irony of that: "With [our tongue] we bless our Lord and Father, and with it we curse people who are made in the likeness of God" (James 3:9). Note that both passages say that we were *made* in God's image.

Scripture does not give us a formal definition of God's image. Rather, it equates the image of God with the new person Christians become through faith in Christ, who has freed us from the curse of sin and death. In Ephesians 4:23,24 Paul urges God's people to "be made new in the attitude of your minds; and to put on the new self, created to be *like God* in true righteousness and holiness." When mankind fell into sin, they lost the ability to be "like God in true righteousness and holiness." As we put on the new self, we grow to become "like God" in that sense.

In a related passage, Paul reveals the close connection between the new people God has created us to be and the image he originally gave us. Paul says, "Put on the new self, which is being renewed in knowledge in the image of its Creator" (Colossians 3:10). Note the word "renewed." To be renewed in something means to reacquire something we once had but don't have anymore. In this verse Paul says that we are renewed in knowledge, the kind of knowledge Adam and Eve had about God when they were created.

Paul explains our renewal in knowledge like this:

> The god of this world has blinded the minds of the unbelievers, to keep them from seeing the light of the gospel of the glory of Christ, who is the image of God. . . . For God, who said, "Let light shine out of darkness," has shone in our hearts to give the light of the knowledge of the glory of God in the face of Jesus Christ. (2 Corinthians 4:4)

When God gives us "the knowledge of the glory of God in the face of Christ," we begin to see things correctly. We see the very image of God, the glory of his love and faithfulness in sending a Savior. The many passages in the New Testament that speak about the knowledge we regain as we put on God's image emphasize that Christ is at the center of all true knowledge. Paul prayed for the Colossians that their

> hearts may be encouraged, being knit together in love, to reach all the riches of full assurance of understanding and the knowledge of God's mystery, which is Christ, in whom are hidden all the treasures of wisdom and knowledge (Colossians 2:2,3).

Paul told the Romans about God's grace: "For those whom he foreknew he also predestined to be conformed to the image of his Son, in order that he might be the firstborn among many brothers" (Romans 8:29). As he guided the congregations he served, Paul expressed in concrete ways what it means to be renewed in the image of Christ and to live as his brothers and sisters:

> We have not ceased to pray for you, asking that you may be filled with the knowledge of his will in all spiritual wisdom and understanding, so as to walk in a manner worthy of the Lord, fully pleasing to him, bearing fruit in every good work and increasing in the knowledge of God. (Colossians 1:9-10)

Peter spoke in similar terms. God is restoring his image in us ("the divine nature") and giving us everything we need to escape the corruption of this world:

> His divine power has granted to us all things that pertain to life and godliness, through the knowledge of him who called us to his own glory and excellence, by which he has granted to us his precious and very great promises, so that through them you may become partakers of the divine nature, having escaped from the corruption that is in the world because of sinful desire. (2 Peter 1:3,4)

We also gain insight into the meaning of God's image by reflecting on what the Spirit of God, who lives in believers, enables us to do: "But the fruit of the Spirit is love, joy, peace, patience, kindness, goodness, faithfulness, gentleness, self-control" (Galatians 5:22,23).

At this point we are faced with a question. Do we still possess the image of God or have we lost it? If we define the image of God as the ability to serve God in righteousness and holiness, we must confess along with Scripture that when Adam and Eve sinned mankind lost God's image.[106] Paul wrote, "I know that nothing good dwells in me, that is, in my flesh" (Romans 7:18), and "The mind that is set on the flesh is hostile to God, for it does not submit to God's law; indeed, it cannot. Those who are in the flesh cannot please God" (Romans 8:7-8). On the other hand, God in speaking to Noah, and James in speaking to us, can be interpreted to say that we still possess the image of God. In both places we are told to respect all human life because all human beings have been created in the image of God. This question has been answered in various ways. Perhaps

---

[106] Note that when Moses made a record of the people who lived between Adam and Noah, he started the list with a reference to the image of God: "When God created man, he made him *in the likeness of God* . . . When Adam had lived 130 years, he fathered a son in *his own* likeness, after his image, and named him Seth" (Genesis 5:1,3). This gives us the impression that Adam did not simply pass down God's image through himself to his son, Seth. Rather, the contrast implies that Adam passed down to Seth a new sinful image he had "created" for himself when he sinned.

it is best simply to use Scripture's way of speaking: We have been created in the image of God. When we put on the new self in Christ, we are being renewed in the image of God, and leave it at that.

We might wish for more information from Scripture. But from what it tells us, we can draw the following conclusions: From the very beginning human beings have not belonged to the animal world. We were created in God's image; animals were not. This is in contrast to evolution, which says that we have all evolved from the same source and that there is no essential barrier between living creatures.

We also learn from Scripture that the image of God is not a list of qualities that might have gradually evolved over time. It is not a sense of morality that evolutionists claim developed over time. Rather, it is something God gave to Adam and Eve at the point when he created them.

The tendency to reduce the definition of the image of God to a list of individual qualities and characteristics surfaces in theistic evolutionary writings. Christian (and Jewish) scholars have offered many suggestions for what should be on that list. Included are qualities such as immortality; the ability to reason; the ability to speak; self-awareness; an awareness of God; the ability to show true, unselfish love; the knowledge of right and wrong; and others. It may, in fact, be that the image of God includes certain qualities and characteristics. But as noted above, Scripture does not list them. For that reason anyone's list is to some degree a matter of speculation.

Defining the image of God as a list of qualities, however, has this effect: It makes it easier for theistic evolutionists to envision God's image as something that evolved. It is no longer a single blessing given to mankind at a specific point in time, namely, when they were created. Rather, it becomes a group of special qualities and characteristics mankind acquired over the eons as they advanced beyond the rest of the animals. Since it cannot be determined which qualities and characteristics are part of God's image, this makes it easier to ignore the topic. In other words, the inability of theologians to agree on what should be on the list makes the image of God a somewhat nebulous concept, easy to dismiss or marginalize.

How Scripture relates mankind's creation in God's image makes it clear that this is one aspect of Scripture's history of the world from beginning to end, a major part of the story of perfection, fall, and restoration. It is incongruous with the theory of evolution. Any hint that we were created in God's image and at the same time had to play a role in the self-centered world of natural selection destroys the meaning of the image of God and of our renewal in Christ. Any hint that the image of God evolved in us through the freedom of choice afforded by evolution flies in the face of God's renewing sinners in his image through the power of the message of his grace in Christ.

4. Mankind was to care for God's creation

God intended ADAM (Scripture's word for human beings, including both Adam and Eve) to play a special role in the creation. When God proposed to create mankind he said, "Let us make man in our image, after our likeness." Immediately after he resolved to create mankind in his image, God went on to say, "And let them have dominion over the fish of the sea and over the birds of the heavens and over the livestock and over all the earth and over every creeping thing that creeps on the earth" (Genesis 1:26).

God said, "And let them have dominion." The Hebrew links the two clauses with a simple "and"—"*and* let them. . . ." The NIV11 translates the "and" a little differently: ". . . *so that* they may rule." This translation contains a bit of interpretation, but it expresses the idea that the image of God would enable mankind to rule his creation. The Lord gifted Adam and Eve with all the qualities and characteristics they needed "so that" they could fulfill the work God gave them. But because they bore his image and were able to serve God in true righteousness and holiness, they were able to use all these gifts perfectly, as God intended.

Obviously, this made them vastly different from the animals. We might put it like this: Animals belong to the class "living creatures." Mankind was also a living creature, but because they were created in God's own image, Adam and Eve also belonged to the class "creator." It's not that they created anything but they were like the one who did. They could care for God's creation with his authority, wisdom, and love.

The Lord used two words to describe mankind's role. First, they were to "have dominion," or rule, over the creation. This word can have a negative connotation, as it does in Moses' warning in Leviticus 25:46: "But you must not rule over your fellow Israelites ruthlessly" (NIV). But it can have a very positive connotation, in which one person rules over something for someone else's good. The psalmist exalts the coming great King of Israel: "May he have dominion from sea to sea, and from the River to the ends of the earth!" (Psalm 72:8).

The second word, "subdue," is used for conquering and subjecting another country, as the Israelites did when they subdued the land of Canaan (Joshua 18:1). It can also refer to the act of subduing another person and making that person a slave (Nehemiah 5:5). It is used in reference to God's love for his people: "He will again have compassion on us; he will tread [subdue] our iniquities underfoot. You will cast all our sins into the depths of the sea" (Micah 7:19).

In a sinful world, sin is usually involved somehow in the act of "ruling over" or "subduing" something. But that would not have been the case in a perfect world. Scripture does not elaborate on just how Adam and Eve would have ruled over this creation. But as we saw in chapter 3, Scripture reveals that God never wavers from his goal of blessing the creation. God always acts in perfect love, truth, and faithfulness toward what he has made. Since they were created in God's image, Adam and Eve would have shared God's intense love for the creation. They would have ruled over God's creation with the goal of doing what was best for it. They would have subdued it in perfect righteousness and holiness.

Mankind is unique among the living creatures God created

Before we turn to theistic evolution's views about the origin of mankind, we'll summarize what Scripture says about it.

Mankind and animals are both "living creatures." According to Scripture, however, human beings are unique. This is demonstrated in various ways. God did not simply command Adam and Eve to appear, as he did with the birds and fish. He did not simply command the earth to produce them, as he did when he created the animals. Like the land animals, mankind was created from the ground. But God did not create them in large numbers, as he did in the case of the animals. He formed a single individual, a man, from the dust of the ground. He then created a mate for the man, a woman, whom he created from Adam's rib. And the fact that Adam could not find a helper suitable for him from among the other living beings God had made, shows that there were no other human beings in existence when he was created. When God brought Adam and Eve together, Adam acknowledged, "This at last is bone of my bones and flesh of my flesh; she shall be called Woman, because she was taken out of Man" (Genesis 2:23).

God turned the form of a man created from inanimate soil into a living being by breathing into the man's nostrils his own divine breath. At that point Adam was now in possession of God's image. There was no lapse of time between when he became a living being and when he received God's image.

Nor was there a period of time between when Adam and Eve were given life and when they received their "souls." Adam's soul is our name for the spirit God gave Adam when he breathed life into him. Although Adam's spirit is referred to by the same term as the spirit of the animals, "living being," God created Adam to be a different category of living being. This is indicated by the use of the important Hebrew word BARA to introduce the creation of mankind, which sets mankind's creation apart from the creation of the animals.

Scripture makes it clear that mankind's spirit lives on after death, either apart from the Lord in hell or with the Lord in heaven. Someday, our spirit will be rejoined with our body. We are not told that about animals—nothing beyond the fact that when animals die, their spirit returns to God who gave it.

God planted two special trees that had implications only for mankind: the Tree of Life and the Tree of the Knowledge of Good and Evil. Adam and Eve were aware of their relation to their Creator, and they understood it would be morally wrong to go against the Creator's will.

Adam and Eve were put on earth for a special purpose. Mankind was to have dominion over the other living creatures that God had made and over the creation in general. Since they possessed God's image, they could fulfill this purpose.

Mankind alone was given the institution of marriage: "Therefore a man shall leave his father and his mother and hold fast to his wife, and they shall become one flesh" (Genesis 2:24). The method God used to create Adam and Eve united the entire human race. We alone know from whom we have descended: "The man called his wife's name Eve, because she was the mother of all living" (Genesis 3:20).

When Adam and Eve fell into sin, God promised to send a Savior from the woman to restore mankind's relationship with God (Genesis 3:15). In the new heavens and earth, animals will share in the blessings of this promise, but the promise was given to human beings alone.

Chapter Five

Who We Are According to Theistic Evolutionists

Sorting out the issues

Those who live on the "edges" of the debate have it easy. If you read Scripture in a straightforward way, you find your description of mankind's origin there. On the other hand, secular evolutionists describe mankind's origin and nature in line with secular evolution without concern for what Scripture says.

But theistic evolutionists have it harder. They must create a middle position. To more easily understand the difficulty of a middle position, we'll begin with a short description of what life is like on the edges.

Life on the edges

Those who accept Scripture as a literal account of Adam and Eve's creation believe this about human origins:

- God created a single human being, Adam. God created Adam's body from the dust of the ground. He then created Eve from Adam's body. Adam and Eve were complete human beings on the day they were created. They understood the institution of marriage. All human beings are physically descended from these two people.

- God brought Adam to life by breathing into Adam his own divine breath. Mankind, therefore, is a body and a spirit (soul). When the spirit leaves the body, the body ceases to live. A person's spirit continues to live on apart from that person's body, and someday the two will be reunited.

- Adam and Eve were created in God's image. They were created righteous and holy and given qualities and characteristics to carry out the role God gave them.

- Mankind was given the responsibility to rule over God's creation. Since Adam and Eve were created in God's image, they could care for God's creation with the same knowledge, wisdom, and love that God himself uses.

Those who accept *pure* Darwinism believe that

- Humans gradually developed over long periods of time through small random variations and the process of natural selection. Human beings are incomplete and are still evolving.

- Humans are comprised completely of matter. Whatever makes human beings "human" is a product of the evolution of matter. The concept of a "soul" separate from the body is an outdated theological idea inherited from Christianity. Humans are animals, just more highly developed. Mankind's creation in "the image of God" and their "original state of perfection" are also outdated Christian ideas.

- Human beings evolved through the same process of struggle and death as did all other living beings. They must compete for scarce resources like every other living thing. Human beings have no command or inherent right to rule over the rest of creation.

Life in the middle

Theistic evolutionists have chosen to walk a middle road. They must merge the sequence of Scripture—a finished and perfect world followed by a fall into sin that resulted in death—with the sequence required by evolution—an evolving world where evil and death have always existed. In chapter 3 we saw that their middle road required replacing Scripture's description of God as separate from evil and good in everything he does, with a description of God in which the meaning of the word *good* is modified and where God uses evil.

In this chapter we are examining the theistic evolutionists' struggle to merge Scripture's teaching on the origin of mankind with that demanded by evolution. Theistic evolutionists must answer this basic question: How did the earliest people, in light of the modern evolutionary interpretation of the fossil evidence, become human beings as they are defined in God's Word? Specifically:

- How did hominins[107]—the animal predecessors of human beings— evolve into human beings (as human beings are described in Genesis 1 and 2)?

- What does it mean that God gave human beings life by breathing his own life into them? How did mankind's spirit become immortal.

- What is the image of God? When did mankind receive God's image?

---

[107]The terms used in the scientific community have changed over the years. *Hominid* has been replaced by *hominin*, which we are using. Hominids are defined as all current and extinct great apes (humans, gorillas, orangutans, and chimpanzees), while hominins are any species of early human life that is more closely related to modern humans than chimpanzees, as well as modern humans themselves.

What does it mean to bear God's image in the context of the evils of natural selection?

- How can an evolving humanity exercise dominion over an evolving creation and subdue it?

Approaching the topic of mankind's origin[108]

Pastors will at times say this to a member struggling with evolution: "The Bible tells us *who* created the universe, but it doesn't tell us *how* he did it." In saying this, they invite their members to believe in evolution if they wish. But in reality they are forcing their members to do more. They are sending them out onto the middle road between Scripture and evolution that is littered with logical potholes and impossible challenges, which, as we will see, even those well versed in the issues find impossible to navigate. Among other things, they are forcing their members to come up with an alternate scenario on how they became human beings.

Variables, scientific and religious

Theistic evolutionists have created a wide range of scenarios to choose from. Their scenarios are based on two variables—(1) on their interpretation of the scientific data and (2) on their religious beliefs.

Scientific variables

The first set of variables is scientific. As theistic evolutionists try to create a scenario for the evolution of man, the only hard data they have at their disposal are: (1) fossil evidence, (2) tools and other objects left behind in locations where the fossils are found, and (3) some indication of the abilities these people had based on how they likely used these tools and objects.

Theistic evolutionists might give the impression that in regard to the fossils they are rallying around firm conclusions accepted by everyone in the scientific community. But this is not true. The scientific community has a range of interpretations of the data. What is more, scientists are continually modifying their own evolutionary scenarios as a result of new discoveries. Theistic evolutionists

---

[108] A note on where we are going: In the next chapter we will concentrate on issues relating to morality. How can Scripture and evolution be combined in regard to the meaning of right and wrong, sin, death, and judgment? And in the final chapter, we will concentrate on the heart of Christianity: How can Jesus' work of giving us freedom through the forgiveness of sins be defined in evolutionary terms?

must wrestle with which interpretations of the fossil evidence they want to use as their starting point.

But that is the easy part. Regardless of how one interprets the fossil evidence, fossils provide no physical evidence to point to a literal Adam and Eve, or even to a community of people who stood out because they had acquired special "human" qualities. Such qualities would have to include a uniquely human body, a human spirit, the image of God, and a God-given command to rule over the creation.

Religious variables

The second set of variables is religious. A theistic evolutionist's position on the origin of mankind is influenced by his or her religious background. Those who identify with liberal Christianity will find less in secular evolution to disagree with, which makes it easier for them to arrive at an evolutionary scenario of the origin of mankind. Topics such as the *soul* and the *image of God* can be relegated to outdated orthodox beliefs or inserted into the discussion with little attempt to define exactly what they are.

Those who accept Scripture's teachings of mankind's unique creation in the image of God, with a God-given command to rule over the creation, and the fall into sin, are more hard-pressed. Their scenarios may include ways in which God intervened in the evolution of hominins. They will speculate on the nature of this intervention and when it might have taken place. Some go so far as to confess that God created a literal Adam and Eve at some point midstream in the course of evolution, but then they struggle with the question of what happened to the hominins.

A theistic evolutionist's position will also be determined by their belief in the nature of Scripture. How much is he or she willing to abandon the belief that Scripture is inspired by God and must be interpreted in a straightforward way? As one reads theist evolutionary literature, it becomes clear that the question is not *if* one departs from a straightforward reading of Scripture—all theistic evolutionists must do that—but *how far* one is willing to go. Belief in evolution forces all theistic evolutionists to take a position on interpreting Scripture that gives them whatever leeway they feel is necessary to have Scripture support their chosen scenario. If you are interested in pursuing the topic of how theistic evolutionists use Scripture, please see the second volume in this set: *One More Elephant: Evolution Versus the Text of Scripture.*

One's opinions about the fossil evidence, one's religious stance—liberal or conservative—and one's approach to reading Scripture are the basic variables that result in the wide range of current theistic evolutionary scenarios of mankind's origin.

Two pitfalls to avoid

Before we look at the scenarios, it will be helpful to identify a couple of potential pitfalls to avoid if you read theistic evolutionary literature. The range of subjects and viewpoints is bewildering. The arguments are often little more than a string of speculation: "If" this is true, then we "might" conclude that such and such is the "likely" scenario. Readers are taken on a journey through the highways and byways of the scenarios suggested by other theistic evolutionists and the choices and compromises each has had to make in arriving at their position. Authors then lay out their own considerations, their reasons for choosing this or that scenario, and they often end with a caveat noting the problems even with the scenario they have chosen.

Here is the first pitfall: We, the readers, are naturally drawn into the debate. We evaluate the material on the author's terms and weigh the options along with them. For example, I might follow an author through the maze of possible solutions for how and when hominins received a human soul. As I read, I am almost unconsciously taking part in the debate. I find myself sympathetic to some of the author's assumptions but critical of others. After seriously working through the arguments, I might agree that the author's position is, in fact, the best option.

It is important always to keep the big picture in mind and keep the elephants in sight. The very act of discussing how hominins received a human soul requires that one accept some basic evolutionary assumptions and reject some of what Scripture says. It implies thinking in terms of the evolutionary structure of history and that competition and suffering have always been in existence. It implies that a loving God would, in fact, have created people through the process of evolution and that he is the source of the suffering involved in the process. Keeping the elephants in mind as we follow an author's evolutionary logic will help us avoid inadvertently being sucked into the debate and becoming too closely involved with its assumptions.

There is a second pitfall: The specialist nature of the creation/theistic evolution debate gives it an aura of complexity. It has been discussed in great detail for over three hundred years. It has been approached from various standpoints—from that of Scripture, of historical theology, philosophy, and of course, current scientific theories. The complexity of these discussions and the depth of knowledge necessary to engage in them make readers wonder if they will ever understand the issues, much less come to their own conclusions about them. Readers are tempted to give up thinking about theistic evolution completely. And that is a dangerous thing.

It is important to realize that coming to grips with the issues is not, as they say, rocket science. In chapter 2 we asked the basic question: How can the Bible's teaching about the history of the world (perfection, fall, restoration) be reconciled with evolution's teaching about the history of the world (suffering and death, no fall, and no restoration)? And in chapter 3 we boiled the issue down to the question: How can the Bible's teaching of God's love be reconciled with the idea that God created a process that relies on competition, suffering, and death? These are simple questions that require little or no technical knowledge of Scripture or of the process of evolution.

Before you continue reading about the origin of mankind, stop here and try your hand at boiling down the debate to a few simple questions. Make a list of what you think theistic evolutionists must answer to merge successfully Scripture and evolution on the origin of mankind. You might think that your questions are too "commonsense" to be worthy of discussion. Don't worry about that. It is the basic, commonsense, "gut-level" questions that must be kept in mind and answered as you move through this topic. Are theistic evolutionists successfully dealing with the important questions, or are they simply ignoring them as they move on to the next question?

As you continue to read, you will find that the theologians, philosophers, and scientists who are writing theistic evolutionary books are wrestling with some of the basic questions on your list. Trust your instinct. If an author does not satisfy you—if they simply let the elephants walk around the room—you have a right to question their thoroughness and to judge their success in completing the theistic evolutionary task.

The spectrum of scenarios for the origin of mankind

Theistic evolutionists offer a variety of scenarios to choose from. Some scenarios better reflect the theory of evolution, while others include more of what Scripture tells us about the origin of mankind. But regardless of which position a theistic evolutionist takes, his or her scenario must include answers to three questions.

(1) How did mankind come into being? Secular evolutionists believe in "reductionism." Reductionism is the claim that the existence of all living things, including mankind, can be explained by (or *reduced* to) the laws of physics and chemistry. God is nowhere in the picture. *Scripture* teaches the opposite, namely, that everything came into being because God told it to come into being. He organized the matter he created, and he sustains all things through the power of his Word.

Theistic evolutionists must answer: Can mankind's origin be reduced to natural laws? Or did God create mankind full-blown in his own image with a special responsibility toward the creatures around them?

(2) Who were the first humans? Secular evolutionists believe that mankind evolved en masse as members of various hominin species, culminating in present-day *homo sapiens*.[109] *Scripture* teaches that all human beings descended from a single pair of people specially created by God: Adam and Eve.

Theistic evolutionists must take a position on questions like these: Were Adam and Eve literal people? Or were they merely symbols of humanity in general? Or might they have represented a small population that God made into human beings? If so, when did God create them and what happened to hominins or the other human beings living around them?

(3) What does it mean to be human? Secular evolutionists teach that a human being is a single unit, without any division of spirit and body. Everything we are—our physical makeup, our ability to think, our self-awareness, and our ability to communicate—emerged through natural laws operating in the process of evolution. This is called the "monistic" position (*mono* means "single").

Scripture on the other hand teaches that in a single act, God created Adam from the dust of the earth, personally gave him life with his own divine breath, and created him in his own image. Mankind was created with two "parts:" a body and a spirit (soul). And the spirit is able to live apart from the body. This is called the "dualistic" position.

Theistic evolutionists must answer: Did God create a single pair that had a body and a spirit? If so, how can this have happened if people evolved? Or did hominins become human beings through a gradual development of human qualities and characteristics over a long period of time through the process of evolution. Which is it? This should be approached as an either/or question with no middle position.

But some adopt a middle position. They suggest that when hominins had evolved to a certain point, God chose two of them or perhaps a small group, and "upgraded" them into human beings as we find them in Genesis 1 and 2.

To blur the boundary line even more, belief in a human soul is presently being lost in historically conservative circles just as it was lost some time ago in liberal churches.[110] What makes it even more complex is that some see the denial of the human soul as affecting the core beliefs of Christianity, while others don't consider it a problem. To liberals, the denial of the soul has little

---

[109] Evolutionists debate whether the various races of human life evolved at the same time in different parts of the world. This is called "polygenesis," which means "origin from many." Or, did mankind evolve from a single population located at a specific place on earth, which then spread out into the world and displaced the other evolving hominin populations? The latter option is more popular today, with the original population thought to have been located in Africa. This is referred to as "monogenesis," or origin from one ("mono") source.

[110] Gheorghe Razmerita, *Theistic Evolution's Struggle for Survival*, p. 150.

affect on their theology. But today, even some in the conservative camp deny the existence of the soul but still claim that their brand of Christianity can be labeled conservative.[111]

A closer look at a number of scenarios[112]

Gheorghe Razmerita describes the two basic options we outlined above: The first is that the creation of humans required "direct interventions of God." By contrast, the second is that "life and human consciousness have emerged out of the evolutionary processes themselves."[113]

Robert Yarbrough describes the general trend today: "The assumption that Adam was an actual historical figure persisted largely unchallenged in the Christian West until the development of modern literary criticism and the rise of biological evolution."[114] He observes, "What is perhaps surprising is that even evangelicals are increasingly losing faith in these classical doctrines. They are looking for new ways to make sense of Adam in Scripture."[115]

William VanDoodewaard organizes theistic evolutionary scenarios into three groups:[116] First, some believe that God at some point in human evolution *gave a soul* to the first couple, Adam and Eve. This took place between 10,000 and 15,000 B.C. (The author notes that this would rule out the inclusion of the Australian aborigines in the human race because their origin is dated to about 40,000 B.C.)

Second, some believe that hominins became human beings because God *established a relationship* with an initial pair or a group of hominins by making

---

[111]Gheorghe Razmerita, *Theistic Evolution's Struggle for Survival.* He includes C. S. Lewis, Derek Kidner, John Stott, and R. J. Berry in this group.

[112]For descriptions of various theistic evolutionary descriptions of the origin of mankind, see Gheorghe Razmerita, *Theistic Evolution's Struggle for Survival.* Razmerita is a Seventh-Day Adventist who rejects the body/soul makeup of human beings. In the context of his belief about the soul, his book attempts to show that dual anthropology (human beings are made up of a body *and a soul*) does not solve the problems inherent in all theistic evolutionary systems, and we agree with his conclusion. He divides the scenarios into those that teach dual anthropology and those that accept a monistic position on the makeup of human beings. His description of the various positions is excellent, and he offers a large number of quotations from primary resources. Also see Gerald Rau, *Mapping the Origins Debate.* He charts the various positions on pp. 35-52 with extended charts on pages 194-205.

[113]Gheorghe Razmerita, *Theistic Evolution's Struggle for Survival.* p. 10.

[114]Robert Yarbrough, "Adam in the New Testament," in *Adam, the Fall, and Original Sin,* ed. Hans Madueme and Michael Reeves (Grand Rapids: Baker, 2014), p. 38.

[115]Hans Madueme and Michael Reeves, ed. *Adam, the Fall, and Original Sin,* p. vii.

[116]William VanDoodewaard, *The Quest for the Historical Adam: Genesis, Hermeneutics, and Human Origins* (Grand Rapids: Reformation Heritage Books, 2015), loc. 7146-7167, Kindle.

them conscious that he exists or by giving them some form of spiritual life. These special hominins provided a link between God and the rest of the hominin population. This new spiritual life may also be called the "image of God." All other human qualities are the result of evolution.

Third, there are those who believe that "Adam and Eve" are merely mythological beings that symbolize all humanity. At some point early in human history, perhaps as early as 150,000 years ago, *God began revealing himself* to large groups of hominins. In this view the "soul" and "image of God" are strictly products of evolution.

Even as VanDoodewaard describes these scenarios, he admits that the attempt is challenging because of "the diversity and fluidity of views." A theistic evolutionist "can easily float between these or other variations." [117]

The following quotations will provide you with a sample of what theistic evolutionists are saying. This is not a list of all possible scenarios, but it will illustrate the range of positions theistic evolutionists are taking. We will start at the more conservative end of the spectrum and work toward the more liberal end.

C. John Collins

C. John Collins' conclusion is a good example of a scenario built on a more conservative theistic evolutionary base. Collins is a professor at Covenant Seminary, the denominational seminary of the Presbyterian Church in America. The theology of Covenant Seminary is based on the Westminster Confession of Faith, which teaches a literal six-day creation. Collins has written a number of books, including a scholarly commentary on Genesis 1-4. We will refer to his book *Did Adam and Eve Really Exist?: Who They Were and Why You Should Care.*

Collins goes further than others in laying out the questions he worked through before he came to his conclusion. This, along with his historically conservative teaching environment, makes his book a good case study of the issues theistic evolutionists in the Evangelical world face when treating the topic of the origin of mankind.

Collins' conclusion is that we should, in fact, care whether or not Adam and Eve existed. Collins points out that the framework of Scripture—a perfect world corrupted by an "alien invader" from the outside—can only be understood in the context of the fall of Adam and Eve. What's more, God's promise of forgiveness and restoration for all people can be understood only if we are descendants of a common ancestor.[118]

---

[117] William VanDoodewaard, *The Quest for the Historical Adam*, loc. 7140.

[118] C. John Collins, *Did Adam and Eve Really Exist?*, p. 134.

Yet Collins accepts evolution. He wants to reconcile what we learn from the human fossil evidence with the origin of human beings according to Scripture—"to explore how the traditional position [regarding Adam and Eve] might relate to questions of paleoanthropology."[119] Collins explores the questions in a logical order.

He begins with Scripture. Not all the details of Scripture's account of the origin of mankind need to be taken literally. Scripture, he says, is more concerned with a "worldview" than a "world picture." By this he means that Scripture is more interested in creating the *stance* we must take to properly understand ourselves and our world rather than in relating the *facts of history*.[120] According to Collins, the purpose of Scripture is to reveal a worldview that we can all identify with, namely—our sense of frustration with the condition of the present world and the feeling that we have lost something. Genesis 1-3 "provides the best explanation for our lives now and for our hunger for things to be better."[121]

Collins' view is that the author of Genesis "was talking about what *he thought* were actual events, using rhetorical and literary techniques to shape the readers' attitudes toward those events."[122] The New Testament authors followed suit: "Hence it is fair to say that the Gospel writers portray Jesus as someone *who believed* both that Adam and Eve were actual people, and that their disobedience changed things for us their descendants."[123]

Once Collins has dismissed a strictly literal reading of Genesis 1-3 and has established his principles for interpreting Scripture, he can begin explaining his position on Adam and Eve. His conclusion is that Adam and Eve were real people. He comes to this conclusion not because a straightforward reading of Scripture requires it, but because he believes the "worldview" of Scripture requires it: Adam and Eve's fall into sin resonates well with the frustrations and longings we all experience.

In discussing the image of God and the human soul, Collins points out that some of God's characteristics described in Genesis 1 and 2 might be included in a definition of his image. Among them are intelligence, language, the appreciation of moral and aesthetic goodness, the cycle of work and rest, and the ability to establish relationships based on love and commitment.[124] Collins softens Scrip-

---

[119]C. John Collins, *Did Adam and Eve Really Exist?*, p. 14.

[120]C. John Collins, *Did Adam and Eve Really Exist?*, p. 134. He explains this position in the first chapter titled "The Shape of the Biblical Story."

[121]C. John Collins, *Did Adam and Eve Really Exist?*, p. 104.

[122]C. John Collins, *Did Adam and Eve Really Exist?*, p. 16 (emphasis added).

[123]C. John Collins, *Did Adam and Eve Really Exist?*, p. 78 (emphasis added).

[124]C. John Collins, *Did Adam and Eve Really Exist?*, pp. 94,95.

ture's teaching on the soul. He admits that Scripture speaks about a "body-soul dualism" but not the kind in which there is an "easy separability of these two elements."[125] Collins nevertheless contends that "the Bible's treatment of [the image of God and the soul] takes for granted some kind of common origin of all human beings in Adam."[126]

Scripture, however, does not provide enough information to answer how Adam and Eve fit into the evolution of mankind. It does not tell us when Adam and Eve lived and what might have been their relation to the hominins living around them. Since Collins accepts evolution, he turns to evolutionary science for help in determining the answers to those questions. Chapter 5 of his book is entitled "Can Science Help Us Pinpoint 'Adam and Eve'?"

Collins first establishes his criteria for keeping speculation from getting out of hand, "to keep the reasoning within the bounds of sound thinking."[127] Before Collins reveals his own conclusion, he describes a number of scenarios suggested by others, using his criteria to evaluate them. Collins' list will give us a feel for the variety of scenarios suggested by theistic evolutionists. The list below is my summary of Collins' descriptions. Additional information can be found in the footnotes.[128]

- Some believe that Adam and Eve were the first members of the genus *Homo*. In evolutionary classification, the genus *Homo* includes a number of species that are now extinct. The only remaining species is *Homo sapiens*, which is the name given to modern humans. But since the first *Homo* is dated at two million years ago, Collins observes, "this leaves a very long time without any specific cultural remains in the paleontological record."[129]

- The first human beings did not come from preexisting hominins. God created Adam and Eve as unique individuals between 70,000 and 50,000 years ago. From them came all human population groups presently existing throughout the world.[130]

---

[125]C. John Collins, *Did Adam and Eve Really Exist?*, p. 95.

[126]C. John Collins, *Did Adam and Eve Really Exist?*, p. 93.

[127]C. John Collins, *Did Adam and Eve Really Exist?*, p. 130.

[128]C. John Collins, *Did Adam and Eve Really Exist?*, pp 122ff. The scenarios are listed in the order Collins lists them.

[129]Collins attributes this observation, not the view itself, to some young-earth creationists and some old-earth creationists, p. 122.

[130]This is the view of the group Reasons to Believe. They teach a series of hominin iterations, each species going extinct and then replaced by God with another. This climaxed in God's creation of Adam and Eve, from whom all humans are descended. They argue that DNA studies

- Around 45,000 B.C., God chose two existing hominins. He gave one of them new genetic information. He then took that information and imparted it to another by using the rib of the first. The human race descended from these two. Collins quotes Gavin McGrath: "God took two hominids to become the first human beings, Adam and Eve (1 Tim. 2:13). In Eve's case, God provided the new genetic information needed to make her human by using some genetic material taken from 'one of' Adam's 'ribs' . . . and these two *alone* are the rest of the human race's progenitors."[131]

- The Adam of Genesis 2-4 was a Neolithic farmer living in the Near East about 10,000 B.C. He and the hominins around him had taken on additional qualities that raised them to the status of *Homo divinus*, "if we may so style Adam." Yet it is difficult to say when the pre-Adamic *Homo sapiens* took on these additional qualities.[132]

- God created an initial pair in his image and gave them headship over the other human beings then in existence (to whom he had also imparted his image). By doing this, he separated human beings from

---

affirm that human beings come from a small group of individuals. This small group, they claim, are the descendants of Adam and Eve.

[131] C. John Collins, *Did Adam and Eve Really Exist?*, p. 123, quoting from Gavin Basil McGrath, "Soteriology: Adam and the Fall," in *Perspectives on Science and Christian Faith* 49:4 (1997), pp. 252-263 (emphasis author's). C. John Collins, *Did Adam and Eve Really Exist?*, p. 95. This position separates Adam and Eve from the animal hominids and creates a scenario where the biblical fall into sin could have taken place..

[132] This position is that of John Stott. He starts with God's command to Adam to care for the garden. Here is a longer quotation from Stott's commentary on Romans:

Adam, then, was a special creation of God, whether God formed him literally "from the dust of the ground" and then "breathed into his nostrils the breath of life," or whether this is the biblical way of saying that he was created out of an already existing hominid. The vital truth we cannot surrender is that, though our bodies are related to the primates, we ourselves in our fundamental identity are related to God.

[In the next paragraph, Stott addresses the question of the hominins who were in existence when God made Adam and Eve:]

What then about those pre-Adamic hominids which had survived natural calamity and disaster (as large numbers did not), had dispersed to other continents, and were now Adam's contemporaries? How did Adam's special creation and subsequent fall relate to them? Derek Kidner suggests that, once it became clear that there was "no natural bridge from animal to man, God may have now conferred his image on Adam's collaterals, to bring them into the same realm of being. Adam's 'federal' headship of humanity extended, if that was the case, outwards to his contemporaries as well as onward to his offspring, and his disobedience disinherited both alike."

From John Stott, *The Message of Romans*, (Downers Grove, IL: InterVarsity Press, 1994), pp. 164-165. Stott is quoting Derek Kidner, *Genesis*, Tyndale OT Commentary (Downers Grove, IL: InterVarsity Press, 1967), p. 30.

the animals. He established a solidarity between the first pair and the other human beings in existence. Because of this solidarity, when Adam fell into sin, all fell into sin with him and were disinherited by God. Adam's sin did not pass down only through physical descent but because of the solidarity of this initial group.[133]

- There was never a time when God made a change in the hominin population. God merely chose a pair of people, or perhaps a group of people, out of a Neolithic farming community and graciously revealed himself to them. They were the first to have a relationship with God. While they should have shared this knowledge with others, they chose to sin and to influence others around them to sin.[134]

- Over eons of time God perfected the animal form that would become human beings. When these beings were ready, God gave them spiritual blessings—self-consciousness, the knowledge of God, the

---

[133]C. John Collins, *Did Adam and Eve Really Exist?*, pp. 124-125. This is Derek Kidner's suggestion, with which Kidner himself finds problems. Collins faults Kidner on two points. The position "is moving us away from the simplicity of the Biblical picture." And although it preserves the unity of mankind, "solidarity in the Bible is not based on legal fiction but on some actual connection." See more about Kidner in a section below.

[134]C. John Collins, *Did Adam and Eve Really Exist?*, pp. 125-128. Here Collins describes Denis Alexanders position. In his book Alexander describes five scenarios for the origin of mankind and their relationship to God. His position (based on Alexander's contention that one of his suggestions, model C, contains the most detailed description) is what Collins is describing above. (See Denis Alexander, *Creation or Evolution*, pp. 234-240 with his evaluation on pp. 240-243.)

Alexander says that after God revealed himself to mankind,

The "man" is therefore viewed as the federal head of the whole of humanity alive at that time. This was the moment at which God decided to start his new spiritual family on earth, consisting of all those who put their trust in God by faith, expressed in obedience to his will. Adam and Eve, in this view, were real people, living in a particular historical era and geographical location, chosen by God to be the representatives of his new humanity on earth, not by virtue of anything that they had done, but simply by God's grace. When Adam recognized Eve as "bone of my bones and flesh of my flesh," he was not just recognizing a fellow *Homo sapiens*—there were plenty of those around—but a fellow believer, one like him who had been called to share in the very life of God in obedience to his commands. The world population in Neolithic times is estimated to lie in the range 1-10 million, genetically just like Adam and Eve, but in model C it was these two farmers out of all those millions to whom God chose to reveal himself. . . .

The text of Genesis 1 makes clear that the whole of humankind without any exception is made in God's image, including certainly all the other millions of people alive in the world in Neolithic times and since. Model C suggests that it was through God's revelation to Adam and Eve that the understanding of what that image actually meant, in practice, was made apparent to them. . . .

So with his model C, the idea is that following on from God's initiative in the lives of Adam and Eve, the way is opened up for any person anywhere in the world to enter God's new international family on earth.

(Denis Alexander, *Creation or Evolution*, pp. 236-239, emphasis added)

ability to make determinations about truth and beauty. But these beings rebelled against God.[135]

Collins concludes this chapter with the admission that these scenarios "leave us with many uncertainties."[136] Collins then gives his own position: "Nothing requires us to abandon monogenesis altogether for some form of polygenesis; rather, a *modified monogenesis*, which keeps Adam and Eve, can do the job."[137] Trying to live in the middle is a messy business. Positing a "modified monogenesis" is an example of this. *Polygenesis* ("a beginning through many") refers to the idea that human beings are descended from more than one ancestor. *Monogenesis* ("a beginning through one") is the scriptural teaching that all human beings have descended from a single pair of people and that Eve was, in fact, "the mother of all living" (Genesis 3:20). If Scripture's teaching of monogenesis is *modified*, that would seem to result in a form of polygenesis. In another book Collins says, "I find it easier to believe that Adam was a fresh creation rather than an

---

[135]C. John Collins, *Did Adam and Eve Really Exist?*, pp. 128-130. This is C.S. Lewis' scenario. See chapter 5 in C.S. Lewis, *The Problem of Pain*, "The Fall of Man." Lewis introduces his scenario for the origin of mankind in these words:

What exactly happened when Man fell, we do not know; but if it is legitimate to guess, I offer the following picture—a "myth" in the Socratic sense, a not unlikely tale.

For long centuries God perfected the animal form which was to become the vehicle of humanity and the image of Himself. He gave it hands whose thumb could be applied to each of the fingers, and jaws and teeth and throat capable of articulation, and a brain sufficiently complex to execute all the material motions whereby rational thought is incarnated. The creature may have existed for ages in this state before it became man: it may even have been clever enough to make things which a modern archaeologist would accept as proof of its humanity. But it was only an animal because all its physical and psychical processes were directed to purely material and natural ends. Then, in the fullness of time, God caused to descend upon this organism, both on its psychology and physiology, a new kind of consciousness which could say "I" and "me," which could look upon itself as an object, which knew God, which could make judgments of truth, beauty, and goodness, and which was so far above time that it could perceive time flowing past (pp. 72,73).

In perfect cyclic movement, being, power and joy descended from God to man in the form of gift and returned from man to God in the form of obedient love and ecstatic adoration. . . . (p. 74).

[136]C. John Collins, *Did Adam and Eve Really Exist?*, p. 131. Other authors present similar lists of options. For example, see James Hurd, "Hominids in the Garden? in *Perspectives on an Evolving Creation*, ed. Keith B. Miller, pp. 222 ff. and Denis Alexander, *Creation or Evolution: Do We Have to Choose?*, p. 233.

[137]C. John Collins, *Did Adam and Eve Really Exist?*, p. 130 (emphasis added). In secular evolutionary literature, polygenesis means that all humans evolved simultaneously within the worldwide hominin population. Monogenesis means that all humans evolved from a small group of hominins living together in a certain place. This is different from how the terms are used in the creation/evolution debate, where monogenesis is the teaching that all human beings descended from one couple, Adam and Eve, and polygenesis is the idea that all human beings evolved from a small group.

upgrade of an existing model."[138] This seems to be a confession of monogenesis. Regardless, in the book we are referring to here, Collins believes that a modified monogenesis "can do the job."[139] Evidently he means doing the job of not allowing evolution to destroy Scripture's worldview and Adam and Eve's place in it.

Collins' retention of Adam and Eve in his theistic evolutionary scenario might be considered a confession of biblical authority. He encourages his readers to wrestle with the issues: "Even so, we must decide whether we accept the authority of Jesus; and that includes his right to have people like Moses, Paul, and John as his authorized messengers, who show us how to interpret the redemptive story."[140] Collins answers in the affirmative. If the Christian message is to remain intact, "it seems to me that Adam and Eve at the headwaters of the human family, and their fall, are not only what Jesus believed but also an irremovable part of that whole story."[141]

Yet Collins goes no further than to offer his personal option—"it seems to me"—that Adam and Eve are a necessary part of the story and that this is what "Jesus believed"—which is different than saying that Jesus knew it to be true.

Derek Kidner

In his commentary on Genesis, Derek Kidner points out that Christians are faced with two stories of the origin of mankind. One is recorded in Genesis. The other is recorded in the fossil evidence. The latter story begins about a million years ago and ends roughly 20,000 years ago. How the two stories can be reconciled is not clear. Christians should realize the provisional nature of both the fossil evidence and the standard interpretation of Genesis.

According to paleontologists, by 20,000 B.C. humans "had already spread widely over the world, displacing another type of hominid, 'Neanderthal Man,' whose own relics, rough as they are, indicate that tools, fire and burial had been in use for long ages before this."[142] According to Scripture, however, mankind came into being "by God's image and breath, nothing less." All humanity descended from Adam, who is listed with other human beings who lived relatively recently. Genesis is not written as myth. Scriptural evidence points to a date for Adam of eight to ten thousand years ago.

---

[138] C. John Collins, *Science and Faith?* (Wheaton: Crossway, 2003), p. 269, Kindle.

[139] C. John Collins, *Did Adam and Eve Really Exist?*, p. 130.

[140] C. John Collins, *Did Adam and Eve Really Exist?* pp. 134,135.

[141] C. John Collins, *Did Adam and Eve Really Exist?* p. 135.

[142] Derek Kidner, *Genesis*, pp. 28,29. This is my paraphrase of Kidner's thinking, which is taken from pp. 28-33.

Kidner suggests that perhaps the difference between science and Scripture lies in how each defines "man." On the basis of the fossil and artifact evidence (tools, painting, etc.), paleontologists believe mankind is very old. Scripture teaches that the first humans are of much more recent origin. So how should the two stories be reconciled? Kidner goes back and forth as he strives to give an answer. Assuming that God made Adam out of a hominin, Kidner writes,

> If . . . God initially shaped man by a process of evolution, it would follow that a considerable stock of near-humans preceded the first true man, and it would be arbitrary to picture these as mindless brutes. Nothing requires that the creature into which God breathed human life should not have been of a species prepared in every way for humanity, with already a long history of practical intelligence, artistic sensibility and the capacity for awe and reflection.[143]

If this was true, after Adam was created there should have been a mixed population. Kidner explains, "On this view, Adam, the first true man, will have had as contemporaries many creatures of comparable intelligence, widely distributed over the world."[144] Adam would have shared the same genetic makeup of the hominins around him. However, when all the other creatures were brought before Adam, he found no one suitable to be his helper. Only after the creation of Eve did Adam find a helper.

So where did these hominins go? They might have been destined to die out after the arrival of Adam as the Neanderthals did. Or, they might have been lost in the flood, leaving only Noah's family. Kidner offers another suggestion. It is at least conceivable that when Adam and Eve were created, God bestowed his image on the hominins living around them. God then made Adam the head of the human race, not in the sense that all humans descended from Adam, but in the sense that Adam was their "federal" head, like the president of a country is the head of its citizens and at times represents them or speaks for them. In this view Adam's sin had a negative effect on the hominins living alongside him, and this effect was passed along to the descendants of these hominins as well as to Adam and Eve's physical descendants. In this way the unity of the human race, even if not its actual physical unity, is preserved. In support of this, Kidner notes that the large group of people already in existence at the time of Cain may have been the hominins who were already alive when God created Adam and Eve. Kidner says he can go along with the traditional answer as to where these people came from, namely that they were Adam and Eve's offspring, but it might

---

[143] Derek Kidner, *Genesis*, p. 31.

[144] Derek Kidner, *Genesis*, p. 31.

be time to reevaluate that position. Kidner admits that this whole scenario is "only tentative"; nevertheless, it is his "personal view."[145]

I wanted to relate Kidner's explanation in some detail. Not every theistic evolutionist seems willing to ask the obvious questions as Kidner does and then build a scenario that takes these questions into account—and then finally admit that it is tentative. All theistic evolutionists should do what Kidner does. They should at least try to answer the questions, construct their own scenarios, and then let their people watch them admit that it is all tentative. Anything less is sticking one's head in the sand and avoiding the obvious.

John Polkinghorne

How might God have changed hominins into human beings like Adam and Eve? Where did the human spirit or soul come from? And how can Scripture's statements about the immortal nature of the human soul fit into the scenarios? The teaching of evolution makes it difficult, if not impossible, even to speculate about these matters.

Likely because of these difficulties, it is becoming more popular simply to reject the Scripture's teaching of the soul and argue that human beings are a unity, nothing more than a unique outcome of chemistry and physics at work in the process of evolution.

John Polkinghorne, an influential scientist and Anglican priest, is a proponent of that idea. He claims that what makes a person *human* arises "not from the injection of something extra from the outside, but from the effects of greater complexity on the inside."[146] Rejecting any idea that God created human beings with a soul, he argues, "If we accept that there are now spiritually conscious human beings, and that there was a time in the past when there were none, then there must have been a time when this property first emerged in humanity."[147]

But what exactly is this emergent property? Polkinghorne writes,

> Clearly, consciousness is possessed by some of the higher animals, but it seems likely that the further power of self-consciousness, with its concomitant ability to form expectations and plans for the future, only dawned with the evolution of the hominid lines leading eventually to *Homo sapiens*. As that self-awareness developed, I suppose that a corre-

---

[145] Derek Kidner, *Genesis*, p. 33.

[146] Quoted in Gheorghe Razmerita, *Theistic Evolution's Struggle for Survival*, p. 97, from John Polkinghorne, *Quarks, Chaos, and Christianity: Questions to Science and Religion* (London: SPCK, 1988).

[147] John Polkinghorne and Nicholas Beale, *Questions of Truth*, p. 71.

sponding spiritual awareness of the presence of God also became part of the experience of these living beings.[148]

Since there is no "detachable spiritual component" and that we are nothing but atoms that are gradually being replaced over time,

> What gives continuity are not the atoms themselves but the almost infinitely complex information-bearing pattern in which they are organized. *The essence of this pattern is the soul.* It will dissolve at death with the decay of the body, but it is a perfectly coherent belief that the faithful God will not allow it to be lost but will preserve it in the divine memory. Thus the ultimate Christian hope is resurrection, God's great eschatological act of the re-embodiment of information-bearing pattern in the environment of the new creation.[149]

The Roman Catholic position

Polkinghorne is an example of a liberal theologian interacting with Scripture's teaching of the human soul. The Roman Catholic Church provides another example. In the first half of the 20th century, some in the Catholic Church had already been working out a system of theistic evolution in which human bodies had evolved.[150] In 1950 Pope Pius XII proclaimed, "If the human body takes its origin from pre-existing living matter, the spiritual soul is immediately created by God."[151] Pius XII was protecting the teaching that human beings have both a body and a soul. The body may have evolved, but every human being has a soul created by God.

Between 1950 and today, the teaching of a soul has largely disappeared from the Catholic Church. It is still an official teaching of the Catholic Church, but it is largely ignored. A Catholic conservative today would likely teach in line with Pius XII's 1950 position. But the church has felt the influence of liberal views.

An article on the Internet contains this comment: "Over recent decades the overwhelmingly dominant view in Catholic academic and educational circles has been heavily weighted against the traditional account of body and soul. In

---

[148] Quoted in Gheorghe Razmerita, *Theistic Evolution's Struggle for Survival,* p. 96, from John Polkinghorne, *Belief in God in an Age of Science* (New Haven, London: Yale University Press 1998), p. 89.

[149] John Polkinghorne and Nicholas Beale, *Questions of Truth,* pp. 22,23 (emphasis added).

[150] See Razmerita's introduction to the theistic evolution of Catholic theologian Ernest Charles Messenger (1888–1951). Gheorghe Razmerita, *Theistic Evolution's Struggle for Survival,* pp. 19-28.

[151] *Humani Generis,* August 12, 1950.

fact any form of 'dualism' with regard to the constitution of human nature has frequently been sneered at as philosophically dated and theologically distasteful."[152] Curtis Jahn, author of *A Lutheran Looks at Catholics*, said that "'soul' is still officially on the books. It is acknowledged by conservatives and largely ignored by liberals. Of course, the adaptation of modern higher critical views of the Bible and of evolution also plays a huge part in this 'development' in Catholic teaching."[153]

"Whatever Happened to the Soul?"

This is the title of a book initiated by several professors from Fuller Theological Seminary. Fuller began as a mainstream Evangelical seminary in 1947. It was built on a conservative foundation (Billy Graham was a member of the board of trustees from 1959 to 1968). It has three schools: the school of theology, the school of psychology, and the school of missions, now called the school of inter-cultural studies. In the late 1990s, faculty members from the schools of theology and psychology began work on a book of essays on the human soul. Ten authors contributed to this book, four of whom were faculty members at Fuller Seminary.

The authors' views on the soul are indistinguishable from the liberal view. They believe that there is no such thing as a human soul and that belief in body/soul dualism is no longer valid in the modern world. Rather, qualities one author calls "soulish" have emerged in human beings during the course of their evolution.

The authors call their position "non-reductive physicalism." This technical sounding term is not too difficult to unpack. "Physicalism" simply means that the human body is nothing more than the physical matter it is made up of. This is essentially the same as what secular evolutionists teach, but with a difference. The difference lies in the word "non-reductive." Secular evolution teaches "reductive physicalism," which means that everything that makes up a human being can be broken down in terms of chemistry and physics. That is, it can be "reduced"

---

[152] https://www.faith.org.uk/article/march-april-2008-body-and-soul-renewing-catholic-orthodoxy. (accessed Nov. 2019)

[153] Personal correspondence with Curt Jahn, author of *A Lutheran Looks at Catholics* (Milwaukee: Northwestern Publishing House, 2014). Jahn notes that Richard McBrien's (liberal) massive (1350 pp.) book *Catholicism* has only a few references in the subject index to "soul." In his hundred-page discussion of "The State of Human Existence" and "The Theology of Human Existence," McBrien includes only a couple of sentences on "dualism," in which he rejects it. He says rather that man *is* body and soul and doesn't go into any more detail as to what that means. Modern Catholicism seems to be heavily influenced by modern materialistic views of psychology, which disavows any existence of the soul (a little ironic, Jahn says, when you think that "psychology" literally means "study of the soul").

to how atoms and molecules interact. "Non-reductive" physicalism differs from this in one way, namely, it contains the idea that as creatures evolve,they become greater than the sum of their parts.

The claim is this: At a certain point in the process of evolution, human brain capacity became large enough to support thinking complex enough to give rise to a group of higher level qualities. The combination of these qualities is what Christians have formerly attributed to the soul. Among these qualities are the ability to be aware of ourselves, to communicate, to reason, and to interrelate with fellow human beings. Included is an awareness of God and a corresponding "spiritual" nature.

Ray Anderson expresses the idea in theological terms: "The human soul is not an immortal substance encased in a mortal body. The life of the person (soul) emerges simultaneously with the bodily form of human existence. Human life has no existence independent of a body."[154] Warren Brown summarizes this idea in evolutionary terms: "A relatively small but critical change in physiology (i.e., the development of a large and complex cerebral cortex) results in the emergence of rather massive differences in human behavior that are evident in the development of culture (language, literature, art, science, technology, moral/ethical sensitivities, and religion)."[155]

Once the human species had arrived at that point, people were able to rise above themselves, so to speak. They could now study the physical processes that enabled them to become what they are, but they *could not reduce* their humanity, their "soulishness," to the lower-level physical process that gave rise to it. In other words, once the whole became greater than the sum of its parts, it became impossible to list the individual steps that went into making it. Warren Brown writes, "The processes of cultural development have so transcended the neurobiological evolution that allowed them, that it becomes *impossible* to imagine human culture [human behavior] to be nothing but neurobiology and genetics."[156]

This leads the authors to redefine various scriptural terms. In his summary chapter, Brown comments on his own earlier chapter, "Cognitive Contributions to Soul": "How do we understand the 'soul' language of Scripture and Christian tradition? I attempted in my chapter . . . [to propose] that *soul* is a *capacity for*

---

[154] Ray Anderson, "On Being Human: The Spiritual Saga of a Creaturely Soul" in *Whatever Happened to the Soul?*, ed. Warren S. Brown, Nancey Murphy, and H. Newton Malony (Minneapolis, Fortress Press, 1998), p. 189.

[155] Warren Brown, "Conclusion: Reconciling Scientific and Biblical Portraits of Human Nature," in *Whatever Happened to the Soul?*, pp. 216,217.

[156] Warren Brown, "Conclusion," p. 217 (emphasis added)..

a particular realm of experience rather than a nonphysical essence inhabiting the body."[157]

In his chapter "Human Nature: One Evolutionist's View," Francisco Ayala describes the emergence of *morality.* He says that the increase of brain capacity enabled human beings to put together a set of functions that enabled them to begin sorting out ethical from unethical actions: "The capacity for ethics, for example, is dependent on an ability to anticipate the consequences of one's behavior, the ability to make value judgments, and the ability to choose alternate behaviors."[158]

Joel Green in his chapter "Bodies—That Is, Human Lives: A Re-Examination of Human Nature in the Bible" defines the *image of God* as the emergent capacity to establish covenant relations "with God and with other humans."[159] Brown summarizes Green's position on why Scripture speaks in terms of a soul separate from the body: "New Testament teachings may well be expressed within first-century habits of language and thought, which were strongly influenced by a Hellenized view of human nature, without the teachings themselves being committed to a dualist view."[160] In other words, in order to communicate to their readers, the New Testament writers wrote in terms of the body-soul ideas of Greek culture, but they didn't necessarily believe those ideas themselves.

Anderson defines the resurrection of the body much like Polkinghorne did: "With the death of the body, the life (soul) of the body also disappears. With the resurrection of the body, the life (soul) of the body reappears."[161] Anderson admits that Scripture does not tell us how "personal self-identity continues through death and resurrection in such a way that it is the very *same* person who dies with a corruptible body and is raised with an incorruptible body."[162] But we can be sure this will happen because of Christ's resurrection.[163]

---

[157] Warren Brown, "Conclusion," p. 221 (emphasis added).

[158] Warren Brown, "Conclusion," p. 216.

[159] Warren Brown, "Conclusion," p. 224.

[160] Warren Brown, "Conclusion," p. 224.

[161] Ray Anderson, "On Being Human: The Spiritual Saga of a Creaturely Soul," in *Whatever Happened to the Soul?*, p. 191.

[162] Ray Anderson, "On Being Human: The Spiritual Saga of a Creaturely Soul," in *Whatever Happened to the Soul?*, p. 193. Michael Ruse also suggests, "God is *not* keeping up a substance but rather information which, at some point, can be reactivated." Michael Ruse, *Can a Darwinian Be a Christian?* (Cambridge: Cambridge University Press, 2001), p. 82 (emphasis author's).

[163] As noted above, John Polkinghorne and Nicholas Beale define the resurrection like this: "Thus the ultimate Christian hope is resurrection, God's great eschatological act of the re-embodiment of information-bearing pattern in the environment of the new creation." *Questions of Truth*, p. 23.

In his conclusion Brown assures us, "Never have the central and important tenets of the Christian faith been damaged, disproved, or significantly changed by looking honestly, humbly, and intently at new advances in science, without dodging their meaning or blushing at their veracity."[164]

Brown concludes the book by pointing out the advantages of the non-reductive physicalist viewpoint. First, when one studies human beings, they "are what you see." There is nothing non-material that has to be factored into one's evaluation of the person. Second, understanding human nature can benefit from both theology *and* science. Science, unlike theology, can only rely on what it sees and is helpless if it must factor into its analysis something it cannot see. Yet non-reductive physicalism speaks of something higher, a soulishness, which theology is able to discuss. Third—and this is only a variation on the first two—a

> complete understanding of human nature remains a grandiose objective. However, when human beings are viewed as whole and undivided, the project is at least theoretically possible. No part of human behavior or experience is *prima facie* excepted as nonmaterial and thus unobservable in principle.[165]

This last statement reveals what is at stake in the discussion of human nature. Only if we deny that we have a soul in addition to our body can science continue its work unhindered. Only a physicalist view of mankind will give science access to every aspect of a human being and allow science to continue its study of the human nature.

This book is now over two decades old. But the approach to human nature described in the book seems to be winning the day among theistic evolutionists. Any attempt to fit a literal Adam and Eve into the scheme of human evolution through a series of hominin species is filled with so much speculation and inconsistency as to be unworkable. And any attempt to retain Scripture's teaching that human beings have a body and soul is to push against the cognitive sciences, all of which begin with a materialistic view of mankind. The only option is to take the view expressed in *Whatever Happened to the Soul?*, the monistic view, that human beings are a single entity.

In his book *Mapping the Origins Debate*, Gerald Rau observes,

> Awareness of God and sinfulness could have arisen slowly in a group of primates over many generations, as there was no single point in time at which pre-humans became human. This interpretation, in accord with Darwinian gradualism and the idea of non-intervention, is the one

---

[164] Warren Brown, "Conclusion," p. 213.

[165] Warren Brown, "Conclusion," p. 228.

espoused by most proponents of evolutionary creation at the present time.[166]

What is lost when mankind's origin according to Scripture is lost.

Scripture's account of the creation of mankind includes four main topics: God created Adam and Eve with unique human bodies; he created Adam and Eve with a unique human spirit—a soul; he created Adam and Eve in his image; and he gave Adam and Eve the task of caring for his creation. Evolution affects all of these topics. We'll take them in order.

God created Adam and Eve with physical bodies

After God finished creating the animals, he turned his attention to mankind. The creation of Adam is set apart from the creation of the animals by the Hebrew word BARA. In Scripture, Adam and Eve's bodies—our bodies—are unique among living beings. Those who accept evolution lose a sense of their uniqueness.

But even more serious, they lose what Jesus meant when he called himself "the Son of Man." Evolution destroys the distinction between mankind and animals. All are linked, if not by physical form, then by a common source of DNA. Theistic evolutionists, in order to be consistent, must teach that when the Son of God became a human being, he linked himself to the entire evolutionary tree of life, not just to human life.

Most theistic evolutionists don't speak much about this. Perhaps it is too embarrassing. But the logic is valid and is not entirely lost in the theistic evolutionary discussion. George Murphy observes:

> The divine condescension that accepted the form of a slave and death on a cross accepted also our bestial ancestry. . . . By his incarnation, cross, and resurrection Christ heals us as members of our evolved species. The flesh which the Word became was not some idealized human nature, abstracted from the evolutionary process, but real historical humanity.[167]

In their rather sarcastic book, Price and Suominen ask, "Mustn't we say that Jesus, as a genuinely human being, was defined by the same animalistic genetic heritage as ours?"[168]

---

[166] Gerald Rau, *Mapping the Origins Debate*, p. 145.

[167] George L. Murphy, "Christology, Evolution, and the Cross," in *Perspectives on an Evolving Creation*, p. 380.

[168] Robert Price and Edwin Suominen, *Evolving out of Eden: Christian Responses to Evolution* (Valley, WA: Tellectual Press, 2013), p. 170, Kindle.

David Clough writes:

> It seems to me that the doctrine of the incarnation need not demarcate an absolute distinction between human beings and the rest of creation. If we have widened our understanding from God becoming a Jewish male human, to a male human, to a human, there seems no barrier to broadening our view one step further in claiming that the incarnation is best understood as God becoming a creature.[169]

It is true that by the power of Christ, the whole creation "will be set free from its bondage to corruption and obtain the freedom of the glory of the children of God" (Romans 8:21). Nevertheless, Jesus came to earth as a human being to save human beings from punishment for sin and alienation from God: "But when the fullness of time had come, God sent forth his Son, born of woman, born under the law, to redeem those who were under the law, so that we might receive adoption as sons" (Galatians 4:4,5). Human beings alone are promised that in Christ our bodies will rise from the dead.

All of this becomes muddled, if not lost, if one doesn't accept Adam and Eve's creation in Genesis 2 as the creation of a being distinct from those he had created before.

God created mankind with a unique human spirit, a soul

To accept evolution is also to deny the unique character of the human spirit. Earlier in this chapter, we saw that the word *soul* is an English translation of the Hebrew word NEPHESH, or *spirit*. Under normal conditions, the word *soul* is easily understood as the human spirit with all its unique qualities. But in the current discussion, the word *soul* tends to confuse matters.

When theistic evolutionists—specifically those who believe that human beings are body and soul—discuss the origin of mankind, the discussion always includes trying to determine when hominins were given a soul, which in turn, was to have made them into human beings. But this is using the word *soul* in a careless way. The soul is just a name for the human spirit. It is not a matter of inserting a "soul" into an animal to make that animal human. Rather, to make an animal into a human being, God would have had to remove the animal spirit from the hominin and then replace it with a human spirit.

Only theistic evolutionists who believe that God created Adam and Eve from scratch in the midst of a large hominin population are free from this problem.

---

[169] David Clough, "All God's Creatures: Reading Genesis on Human and Nonhuman Animals," in *Reading Genesis After Darwin*, ed. Stephen Barton, C. and David Wilkinson (Oxford: Oxford University Press, 2009), p. 155.

But their position raises the other problems we saw men like C. John Collins wrestling with above: How did the creation of Adam with a human spirit affect the hominins around him who were still animals? Did God also give these hominins a human spirit? Did they become moral beings at that point? And what happened to these hominins, an especially troublesome question if they now had a human spirit? And if the hominin population became extinct, did Adam and Eve and their descendants have anything to do with that?

Every scenario that involves God using hominins as stepping-stones to the creation of human beings soon starts to become unworkable. It is more logical to hold the monistic position and say that animal spirits evolved soulish qualities, which is what more and more theistic evolutionists in the Evangelical world are doing.

Evolutionary monism takes away Scripture's understanding of reality and its teaching about future events. To get a sense of this, consider Jesus' words to the thief on the cross: "Truly, I say to you, today you will be with me in Paradise" (Luke 23:43). In the context of the predominant evolutionary view of the soul, Jesus would have meant, "Truly, today your body will go into the grave, but take heart, until the Last Day you will remain in God's memory in Paradise."

We are body and spirit, but our spirit is the "I" in a Christian's thinking about salvation. "I" came to faith in Christ here in time. "I" will go to heaven and not to hell when my body and spirit separate at the end of my time here. "I" will be reunited with my body on the Last Day and spend eternity with the Lord in the same body I have now.

God created mankind in his image

Theistic evolutionary literature usually contains a discussion about when God might have given his image to evolving hominins. Sometimes there is even a discussion about the meaning of God's image,

But what is almost never discussed is that God's creating mankind through the process of natural selection means that God's image has a dark side. If God is willing to use the evils of natural selection to create us, then his image is not just a reflection of goodness and love, but also of the willingness to use evil if it serves a higher good. To put this a little differently, if mankind was made in the image of God, but according to God's method of creating they must engage in the self-centered and ruthless competition of natural selection, then the qualities of self-centeredness and ruthlessness must be qualities found in the One whose image we bear.

Some theistic evolutionists see the problem. Barton and Wilkinson ask, "In what way, if any, can a creature that has evolved through processes of natural selection be seen as 'created in the image of God'?"[170] Giberson and Collins ask the same question, "Can we be both the product of evolution and created in the image of God?"[171] To take it a step further, if the image of God has a dark side, what does this mean for Christians who are being renewed in the image of God?

In Scripture, the term "image of God," which theistic evolutionists so casually toss into the evolutionary framework, can only be understood in the framework of Scripture. God's love for people who fell into sin, our renewal in Christ, and the perfect future God has in store for his people—all this is lost if God forces us to play a role in the process of natural selection.

We will continue this line of thought in our discussion of how theistic evolutionists must define morality, which is the topic of the next chapter.

God gave mankind the responsibility to care for his creation

This final topic is largely ignored in theistic evolutionary literature. It is not hard to see why. It is impossible to say how God could give mankind dominion over creation even while we are evolving along with it. It is impossible to explain how mankind could care for God's creation and at the same time evolve at the expense of the living creatures around us. In that case, God's command to rule over his creation and subdue it could not include caring for it in love. It would mean giving mankind the right to exploit it for their own benefit.

What is more, even if Adam and Eve in love wanted to help the creation, how could they rule and have dominion over the plants and living creatures if those beings were also consigned by God to develop through the normal evolutionary process? In other words, how does one rule over and subdue a creation forced to survive at the expense of others?

Although we still have God's command to rule over his world, to a great extent we are hamstrung in our efforts because of the temporary curse God put on his creation. But it is quite another thing to claim that from the beginning God commanded us to care for a world consigned to competition, self-centeredness, and death—which is what theistic evolutionists must say.

Elephants in the room

After struggling to combine Scripture and evolution on the origin of mankind, theistic evolutionists must admit that all the scenarios "leave us with many

---

[170] Stephen Barton and David Wilkinson, ed., *Reading Genesis After Darwin*, p. 17.

[171] Karl Giberson and Francis Collins, The Language of Science and Faith, p. 201.

uncertainties."[172] It would have been better to say that they leave us with many impossibilities. A firm commitment to evolution forces one to turn impossibilities into mere uncertainties.

In one place where John Collins was discussing the attempts of certain linguists to explain the origin of human language, he rather sarcastically characterized their logic like this: "I can get myself into the frame of mind in which this story looks feasible; therefore we should treat the feasibility as established."[173] That sentiment could apply to the entire program of creating evolutionary scenarios to describe the origin of mankind: "If I can imagine a scenario being true, I have the right to argue that it is."

After describing the various ways theistic evolutionists try to picture mankind's origin, Razmerita says, "Unrelenting and irremediable internal incoherencies plague all theistic evolutionary systems and the theistic evolutionary approach as a whole," and none of them provide "a viable model of reconciliation between the scientific evolutionary worldview and the biblical doctrine of creation."[174]

In the two previous chapters, we identified a number of elephants in the room. To keep them in mind, we'll repeat them:

- **The basic framework of the world's history as taught in Scripture is wrong.**

- **The evil associated with creation by evolution came from God.**

- **God, whom Scripture says *is love*, used the evils of natural selection over billions of years to create living beings.**

- **The process of evolution—which locks mankind into a system of self-interest, competition, and death—leads to freedom.**

In this chapter three more elephants have entered the room:

- **Scripture's description of the origin of mankind is wrong.**

- **God must be evil because his image defined human beings and he requires human beings to take part in the evils of natural selection.**

- **God commanded mankind to rule over the earth in love, and then he made it impossible for mankind to fulfill that command.**

---

[172] C. John Collins, *Did Adam and Eve Really Exist?*, p. 131.

[173] C. John Collins, *Did Adam and Eve Really Exist?*, p. 98.

[174] Gheorghe Razmerita, *Theistic Evolution's Struggle for Survival*, p. 154.

Chapter 6

Right and Wrong. Sin, Death, and Judgment

According to Scripture

Introduction

This chapter deals with a range of topics related to the subject of good and evil: How do we determine right from wrong? What is sin? What is death? What does it mean that God judges sin? Theistic evolutionists understand the importance of these questions. We'll first see what Scripture teaches about these topics.

Right and wrong

Satan wants to redefine the meaning of right and wrong

Satan's temptation of Eve can be viewed as his attempt to change the definition of right and wrong. God said it was wrong if they ate from the Tree of the Knowledge of Good and Evil. Satan said God was withholding from them valuable truths about life. God said they would die if they ate from the tree. Satan said that if they ate, they would be more alive than ever.

There was an element of truth in what Satan said. God, of course, is well aware of good and evil. When he forced Adam and Eve out of the Garden of Eden, God assessed the matter like this: "Behold, the man has become *like one of us* in knowing good and evil" (Genesis 3:22). But that is where the comparison ends. God knows good and evil, but he has nothing to do with evil. For Adam and Eve, knowing good and evil was different. The perfection in which they had been created was gone, and the evil they had not known before now dominated their lives.

God did not want mankind to remain in that state. He wanted Adam and Eve restored to what they had been when he created them. He promised a Savior (Genesis 3:15), and then he made it impossible for Adam and Eve to eat from the Tree of Life and live forever under the domination of evil.

Right and wrong can be defined

In Scripture right is not a vague, open-ended idea. Wrong is not a matter of opinion. Paul defined the image of God as the ability to know right and wrong: "Put off your old self, which belongs to your former manner of life and is corrupt through deceitful desires, and to be renewed in the spirit of your minds, and to put on the new self, *created after the likeness of God in true righteousness and holiness*" (Ephesians 4:22-24).

In chapter 3 we saw that God's goodness can be defined in concrete ways; what it means to live a morally good life can also be defined in concrete ways. In Galatians 5 Paul listed the wrong things the sinful nature prompts us to do:

> Now the works of the flesh are evident: sexual immorality, impurity, sensuality, idolatry, sorcery, enmity, strife, jealousy, fits of anger, rivalries, dissensions, divisions, envy, drunkenness, orgies, and things like these. I warn you, as I warned you before, that those who do such things will not inherit the kingdom of God. (Galatians 5:19-23)

Paul contrasts this with what God wants us to do, and through his Spirit enables us to do: "But the fruit of the Spirit is love, joy, peace, patience, kindness, goodness, faithfulness, gentleness, self-control; against such things there is no law. . . . Let us not become conceited, provoking one another, envying one another" (Galatians 5:22,26).

The entire Scripture assumes that the distinction between right and wrong is not situational or a matter of culture. Cain's murder of Abel was as wrong then as it would be today. In the years before the flood, God saw "that the wickedness of man was great in the earth, and that every intention of the thoughts of his heart was only evil continually" (Genesis 6:5). God spelled out his will in concrete statements to the people of Israel in the Ten Commandments. Later, when a man asked Jesus what he had to do to inherit eternal life, Jesus responded with a list drawn from the Ten Commandments: "You know the commandments: 'Do not murder, Do not commit adultery, Do not steal, Do not bear false witness, Do not defraud, Honor your father and mother'" (Mark 10:19). Jesus then led this man to realize he had not kept the most basic commandment of all: to love the Lord above all things.

The book of Psalms begins with the distinction between the righteous and the wicked: "Blessed is the man who walks not in the counsel of the wicked, nor stands in the way of sinners, nor sits in the seat of scoffers; but his delight is in the law of the LORD, and on his law he meditates day and night" (Psalm 1:1,2). God's Old Testament prophets centered their message on right and wrong and on God's promise of a Savior from the guilt of sin. They renounced deeds done against God's will. They promised God's blessings on those who repent and follow his will.

In the Sermon on the Mount (Matthew 5-7), Jesus addressed the religious leaders of his day who were in the habit of modifying the law based on how much of it they could actually keep. Jesus revealed the full scope of the law, which no one can keep. And he assured the crowd that he would keep God's law to its full extent in their place: "Do not think that I have come to abolish the Law or the Prophets; I have not come to abolish them but to fulfill them. For truly, I say to you, until heaven and earth pass away, not an iota, not a dot, will pass from the Law until all is accomplished" (Matthew 5:17,18).

Throughout Scripture it is stated or assumed that the meaning of right and wrong originates with God. God gave the people of Israel his laws on Mount Sinai, "written with the finger of God" (Exodus 31:18). God told the Israelites, "You shall be holy, for I the LORD your God am holy" (Leviticus 19:2), and Peter quoted these words as encouragement to the Christians of his day: "As obedient children, do not be conformed to the passions of your former ignorance, but as he who called you is holy, you also be holy in all your conduct, since it is written, 'You shall be holy, for I am holy'" (1 Peter 1:14-16).

All human beings know the difference between right and wrong

God created human beings in his image. Those who have become righteous through forgiveness in Christ are being re-created in the image of God "in true righteousness and holiness" (Ephesians 4:24). Even after Adam and Eve fell into sin, God enabled them to retain the knowledge of right and wrong. All people know the difference.

Cain knew it was wrong to murder his brother. And he was afraid of those living around him who knew about the murder he had committed.

Abraham thought the people of Egypt were a bunch of thugs who would take his beautiful wife and kill him. But it was quite the opposite. The pharaoh knew that adultery was wrong and was angry with Abraham for passing off Sarah as his sister. So did a Philistine king, Abimelech, whom Abraham also tricked into thinking that Sarah was his sister and available for anyone to take as his wife. Abimelech rebuked Abraham for his lie: "And how have I sinned against you, that you have brought on me and my kingdom a great sin?" (Genesis 20:9).

When God gave the Israelites his law, even the unbelieving nations could see that those laws were special. Moses encouraged the Israelites: "Observe them [these laws] carefully, for this will show your wisdom and understanding to the nations, who will hear about all these decrees and say, 'Surely this great nation is a wise and understanding people.' . . . And what other nation is so great as to

125

have such righteous decrees and laws as this body of laws I am setting before you today?" (Deuteronomy 4:6,8).

In Romans 1:18–2:16, Paul tells us what all people know even apart from God's revelation in Scripture. In these verses Paul is describing non-Jews, who did not have the Old Testament Scriptures. None of them had to be told there is a Creator. All of them were able to conclude they should worship the God who created all things, rather than worship something he created.

> For the wrath of God is revealed from heaven against all ungodliness and unrighteousness of men, who by their unrighteousness suppress the truth. For what can be known about God is plain to them, because God has shown it to them. For his invisible attributes, namely, his eternal power and divine nature, have been clearly perceived, ever since the creation of the world, in the things that have been made. So they are without excuse. (Romans 1:18-20)

Because they suppressed what they knew about the Creator and worshiped idols, God turned them over to their sinful lusts and desires and let them experience the result of their sins. After listing specific wrongs people do, Paul made it clear that they were sinning against their own better knowledge: "Although they know God's righteous decree that those who do such things deserve death, they not only continue to do these very things but also approve of those who practice them" (Romans 1:32).

A few verses later, Paul made the same point. He pointed out that non-Jews don't have the law God gave to the Israelites, but they do have the law: "For when Gentiles, who do not have the law, by nature do what the law requires, they are a law to themselves, even though they do not have the law. They show that the work of the law is written on their hearts" (Romans 2:14,15). God has even given all people a conscience, which is simply a voice, a feeling, that tells them when they are doing what they know is right or doing what they know is wrong: ". . . their conscience also bears witness, and their conflicting thoughts accuse or even excuse them" (Romans 2:15).

In another place Paul referred to the honorable way he administered an offering for the people in Judea. People in general understand the temptation to steal, and Paul didn't want to open himself up to suspicion: "For we aim at what is honorable not only in the Lord's sight *but also in the sight of man*" (2 Corinthians 8:21).

In this fallen world, sinful human beings sometimes have trouble deciding the good and right way to act. But that is due to us—because our conscience has been dulled or because we have followed teachings that conflict with what we know is right and wrong.

126

Actions that go against God's law are called "sin"

When people do something that goes against God's will, they have done wrong. Scripture calls that by a number of words, one being *sin*. The apostle John wrote, "Everyone who makes a practice of sinning also practices lawlessness; sin is lawlessness" (1 John 3:4). James wrote along the same lines and added the fact that all sin is serious: "But if you show partiality, you are committing sin and are convicted by the law as transgressors. For whoever keeps the whole law but fails in one point has become accountable for all of it" (James 2:9,10).

The Old Testament uses various words for sin, which are translated with rather picturesque English words. *Transgression* is from the Latin and means "to step over" something. The English word *trespass* is more familiar to us. A "no trespassing" sign warns against stepping over a boundary, in this case the boundary between right and wrong. *Iniquity* refers to an act that is "not equal" to one of God's laws. *Sin* itself is an Old English word that means "moral wrongdoing."

David used them all when he confessed, "I acknowledged my sin to you, and I did not cover my iniquity; I said, 'I will confess my transgressions to the LORD,' and you forgave the iniquity of my sin" (Psalm 32:5). David confessed that sin brings *guilt*, another Old English word. In Scripture guilt refers to more than guilty feelings. Guilt is a debt that a person owes to someone against whom they have sinned. In Psalm 32, David asked God to *forgive* the guilt of his sin. Forgive is another Old English word that means to "allow" or "remit" a debt. David was saying, "Lord, I owe you for that sin I committed. Please release me from that debt."

All Scripture is based on these truths: Sin is an act against God's law. Sin carries a penalty that a human being cannot pay. And we ask God to take that penalty away.

Death began in Eden when Adam and Eve broke God's command

A penalty—a burden of guilt—was attached to sinning against the first commandment God gave mankind. God told Adam and Eve that if they ate from the Tree of the Knowledge of Good and Evil, they would die: "You may surely eat of every tree of the garden, but of the tree of the knowledge of good and evil you shall not eat, for in the day that you eat of it you shall surely die" (Genesis 2:16,17). Adam and Eve ate from the tree, and they received the sentence of death.

In Scripture the word *death* refers to separation. It can refer to physical death (when body and spirit separate), to spiritual death (when a person is separated from God), or to eternal death (when a person is separated from God eternally). It is clear that the penalty attached to eating from the tree included all three.

Some theistic evolutionists limit God's punishment on Adam and Eve to spiritual death. But God was clearly referring to physical death when he said to Adam, "By the sweat of your face you shall eat bread, till you return to the ground, for out of it you were taken; for you are dust, and to dust you shall return" (Genesis 3:1). Also, God kept Adam and Eve from eating of the Tree of Life. God explained why he did this: "Behold, the man has become like one of us in knowing good and evil. Now, lest he reach out his hand and take also of the tree of life and eat, *and live forever* . . ." (Genesis 3:22). If "death" refers to spiritual death, and "live forever" refers to spiritual life, then God would be saying that he did not want Adam and Eve to be reunited with him and to have their spiritual life restored by eating from the Tree of Life. Yet God had already given Adam and Eve the promise that in the future someone would crush Satan's head. By faith in this promise, Adam and Eve had already become spiritually alive. Their physical death would now become the doorway to life in God's presence. Eating from the Tree of Life would keep that from happening.

The entire New Testament echoes this truth. Paul tells us that sin and death began in the Garden of Eden and was passed down to all people: "Therefore, just as sin came into the world through one man, and death through sin, and so death spread to all men because all sinned" (Romans 5:12). But Jesus promised, "Truly, truly, I say to you, whoever hears my word and believes him who sent me has eternal life. He does not come into judgment, but has passed from death to life" (John 5:24). That's the blessing God wanted for Adam and Eve and their descendants.

God judges sin

Our conscience and Scripture reveal that we are accountable to God for the wrongs we do. Guilt—not merely the feeling but especially the penalty—must be dealt with.

In Eden

Genesis 3 is a litany of accountability. God came looking for Adam and Eve in the Garden. They hid from him because they were naked. Adam and Eve felt shame over the thoughts going through their minds when they saw each other's nakedness. God asked them, "Who told you that you were naked? Have you eaten of the tree of which I commanded you not to eat?" (Genesis 3:11). Adam passed the blame on to Eve. Eve passed it on to the serpent. God held the serpent accountable and revealed that someday his head would be crushed. With that promise, Adam and Eve's fear of accountability to God was gone. The suffering

God brought into their lives would remind them that God is serious about sin. They would seek rest in God's promise.

In the early world

God sent the flood as a judgment on sin: "The LORD saw that the wickedness of man was great in the earth, and that every intention of the thoughts of his heart was only evil continually. And the LORD regretted that he had made man on the earth, and it grieved him to his heart. So the LORD said, 'I will blot out man whom I have created from the face of the land'" (Genesis 6:5,7). Peter in no uncertain terms described the flood and the destruction of Sodom and Gomorrah that came later as God's judgment on those who lived in sin and rebellion against him: "If he did not spare the ancient world, but preserved Noah, a herald of righteousness, with seven others, when he brought a flood upon the world of the ungodly; if by turning the cities of Sodom and Gomorrah to ashes he condemned them to extinction, making them an example of what is going to happen to the ungodly. . . ." (2 Peter 2:5,6). If that is true, "then the Lord knows how to rescue the godly from trials, and to keep the unrighteous under punishment until the day of judgment" (2 Peter 2:9).

Moses

When God gave the Mosaic Law, he did not invite the people of Israel to a picnic and poetry reading. God came down on Mount Sinai in a way appropriate for the perfect Lord to stand before sinful human beings for the purpose of giving them his law.

> There were thunders and lightnings and a thick cloud on the mountain and a very loud trumpet blast, so that all the people in the camp trembled. Then Moses brought the people out of the camp to meet God, and they took their stand at the foot of the mountain. Now Mount Sinai was wrapped in smoke because the LORD had descended on it in fire. The smoke of it went up like the smoke of a kiln, and the whole mountain trembled greatly. And as the sound of the trumpet grew louder and louder, Moses spoke, and God answered him in thunder. (Exodus 19:16-19)

While Moses was on top of the mountain receiving God's law, the people became curious and started to approach the mountain. But the people's curiosity was not compatible with the serious nature of the Law. The LORD said to Moses, "Go down and warn the people, lest they break through to the LORD to look and many of them perish" (Exodus 19:21).

Jesus

It is impossible to remove the theme of judgment from Jesus' message. In a parable picturing the Last Day and the wedding feast of heaven, a man showed up without a wedding garment. God asked, "'Friend, how did you get in here without a wedding garment?' And he was speechless. Then the king said to the attendants, 'Bind him hand and foot and cast him into the outer darkness. In that place there will be weeping and gnashing of teeth'" (Matthew 22:12,13). In the parable of the rich man and Lazarus, the rich man is pictured suffering the pain of hell (Luke 16:19-31). The parable of the sheep and the goats, in which Jesus pictured the final judgment, ends with these words: "And [the unrighteous] will go away into eternal punishment, but the righteous into eternal life" (Matthew 25:46).

Paul

Paul warns us about our accountability for the sins we commit: "Do not be deceived: God is not mocked, for whatever one sows, that will he also reap. For the one who sows to his own flesh will from the flesh reap corruption, but the one who sows to the Spirit will from the Spirit reap eternal life" (Galatians 6:7,8).

Paul taught Timothy how to choose congregational leaders wisely. He wanted Timothy to do nothing that would jeopardize the faith of a new Christian: "He must not be a recent convert, or he may become puffed up with conceit and fall into the condemnation of the devil" (1 Timothy 3:6).

In Christ we are no longer accountable for our sins. Paul encouraged us to give thanks to the Father "who has qualified you to share in the inheritance of the saints in light. He has delivered us from the domain of darkness and transferred us to the kingdom of his beloved Son, in whom we have redemption, the forgiveness of sins" (Colossians 1:12-14).

If there were no accountability, God's Son would not have had to come to earth. This will be the subject of the next chapter. But we get a taste of that as we listen to the hymn writer reflect on the crucifixion:

> If you think of sin but lightly
> Nor suppose the evil great,
> Here you see its nature rightly,
> Here its guilt may estimate.
> Mark the sacrifice appointed;
> See who bears the awful load—

'Tis the Word, the Lord's Anointed,
Son of Man and Son of God.[175]

---

[175] *Christian Worship: A Lutheran Hymnal* (Milwaukee: Northwestern Publishing House, 1993), 127:3.

Right and Wrong. Sin, Death, and Judgment

According to Theistic Evolutionists

Introduction

In this chapter we are dealing with a number of topics that in Scripture are closely related: right and wrong, sin and death, and God's judgment on sin. Here again, theistic evolutionists must work toward a middle position between secular evolution and a straightforward reading of Scripture.

Life on the edges is quite clear. Scripture describes the situation like this:

- God defines right and wrong, which is nothing other than a description of God's own holiness.

- Even now, all people have a basic knowledge of right and wrong. They know when they are doing right and when they are doing wrong.

- Adam and Eve had been created holy, but at Satan's prompting they sinned.

- As children of Adam and Eve, all people share in Adam's guilt and sinful nature.

- Death first came into the world when Adam and Eve sinned.

- Unless people repent, God will judge them for their sins.

We note the tremendous gulf between Scripture and secular evolutionists:

- Right and wrong are loosely defined by the process of evolution itself. Right is whatever helps a species evolve, and wrong is whatever hinders that species' evolution.

- A sense of morality comes from one's genetic makeup and to some extent from the culture in which a person lives.

- There was no first pair of human beings who brought into the world what Christians call "sin," "original sin," and "guilt." These are outdated religious terms, largely without meaning.

- Death is a natural process, necessary for the evolution of species.

- Even if a person believes in God, it makes little sense to say that God judges people for doing what evolution calls on them to do.

Theistic evolutionists must find a middle road between these two positions.

Right and wrong

The so-called soft sciences, sciences like psychology and sociology, study the topics we are covering in this chapter. They explore these topics to understand how people perceive them and how these perceptions affect human behavior.

Scripture teaches that all people have the "things required by the law"[176] (Romans 2:14 NIV84) written in their hearts. We all have a conscience that testifies to whether or not we are following that law. We know that God exists, and we sense that God will judge sin (Romans 1:32). Scientists observe the truth of what Paul writes in these verses. Since these beliefs have an effect on people's thinking and emotions, secular scientists want to understand why people share them. They search for insights in the process of evolution.

Theistic evolutionists, however, must construct a middle road between what Scripture teaches about these topics and what scientists believe they have discovered through their study of evolution. What might such a middle road look like?

It is relatively easy to speculate about the fossil evidence purported to have been left by humans as they evolved. But it is much harder to speculate on matters where no hard evidence exists. On the topics of this chapter theistic evolutionists have only the words of Scripture and the bare idea of evolution to work with. They have no hard evidence on which to attempt to build a middle road.

I tried to locate theistic evolutionary discussions about how such things as a sense of right and wrong, the human conscience, and a sense of God's judgment on sin might have evolved. I found little material in the books I read. "Perhaps these discussions exist," I thought, "but I just haven't found them."

However, Tapio Poulimatke, in his chapter about theistic evolutionists and morality in the recent book *Theistic Evolution,* finds the same lack. He offers this summary:

> Although theistic evolutionists assume that the idea of moral conscience as an expression of God's design for humans is fully compatible with various naturalistic explanations of the origin of moral conscience, they fail to specify a natural process that could plausibly do the job. In this respect theistic evolutionism amounts to little more than the statement that they do not see a logical problem in assuming that God could have used a natural process.[177]

---

[176]There is a distinction between Paul's phrase "things required by the law" and God's description of what will happen through the new covenant God wold someday establish with all people: "I will put my law in their minds and write it on their hearts" (Jeremiah 31:33 NIV84). The second phrase refers to the new life God has given Christians, while Paul's phrase "things required by the law" (literally, "the works of the law") likely refers to a simple knowledge of right and wrong.

[177]Tapio Poulimatke, "The Origin of Moral Conscience: Theistic Evolution Versus Intelligent

Poulimatke's point is that theistic evolutionists are simply borrowing views on the evolution of morality from secular evolutionists and then claiming that *God* could have used these natural processes to create mankind as moral beings. Accordingly, the border line between how secular evolutionists analyze these topics and how theistic evolutionists analyze them is rather thin.

The evolution of morality

If Poulimatke is correct and theistic evolutionists are basing their discussion of morality on the work done in the secular world, we should begin by looking at how secular evolutionists describe the origin of morality.

As mentioned above, secular evolutionists are aware that people have a sense of right and wrong, a sense of guilt, and even the sense that God will punish or reward them for what they do. What people sense about these matters plays an important role in how they behave. Therefore, it is important to study these matters and suggest how they evolved.

This has resulted in a variety of disciplines that study human behavior from various angles. Some disciplines focus on the human body, especially the brain and the nervous system. Others focus on the behavior itself.

The attempt to understand human behavior in evolutionary terms has resulted in a new discipline that arose in the last half of the 20th century. This discipline is called sociobiology. It was fueled by E. O. Wilson's 1975 book *Sociobiology: The*

Design" in *Theistic Evolution*, ed. J.P. Moreland, Stephen C. Meyer, Christopher Shaw, Ann Gauger, and Wayne Grudem (Wheaton: Crossway, 2017), p. 731. This quote is found in the following context (pages 731, 732):

> Theistic evolutionists generally agree that Darwinian evolution is not able to establish the origin of actual moral obligations. All that the evolutionary story can possibly do is to explain how we acquired moral beliefs and emotions. The problem for theistic evolutionists is, however, that current evolutionary accounts fail even in the latter task: they fail to explain the origin of moral conscience. The human capacity to discern moral truths cannot be reduced to a product of the kind of combinatorial processes that are available to a Darwinian account of evolution. Although theistic evolutionists assume that the idea of moral conscience as an expression of God's design for humans is fully compatible with various naturalistic explanations of the origin of moral conscience, they fail to specify a natural process that could plausibly do the job. In this respect theistic evolutionism amounts to little more than the statement that they do not see a logical problem in assuming that God could have used a natural process. Although theistic evolutionists usually adhere to the theories prevalent in evolutionary science and claim that God used evolutionary mechanisms to attain his purposes, the origin of morality presents a special problem. Morality is generally experienced as involving a transcendent source of obligation, which seems to assume a divine Lawgiver. As C. Stephen Evans argues in detail, moral obligations are "objective, motivating, binary in nature, universal, overriding, and allow us to bring deliberation to closure." (Poulimatke is citing C. Stephen Evans, *God and Moral Obligation* (Oxford: Oxford University Press, 2013), p. 181.)

New Synthesis (the 25th anniversary edition was published in 2000). Sociobiology is a "new synthesis" in the sense that it wants to combine biology and sociology into a single discipline; it is a discipline "engaged in discovering the biological foundation of social behavior."[178]

When *sociobiologists* study human beings, they do more than just observe, record, and try to find patterns of behavior. They work to interpret all behavior *as a product of evolution.* Peter Bowler writes, "The science of sociobiology explains all animal behavior, including human social behavior, in terms of instincts generated by natural selection acting among groups of genetically related individuals."[179] The evolutionary struggle to survive, the incessant competition for scarce resources, and the desire to do what is necessary to keep one's genes viable (as subconscious as that may be)—all of this, they believe, must have guided and directed the evolution of our genes and ultimately determined (or at least heavily influenced) our social behavior.[180] Sociobiologists are confident that given enough time, they will discover how the physical matter that evolved into the human body also evolved into such things as consciousness and the emotions and desires that lead to various forms of human behavior.

Altruism versus Christian morality

In Christianity, God's righteousness is the measure of right and wrong. In sociobiology, the process of natural selection and the need to keep one's genes viable for the next generation is considered to be the measure of right and wrong.

By definition, the process of natural selection does not breed kindness to other people. For evolution to progress, creatures that carry superior genes must kill off those that carry inferior genes. Richard Dawkins, a well-known secular evolutionist, says that the goal of a person's genes is to survive and be present in the next generation. This requires a ruthless concern for oneself.

Nevertheless, evolutionists recognize that living beings do help each other in various ways. Evolutionists recognize this. They call such behavior "altruism." But there is a problem with this. In his essay on the evolution of the human soul,

---

[178] Francisco Ayala, "Human Nature: One Evolutionist's View," in *Whatever Happened to the Soul?*, ed. Warren Brown, Nancey Murphy, and H., Newton Malony, p. 46.

[179] Peter Bowler, *Monkey Trials and Gorilla Sermons: Evolution and Creation from Darwin to Intelligent Design* (Cambridge: Harvard, 2007), loc. 284, Kindle.

[180] In the field of sociobiology, there is tension between the genes and culture. How much do our genes and how much does our culture determine our behavior? *Evolutionary psychology* is a field related to sociobiology. Evolutionary psychology claims that everything starts with genes and that human cultures evolved under their influence. But at some point the genes turned a certain amount of control over human behavior over to the cultures that evolved under their influence. In other words, at some point, culture and not genes began to determine behavior.

Warren Brown explains, "One of the problems in the evolution of behavior that has prompted much discussion over the last few decades is how altruism might have survived natural selection. . . . Altruism implies one organism doing what is more beneficial for the survival of another at the expense of itself."[181]

To explain the evolution of altruism, Brown notes that sociobiologists appeal to the concepts of "kin selection" and "reciprocal altruism." *Kin selection* means that within one's natural or social kinship, genes have determined that it is advantageous to sacrifice oneself, even to give one's life for a relative. Parents might sacrifice themselves for their children, or a soldier might give his life for a "brother" on the battlefield. *Reciprocal altruism* has a wider scope. Within the general population, it has become clear by experience that it is advantageous for one species to help another provided that the other species reciprocates (something that is often observed in nature). This knowledge has become embedded in the genes of both species and determines their mutually beneficial behavior. All forms of altruism, therefore, are acts of kindness practiced for one's own benefit. Peter Bowler says, "Morality is just another product of what Dawkins calls the 'selfish gene.'"[182]

Sociobiologists recognize, however, that *human* altruism has risen to a higher level than animal altruism. Altruism in humans has become more than a collection of genetically determined self-centered responses. This conclusion does not surprise us. Scripture tells us that human beings know God's law, realize when they have sinned, and know they deserve God's judgment. This results in a sense of responsibility toward those around us.

Sociobiologists attempt to integrate this into the process of evolution. Ruse explains that all people, including sociobiologists, accept the fact that "the key component in ethics—especially ethics at the substantive level—is the fact that we feel the obligation to promote (through our actions) the good, meaning that *we feel the need to act kindly toward others simply because this is the right thing to do.*" We have moral sentiments, and "they are genuine. . . . Each and every one of us knows the tug of moral obligation."[183]

Ruse describes the difference between human altruism and animal altruism ("Mother Theresa altruism" versus "ant altruism," as he calls them). In the case of ants, they help each other simply for "biological returns." Since a queen ant

---

[181] Warren Brown, "Evolution, Cognitive Neuroscience, and the Soul," in *Perspectives on an Evolving Creation,* ed. Keith B. Miller, p. 521.

[182] Peter Bowler, *Monkey Trials and Gorilla Sermons: Evolution and Creation From Darwin to Intelligent Design,* loc. 284.

[183] Michael Ruse, *Can a Darwinian Be a Christian?,* p. 191 (emphasis added).

can produce millions of offspring, it makes little difference if many of them are lost. Therefore, biological altruism is enough for the needs of their species.

Human altruism is also a product of evolution because human beings also "need to cooperate to survive."[184] But since human beings have a relatively small number of offspring, humans had to develop "more sophisticated mechanisms" to motivate and control themselves so they "can respond to change and challenges" that threaten their offspring.[185]

Or perhaps human beings, Ruse suggests, have a "super brain," which is able to handle every situation by "calculating carefully the costs of any social interaction and acting positively only if it is in our self-interest."[186] However, this should not be viewed as evil or selfish. It is merely a mutual way of working together for the good of the human species.

But even this does not adequately describe human nature with its sense of morality. So sociobiologists must take the matter a step further. They speculate that our selfish desires are a barrier to our evolution; because human beings are social creatures, our natural selfishness itself must somehow be overcome for the good of the human species. Therefore, out of necessity, humans have evolved something to break through this barrier. This something is "the feeling that we 'ought' to do certain things, even though our nature is against it. . . .We need something as powerful as this, or [human] 'altruism' will not be achieved."[187] Ruse writes,

> The sociobiological claim is that in the case of humans, we are genetically predetermined to think in certain ways, so that in specified situations we will incline to act in certain ways. And *the genetic predetermination manifests itself as a moral sense: an awareness of certain rules or guides which are binding upon us—the prescriptions of normative ethics.*[188]

Why do human genes, selfish as they are, not necessarily produce selfish people?[189] The explanation boils down to the idea that evolution has made unselfish actions a tool for its own goals: "The claim is that in order to make us good *biological* 'altruists,' natural selection has made us *moral* altruists.[190]

---

[184] Michael Ruse, *Can a Darwinian Be a Christian?*, p. 192.

[185] Michael Ruse, *Can a Darwinian Be a Christian?*, p. 193.

[186] Michael Ruse, *Can a Darwinian Be a Christian?*, p. 193.

[187] Michael Ruse, *Can a Darwinian Be a Christian?*, p. 195.

[188] Michael Ruse, *Can a Darwinian Be a Christian?*, p. 194 (emphasis added).

[189] Michael Ruse, *Can a Darwinian Be a Christian?*, p. 195.

[190] Michael Ruse, *Can a Darwinian Be a Christian?*, pp. 194,195 (emphasis added).

It should be clear that we are really no further than we were when we started: Even unselfishness has evolved for selfish reasons.

A straightforward reading of Scripture explains that our moral sense and feeling of obligation to help our fellow human beings comes from God and is ultimately directed back to serving him. Secular evolutionists, on the other hand, explain our sense of morality and obligation to help others as a product of natural selection which is ultimately directed back to us and our need to compete successfully.

The theistic evolutionists' predicament

Can theistic evolutionists offer an alternative? Their acceptance of evolution constrains their options. If evolution is true, then a sense of right and wrong had to have evolved. It seems they have little choice but to think like sociobiologists. But how they can talk about morality in a way that gives God a role in defining right and wrong? And if God is in some way given a place in the process, how can God's own righteousness and love provide the pattern for human morality, as self-centered as it must be in the context of natural selection?

It seems that theistic evolutionists are at a loss as to how to answer that question. As Poulimatke observed, theistic evolutionists simply assume that morality can be explained in evolutionary terms, and they fail to offer their own alternative.

The theistic evolutionists' predicament parallels what we saw in the previous chapter on the origin of human beings. As we saw, theistic evolutionists have two basic options to describe the origin of human beings. (1) They can create scenarios in which God at a certain time miraculously created Adam and Eve (or at least a small population of human beings) in his image and with a human soul, from whom all human beings descended, or (2) they can say that hominins gradually evolved human qualities, and through that process became what we call human beings.

Theistic evolutionists have the same two options in regard to the origin of the sense of right and wrong and our feeling that we ought to do the right. They could conceivably think in terms of option 1, that is, that God created Adam and Eve or a select group of people and then implanted in them the knowledge of right and wrong and a sense that they should do the right. If someone wanted to take that position, they would *avoid* having to figure out how a sense of morality evolved. But, as we saw in the last chapter, that option contains so many problems and unanswered questions that many, even in the Evangelical world, have abandoned it. The attempt to use something like option 1 to explain the origin of morality is fraught with even more problems. There is nothing concrete to look at, no bones or artifacts to examine. They are dealing with thoughts and emotions. And the one thing they can see, namely, the bodies of people who died, throws the matter into complete confusion.

It seems that theistic evolutionists are going down the same road in regard to the origin of morality as they have followed in regard to the origin of human beings. They are not making the claim that at some point God turned hominins into moral creatures. Rather, they are deferring to option 2, which makes all aspects of the origin of human beings a product of the forces of physics and chemistry (even if at some point human beings became more than the sum of their parts). In line with secular sociobiologists, they are adding morality and the human sense of right and wrong to the list of qualities that evolved as hominins became human beings.

Evolution makes an absolute definition of right and wrong impossible

But how and when was the idea of right and wrong conceived; what does it mean to live morally in the context of evolution? Before we start looking at these topics, I have to offer a disclaimer. We are entering some very muddy waters, even more muddy than theistic evolutionist attempts to figure out the origin of the human soul and questions related to the image of God. We will see men and women struggling with truths central to our existence here in time and to the end of existence in the world. I can only encourage you to look at the arguments and ask yourself what they do to the Christian faith.

We start with Michael Ruse, who is thinking about the relationship between God and Darwinian evolution as a religious philosopher. He is helpful because he lays out the matter in clear terms. According to Ruse, right and wrong cannot be reduced to a code; it did not come from God as an expression of his will, as revealed in Scripture. Rather, it was revealed as life unfolded in the process of evolution. He points out that the female praying mantis may eat her husband. But that is natural for her; it would not be natural for us. God intends for us to do

> that which is within the limits of our evolved nature.... The progress of evolution was part of God's plan, God's intention. It is not a matter of fact, but a matter of divine desire. And as such, it gains moral value.... Biological progress stands behind our ultimate moral obligations, and behind this stands God.[191]

Ruse is saying that right and wrong are determined by what is natural in the context of evolution. Since God chose to use evolution to create living creatures, whatever fosters the progress of biological evolution is moral: "The Darwinian

---

[191] Michael Ruse, *Can a Darwinian Be a Christian?*, p. 185.

who is a Christian justifies his or her position here by reference to the way in which God has made things of positive value."[192] That is, as we look around us, we can see the many things of positive value that God has given us through the process of evolution. Therefore, "one's morality is being constrained and defined by what one takes to be the process and product of evolution."[193] (As an aside, this is the same tack taken by theistic evolutionists to explain how an evolving creation and its creator can be called "very good." Evolution determines that.)

Ruse says that right and wrong are determined by one's understanding of evolution and is subject to change as evolution is better understood: "If you can show that modern biology demands rethinking empirical claims (say, about birth control), then one's moral position might likewise be rethought."[194]

As mentioned, Ruse is arguing the matter philosophically. But what about those who closely identify with Christianity? Can they break his logic and provide a middle road that contains the idea of God's unchanging will that applies to all people of all time? What follows is a loosely organized collection of quotations from modern theistic evolutionists that illustrate the nature of right and wrong when determined in the context of evolution. Here's where the waters get muddy.

Sociobiologist Patricia Williams, whose book was published by Fortress Press of the Evangelical Lutheran Church of America, pulls no punches in explaining how sociobiology affects our understanding of sin: "We sin because we have natural, evolutionarily necessary desires that may become inordinate, especially in environments different from that in which our ancestors evolved."[195]

Therefore, according to Williams, punishment for sin is an illusion: "We do not suffer because God is punishing Adam and Eve's sin in us. Adam and Eve were never historical people, merely symbolic figures in a symbolic narrative."[196] According to Williams, God is benevolent, not vindictive: "The aspects of human life Genesis 3 presents as cursed are natural aspects of our evolutionary and primate heritage. They may be construed as blessings. They are not punishments for sin. With this realization, gone is the punitive God of Genesis 3. . . ."[197]

The power of evolution to provide human beings with choices has given rise to morality: "Morality develops naturally. It arises from our ancestral heritage and our efforts to live together, not through an externally imposed set of rules.

---

[192] Michael Ruse, *Can a Darwinian Be a Christian?*, p. 203.

[193] Michael Ruse, *Can a Darwinian Be a Christian?*, p. 202.

[194] Michael Ruse, *Can a Darwinian Be a Christian?*, p. 203.

[195] Patricia Williams, *Doing Without Adam and Eve: Sociobiology and Original Sin* (Minneapolis: Fortress Press, 2001), pp. 157,158.

[196] Patricia Williams, *Doing Without Adam and Eve: Sociobiology and Original Sin*, p. 158.

[197] Patricia Williams, *Doing Without Adam and Eve: Sociobiology and Original Sin*, p. 157.

With our evolution, a remarkable capacity for morality enters the universe. Like God, we know good from evil. As God creates a moral universe, *so do we.*"[198]

Williams ascribes the emergence of Christian love (even using the Christian term *charity*) to human evolution: "Charity is not natural to us, although it can arise in us by naturalistic means. . . . Charity is rooted in [our natural, evolved] abilities and inclinations, but to reach fruition, it must be nurtured."[199]

Human death is evil only because it cuts short our time to develop, create, and plan for the future. Human death is justified, however, because "having these things and experiencing death as an evil is far better than not having these things."[200] Williams concludes her discussion of evil:

> The source of evil is not some divine opponent of God. The source of evil is not even human sin. Rather, the sources of evil lie in attributes so valuable that we could not even consider eliminating them in order to eradicate evil. Presumably, neither would God. If the universe is to have the goods it does, evil cannot be abolished. God has structured the universe so that these greater goods more than compensate for evil. The fact that evil is more than compensated is enough to justify its existence.[201]

We'll show how this affects Williams' view of Jesus' work in the next chapter.

Warren Brown, the Fuller Seminary professor quoted earlier who argues that the human "soul" is a product of evolution, explains the origin of morality like this: God created mankind in a universe governed by the fundamental law that "survival benefits accrue from cooperation, and what is good for one is generally good for all."[202]

Reacting to claims that God is acting "immorally" in using the suffering of evolution as his tool of creation, John Munday writes,

> We maintain that to require God to justify his actions is arrogant hubris. God does not have to morally defend anything he does. It is the Creator's prerogative to set up creation according to his will and pleasure. We must conform our notion of love and morality to his. Why presume

---

[198] Patricia Williams, *Doing Without Adam and Eve: Sociobiology and Original Sin*, p. 166 (emphasis added).

[199] Patricia Williams, *Doing Without Adam and Eve: Sociobiology and Original Sin*, p. 158.

[200] Patricia Williams, *Doing Without Adam and Eve: Sociobiology and Original Sin*, p. 178.

[201] Patricia Williams, *Doing Without Adam and Eve: Sociobiology and Original Sin*, p. 179.

[202] Warren Brown, "Evolution, Cognitive Neuroscience, and the Soul," in *Perspectives on an Evolving Creation,* ed. Keith B. Miller, p. 523.

> his love and his morality should preclude all suffering of man and beast, and that it is always wrong for the innocent to suffer? [203]

This, of course, rejects Scripture's history of the world that includes a fall into sin and entrance of evil from the outside. And it rejects how God uses suffering as we have seen that described in chapter 3.

Robin Collins attempts to define sin in the context of evolution:

> Within an evolutionary framework, these inclinations that tempt us to evil can be seen as partly involving those inclinations toward self-pres-ervation, self-interest, aggression, and kinship interest that result from natural selection. *Such inclinations are not themselves evil since they can often lead to beneficial actions, such as keeping oneself alive.* But they pro-vide the temptation or basis for evil action. It is our choosing to follow these temptations over the good that often results in actual evil. . . .[204]

Collins is saying that the acts of selfishness that people do as participants in the process of natural selection are okay. But as beings who possess self-con-sciousness, an act can become selfish and evil if it goes beyond the requirements of evolution. (Imagine using that logic to counsel someone who has temper problems or is a compulsive spender: "It's fine to be aggressive and to hoard things to preserve yourself. That's how God enabled you to evolve. But you must determine if your self-awareness is fostering the kind of aggression and greed that God never intended people to use in natural selection.") Following this logic, it is impossible to know if we are doing good or evil.

Francisco Ayala slices it another way. He says that "the capacity for ethics is a necessary attribute of human nature, and thus a product of biological evolution," but that "moral norms are products of cultural [not biological] evolution."[205] In other words, our sense of morality evolved, but the actual definition of right and wrong is dictated by one's culture.

Even relatively conservative theologians cannot avoid trouble defining sin in the context of evolution. C. John Collins, whose views on Adam and Eve we looked at in the last chapter, offers an interesting quote from Norman T. Wright's 2002 commentary on Romans, which Collins says deserves "serious reflection":

---

[203] John Munday, "Animal Pain: Beyond the Threshold?" in *Perspectives on an Evolving Cre-ation,* ed. Keith B. Miller, p. 444.

[204] Robin Collins, "Evolution and Original Sin," in *Perspectives on an Evolving Creation*, ed. Keith B. Miller, p. 486 (emphasis added).

[205] Francisco Ayala, "Human Nature: One Evolutionist's View," in *Whatever Happened to the Soul?,* ed. Warren Brown, Nancey Murphy, and Newton Malony, p. 41.

What "sin" would have meant in the early dawn of the human race it is impossible to say; but the turning away from open and obedient relationship with the loving creator, and the turning toward that which, though beautiful and enticing, is not God, is such a many-sided phenomenon that it is not hard to envisage it at any stage of anthropoid development.[206]

Wright does not explain, however, how hominins "at the early dawn of the human race" could have had an "open and obedient relationship with the loving creator" or how they discovered what it meant to obey God.

A theistic evolutionist who wants to do justice to both Scripture and evolution cannot but conclude that God has two standards of morality. He has one standard for himself that he uses when he creates through evolution (which is revealed in the process of evolution itself), and he has another standard for us to use when making decisions on how to serve him and show love to our fellow man (which is the one revealed in Scripture).

Evolution denies mankind's fall and original sin[207]

According to evolution it is impossible to say that human beings *became* sinful. They always were sinful. Michael Ruse puts it bluntly: "Original sin is part of the biological package."[208] Or as Richard Mortimer puts it, theistic evolutionists replace original sin with "evolved instincts."[209]

T. A. Noble describes the problem:

The major problem with the doctrine of the Fall arising in the modern era is how to cope with the difficulty of assigning it a place in history or prehistory, which Pauline doctrine seems to require. The alternative, taken by many in the light of the story of human origins established by

---

[206] C. John Collins, *Did Adam and Eve Really Exist?*, p. 87. Quoting N. T. Wright's "Romans," in *The New Interpreter's Bible*, ed. Leander Kek et al. (Nashville: Abingdon, 2002), 10:393-770 at 524ab (the reference here is to an earlier printing where the quotation was at 526ab).

[207] In this discussion the phrase "original sin" is used in reference to a person's sinful nature, not the guilt of Adam's sin that was passed down to all people as Paul describes it in Romans 5:12-14. Most theistic evolutionists use the term in the first sense and rarely discuss the implications of evolution for the second sense.

[208] Michael Ruse, *Can a Darwinian Be a Christian?*, p. 210.

[209] Richard Mortimer, "Blocher, Original Sin and Evolution," in *Darwin, Creation and the Fall: Theological Challenges*, ed. R. J. Berry and T. A. Noble (Nottingham: Apollos [InterVarsity Press], 2009), p. 187.

modern science, is to reinterpret and dispense with the idea that the Fall was an event.[210]

Noble concludes that we simply cannot reconcile evolution and Scripture in regard to the fall into sin and the advent of death. On how to reconcile what evolution and Scripture say about death he writes, "We must be prepared to accept that there are things we do not yet know and that in the meantime we have to hold the two stories in tension."[211] He concludes his essay on the same note: "If there are tensions with the story told by modern science, we must not fall into the trap of conflating the two stories but live with the tension while working at ways of resolving it. . . . We may not be able to see the resolution of the tension until the kingdom comes in glory and power."[212]

Where Noble sees a "tension" that might someday be resolved with more information, Robin Collins, like many theistic evolutionists, sees an unresolvable contradiction. He proposes that Genesis 1-3 should be read both as the history of human evolution *and also* as a picture of an ideal state "that was never achieved, an ideal picture of an ideal relationship with God."[213] He calls this the historical/ideal (HI) view. According to this view, Adam and Eve in their perfect state represent a yet unrealized ideal. And into this he weaves a way to view the fall into sin and a role for Adam and Eve. Adam and Eve played a role

> of representing "everyperson"—that is, each one of us—and that of representing the first hominins, or group of hominins, who had the capacity for free choice and self-consciousness. With this capacity for self-consciousness and free choice, the HI view hypothesizes that these hominins also became aware of God and God's requirements, but more often than not rejected them. One could even imagine that this awareness was particularly clear, uncluttered by the spiritual darkness that eventually clouded the minds of the human race because of its turning away from God. . . . So, in this sense, these first ancestors were in what could be considered an original state of "justice and holiness," free from bondage to sin. Nonetheless they were subject to various temptations arising both from the desires and instincts they inherited from their evolutionary past and from various new possibilities for self-centered-

---

[210] T. A. Noble, "Original Sin and the Fall: Definitions and a Proposal," in *Darwin, Creation and the Fall: Theological Challenges*, ed. R. J. Berry and T. A. Noble, p. 99.

[211] T. A. Noble, "Original Sin and the Fall: Definitions and a Proposal," p. 123.

[212] T. A. Noble, "Original Sin and the Fall: Definitions and a Proposal," p. 129.

[213] Robin Collins, "Evolution and Original Sin," in *Perspectives on an Evolving Creation*, ed. Keith B. Miller, p. 470.

ness, self-idolization, self-denigration, and the like that came with their new self-consciousness.[214]

In Robin Collins' view, original sin is a combination of "(1) the sinful choices of these hominins, (2) the continuing sinful choices of the succeeding generations including ourselves as we come to self-consciousness, and (3) the resulting bondage to sin and spiritual darkness that is inherited from our ancestors and generated by our own choices."[215] However, original sin is not a "distortion of human nature," but is similar to other things we *inherit* like genetics and culture, only that it has its own spiritual dimension.[216]

R. J. Berry and T. A. Noble describe the fall as the failure of the hominins who had received God's image to rise from hominin to human, that is, to attain the moral greatness the new human beings were meant to exemplify. They explain:

> But our best hypothesis about human moral experience and sin might run something like this. Our pre humen ancestors cannot be called immoral (let alone "sinful") on the grounds that they killed, deceived, behaved promiscuously, and so on. But when God created the first humans, apes now in God's image, or *Homo divinus* as John Stott has called them, these creatures, since they were now brought into this unique relationship to God, became moral agents. Although they shared many inherited—including behavioral—traits with their ancestors and animal relatives, this did not mean that they were dependent on or determined by them. . . . But the new relationship to God, being in his image, which led to new moral possibilities and responsibilities, was followed by a failure to believe and obey God, and consequently a failure to grow into the spiritual and moral greatness we were meant to exemplify.[217]

Catholic theologian Denis Edwards, who himself dismisses the idea of original sin, surveys some Catholic theistic evolutionists' ideas. Some theologians, (and not just from the Catholic church) consider the fall as an "upward fall." This sounds odd to anyone who reads Genesis 3 with any degree of literalism.

---

[214] Robin Collins, in *Perspectives on an Evolving Creation*, ed. Keith B. Miller, p. 470.

[215] Robin Collins, "Evolution and Original Sin," in *Perspectives on an Evolving Creation*, ed. Keith B. Miller, p. 470.

[216] Robin Collins, "Evolution and Original Sin," in *Perspectives on an Evolving Creation*, ed. Keith B. Miller, pp. 470,471.

[217] R. J. Berry and T. A. Noble, "Epilogue: The Sea of Faith: Darwin Didn't Drain It" in *Darwin, Creation and the Fall, Theological Challenges*, R. J. Berry and T. A. Noble, T. eds., pp. 200,201. It is interesting that God's image is supposed to lead to *new* moral possibilities and responsibilities. If this is really a description of God's image, one wonders how this description might be applied to God's way of acting.

To explain how an upward fall might happen, Edwards reviews the thoughts of Catholic theologian Gabriel Daly. Daly's view is couched in the Catholic understanding of grace as God's healing power, which he deftly turns into an evolutionary concept. The "fall" is "the movement from one level of evolution to another . . . an alienation from peace at one level in order to attain it at a higher level." [218]

Grace comes to the aid of human beings as they move from one level of evolution to the next. Throughout the process of evolution, human beings "go forward 'weighed down by a genetically produced nostalgia' for their animal past." Humans retain from the previous level "the appetites, instincts, drives, and energies that bring satisfaction to other animals." But they "are not enough to bring peace" to the human being at a new level of self-awareness. Nevertheless, the old appetites and desires remain "in the human being alongside the newly developed awareness of right and wrong." This way of thinking provides an evolutionary explanation for the human urge to sin. These urges are what the classical doctrine of original sin has called the "tinder of sin" (*fomes peccati*), or what is behind what we normally think of when we hear the word *temptation*.

Edwards asks if the instincts and drives that are proper to nonhuman primates become sin when they are found in self-aware human beings. Daly's response is that they are not sin, since they come from the hands of the Creator. But they can become the instruments of sin if they are not shaped and healed by grace.

But do people sin when they revert to the instincts of an earlier level? No. After all, the "sins" they were committing at an earlier stage of their existence were tools God was using to enable them to evolve upward.

Because of its very nature, evolution negates any idea of a fall into sin as recorded in Scripture. And it goes a long way toward redefining sin. Gheorghe Razmerita, arguing against theistic evolution, states what should be obvious in an upward evolving world, that "the idea of a 'fall' is inappropriate, since humanity has never been so close to its highest level of consciousness, morality, and responsibility as now." [219]

Death cannot be considered an act of judgment

Malcolm Jeeves and R. J. Berry write, "Physical death should not be equated with evil; it was part of God's plan from the beginning." Lamoureux acknowledges the problem: "The greatest challenge for evolutionary creation is to explain biblical passages that refer to a causal connection between the sin of Adam and

---

[218] Quotations in this and the next paragraph are from Denis Edwards, *The God of Evolution*. See loc. 615-619 for the section on Gabriel Daly.

[219] Gheorghe Razmerita, *Theistic Evolution's Struggle for Survival,* p. 123.

the origin of physical death."[220] It is, in fact, impossible. Lamoureux handles the problem by assigning Genesis 1-11 to the category of ancient beliefs.[221]

Evolutionists teach that natural selection requires the presence of death, and so death has always existed in the world. Some theistic evolutionists compromise on this issue and teach that mankind began to die only after Adam and Eve sinned. But they know they cannot compromise on the death of animals; for evolution to have happened, animals had to have died from the start. Verne Poythress writes:

> I conclude that we do not have any firm basis for saying that animal death started only after the fall of man. Again, we must beware of presuming to dictate to God what kind of world he had to create. It had to be 'very good' in his sight; but that is not the same as saying that it must match what some of *us* may think ideal.[222]

Cliché: Mankind began to die after the fall into sin. But animals have always been dying.

It is true that Scripture does not specifically say that animals began to die when mankind began to die. But it is impossible to accept Scripture's account of creation and believe that God created animals with the intention that they should die. In Scripture human death is always viewed as something evil, which needs to be overcome. To say that animal death is a good and necessary part of God's method of creating the animals is illogical.

It is sometimes argued that in order to understand God's threat of death, Adam and Eve had to be seeing death around them. But this is pure speculation. It implies they did not understand that God had given life to their bodies through his spirit and that if he withdrew his spirit, their bodies would be powerless, that is, dead. And even if they witnessed animal death, it would be impossible for them to learn from that what human death might mean—the death of people created in God's image with an immortal soul.

But this cliché is really a non issue. A person cannot accept one

---

[220] Denis Lamoureux, *Evolutionary Creation*, p. 305.

[221] Those who agree that Genesis 1-3 contain some actual history often claim that human "death" in that chapter refers not to physical death but to spiritual death. But when God told Adam that he came from the ground and would return to the ground, it is clear that God was describing physical death.

[222] Verne Poythress, *Redeeming Science* (Wheaton: Crossway, 2006), p. 122 (emphasis author's).

piece of evolution and disregard other pieces at will. The supposed fossil evidence includes human as well as animal remains. And the idea that God created two perfect human beings in the midst of a huge hominin population dying all around them forces us into the jungle of impossible questions and contradictions we looked at in the last chapter on the origin of mankind.

This argument is nothing other than a last-ditch attempt to teach evolution while at the same time teaching that death came into our lives after Adam and Eve sinned. If a person wants to teach that God exempted Adam and Eve from death and created them in a special way outside the process of evolution, why not just accept a six 24-hour-day creation.

In Scripture death came into the world as God's judgment on Adam and Eve because they sinned; they refused to obey the command he gave them. Paul wrote: "For the wages of sin is death" (Romans 6:23). And in 1 Corinthians 15 he links sin and death: "The sting of death is sin, and the power of sin is the law" (verse 56). The process of evolution nullifies this part of Scripture's message, which is so prominent from the beginning of Scripture to the end.

But how can it be otherwise? Natural selection makes necessary the whole range of self-centered and rebellious actions God speaks against in his Word. How can these acts be called sinful? Evolution teaches that death is part of the natural order of things. How can it be bad, much less a penalty for sin?

For that reason, the teaching of judgment receives little attention in theistic evolutionary literature. And when it does, it is only to dismiss it as a remnant of ancient religious thought. Denis Alexander simply denies Genesis 3: There is no "suggestion that the earth itself was cursed . . . or that anything physically changed in either the earth or in the heavens as a consequence of the Fall." According to Alexander, the ground was cursed because, on account of sin, Adam "would no longer be a really effective earth-keeper, looking after the *adamah* [the earth] as he should."[223] In this view, the curse is nothing more than Scripture's observation that Adam's sin would make him an inept farmer and that the land would suffer because of his lack of skill.

Catholic theologian Jack Mahoney states the matter clearly: "Whereas in traditional Christianity death has always been perceived as a penalty, in evolution through natural selection the death of individuals, not just of humans, it [death] is rather seen as a biological necessity and a requirement. Without individual death there would be no natural selection among the variety of random

---

[223] Denis Alexander, *Creation or Evolution,* p. 262.

evolutionary developments that occur over time, no processes of variation and specializing, and no surviving in response to environments."[224]

Denis Alexander cannot see death as anything other than God's tool of blessings. The following quotation is an example of how belief in evolution affects one's ability to approach Scripture with any degree of logic. Alexander writes, "Physical death is intrinsic to the purposes of God for human life on this earth, and we cannot inherit the kingdom without going through its portal."[225] This means that since God uses death to create us through the process of evolution, it is only natural that he would use death to take us to heaven. But this logic destroys the central message of Scripture. God sent his Son to overcome sin and the curse of death. Only because Christ defeated death's power to usher people into hell does God use death as our portal to heaven.

Alexander is not alone in arguing this way. Daniel Harrell compares the blessings of Jesus' death on the cross with the death required by evolution: "Death becomes the gateway to eternal life it was supposed to be in the first place—foreshadowed by evolution's own use of death as the gateway to biological new life."[226]

These authors are using the logic demanded by evolution, not the logic of Scripture.

Some theistic evolutionists do see the elephants in the room

Peter Enns, former professor at Westminster Theological Seminary, sees the problems of combining natural selection with Scripture's teachings of sin and death:

> The very nature of what sin is and why people die is turned on its head. Some characteristics that Christians have thought of as sinful—for example, in an evolutionary scheme the aggression and dominance associated with "survival of the fittest" and sexual promiscuity to perpetuate one's gene pool—are understood as means of ensuring survival.

> Likewise, death is not the enemy to be defeated. It may be feared, it may be ritualized, . . . but death is not the unnatural state introduced by a disobedient couple in a primordial garden. Actually, it is the means that promoted the continued evolution of life on this planet and even ensures workable population numbers. Death may hurt, but it is evolution's ally.

---

[224]Jack Mahoney, *Christianity in Evolution* (Washington, D.C.: Georgetown University Press, 2011), page 63. Kindle.

[225]Denis Alexander, *Creation or Evolution: Do We Have to Choose?*, p. 267.

[226]Daniel Harrell, *Nature's Witness: How Evolution Can Inspire Faith*, p. 119.

Evolution, therefore, cannot simply be grafted onto evangelical Christian faith.[227]

Madueme and Reeves write: "If we remove a historical Adam and fall from the theological picture, then sin becomes a side effect of evolution, a part of the natural ontology of created human beings. . . . The creator God is rendered ultimately responsible for sin."[228]

Others see the problems that evolution causes for how we view right and wrong, and how we define sin. Robert Price and Edwin Suominen mock Christians who read Scripture in a straightforward way. But they also mock theistic evolutionists for trying to find a compromise position:

> You are here because you had ancestors who did what it took to survive and reproduce in a very harsh world. It's as simple as that! What you inherited from them is not some taint of sin, but the very traits that allowed them to produce you. . . . Those actions that have been labeled as "sin" do not arise from any subsequent corruption of our nature, but from our very nature itself as the descendants of reproductive survivors in a harsh and brutal world.[229]

Cornelius Hunter describes the problem evolution causes for God's right to judge human beings: "How can God be so aloof from his creation, allowing even his creatures to be the result of blind ethical forces, yet simultaneously be the source of our moral law and ultimate judge of our actions?"[230]

Conclusion

I approached this writing project with the expectation that there was a group of relatively conservative evangelical theologians who accepted evolution but who would attempt to read Scripture in a straightforward way.

I was being naïve. It soon became clear that the very act of accepting evolution as God's tool of creation puts an author in the position of trying to fit a square

---

[227] Peter Enns, *The Evolution of Adam: What the Bible Does and Doesn't Say About Human Origins* (Grand Rapids: Brazos [Baker] Press, 2012), p. 147 (paragraph divisions mine).

[228] Hans Madueme and Michael Reeves, "Threads in a Seamless Garment: Original Sin in Systematic Theology," in *Adam, the Fall, and Original Sin,* ed. Hans Madueme and Michael Reeves, pp. 210, 211.

[229] Robert Price and Edwin Suominen, *Evolving Out of Eden: Christian Responses to Evolution,* pp. 190, 191.

[230] Cornelius Hunter, *Darwin's God: Evolution and the Problem of Evil* (Grand Rapids: Baker, 2001), p. 138.

peg into a round hole. An author who accepts evolution must get out his knife and whittle Scripture into a shape that will fit into the teaching of evolution.

The discussion of a six-day creation versus theistic evolution has become a matter of rhetoric and compromise. But in truth it is a matter of opposites. If God is the Creator of the evolutionary process, we can never see him as the God of Scripture, complete in love and mercy, and righteous when he judges. God himself becomes responsible for the evil in the world. The meaning of right and wrong is not determined by God's revelation of his will in Scripture, but by whatever contributes to the process of evolution. The concept of "sin" becomes vague and subject to human definition. We have no basis on which to diagnose the problem of evil and seek a remedy. Once the link between evolution and death is created, the link between sin and death is severed. The idea that sin is serious and that God will judge sin is lost—or it would be lost except for the fact that the works of the law are still written in our hearts and that we still have the testimony of our conscience.

Elephants in the room

In the previous lessons, we identified a number of elephants in the room. To keep them in mind, we'll repeat them:

- **The basic framework of the world's history as taught in Scripture is wrong.**
- **The evil associated with creation by evolution came from God.**
- **God, whom Scripture says *is love*, used the evils of natural selection over billions of years to create living beings.**
- **The process of evolution—which locks mankind into a system of self-interest, competition, and death—leads to freedom.**
- **Scripture's description of the origin of mankind is wrong.**
- **God must be evil because his image defined human beings, and he requires human beings to take part in the evils of natural selection.**
- **God commanded mankind to rule over the earth in love, and then he made it impossible for mankind to fulfill that command.**

From this chapter we discern several more elephants:

- **The requirements of evolution, not the will of God, define morality.**

- Sin cannot be equated with evil because God's tool of natural selection requires it. At best, sin can only be defined as causing others more suffering than is necessary.

- Death is good and natural.

- God cannot judge evolving creatures for doing what he requires them to do.

In the final chapter, "What Jesus Did for the World," we will find evolution forcing itself into the deepest corner of our faith. If right and wrong cannot be defined, why was it necessary for Christ to keep God's law in our place? If God used death to create us, why did Christ have to overcome it by means of his death and resurrection? If imperfection and struggle are normal, then the world is not living under God's temporary curse and talk of its "restoration" when Jesus returns is a contradiction in terms.

Chapter 7

What Jesus Did for the World

According to Scripture

In the previous chapters we explored foundational truths that lie at the center of the Christian faith. Everything Jesus did for us rests on these truths.

The world was perfect. It fell into sin. Someday God will restore it.

Jesus created a world in which there was light

The gospel writer John tells us,

> In the beginning was the Word, and the Word was with God, and the Word was God. He was in the beginning with God. All things were made through him, and without him was not any thing made that was made. In him was life, and the life was the light of men. The light shines in the darkness, and the darkness has not overcome it. (John 1:1-5)

John calls Jesus "the Word." In the beginning, Jesus was "with" God. In fact, as John says, Jesus was God. God created the world "through him." John describes Jesus' creating activity from two standpoints. First the positive—everything that was made was made through him. Then the negative—without him nothing was made.

Jesus came to give light to the world. He came to give the world the light it had lost. After all, if Jesus is light, and God made the world through him, God would have created the world and the people in it to enjoy the light of his presence and blessings. But the light in which he created the world was lost. Christ came to restore that light.

By nature we do not understand or want to accept the light. But, as John says, "To all who did receive him, who believed in his name, he gave the right to become children of God, who were born, not of blood nor of the will of the flesh nor of the will of man, but of God" (John 1:12,13).

Jesus came to destroy Satan

The light was lost because Satan led Adam and Eve into sin. It was replaced with darkness. Every one of us were born in the darkness of unbelief, under the dominion of sin, and on the path to eternal death with Satan. Jesus reversed all this. He came to fulfill the promise God made in Genesis 3:15 that a child of the woman would undo the results of Satan's temptation of Adam and Eve.

Jesus said, "Now is the judgment of this world; now will the ruler of this world be cast out" (John 12:31). Not only will Satan be judged. This world, which operates under Satan's influence, will also be judged and condemned along with him. When he was just hours away from his crucifixion, Jesus said, "The prince of this world now stands condemned" (John 16:11). Once the guilt of sin was gone, Satan lost his right to accuse people before God and claim that we must suffer God's judgment along with him. Paul said that Jesus' work "disarmed" Satan:

> He forgave us all our sins, having canceled the written code, with its regulations, that was against us and that stood opposed to us; he took it away, nailing it to the cross. And having disarmed the powers and authorities, he made a public spectacle of them, triumphing over them by the cross. (Colossians 2:13-15)

The writer of Hebrews explained that God's Son died and rose again so that "through death he might destroy the one who has the power of death, that is, the devil, and deliver all those who through fear of death were subject to lifelong slavery" (Hebrews 2:14,15).

Jesus described his own kingdom, that is, his right to rule over all creation, as the antithesis of Satan's kingdom. When some religious leaders accused Jesus of driving out demons by the power of Satan, Jesus replied, "If Satan . . . is divided against himself, how will his kingdom stand? For you say that I cast out demons by Beelzebul. . . . But if it is by the finger of God that I cast out demons, then the kingdom of God has come upon you" (Luke 11:18,20).

Someday Jesus will return and give Satan his final death blow. John saw a vision of that: "Then I saw heaven opened, and behold, a white horse! The one sitting on it is called Faithful and True, and in righteousness he judges and makes war" (Revelation 19:11). Then John saw Satan's end: "Fire came down from heaven and consumed them, and the devil who had deceived them was thrown into the lake of fire and sulfur where the beast and the false prophet were, and they will be tormented day and night forever and ever" (Revelation 20:9,10).

Jesus undid the curse of sin

God's commandment not to eat from the Tree of the Knowledge of Good and Evil gave Adam and Eve a way to serve him. Satan, however, turned that command into a way to sin against him. Their sin brought God's curse on the world:

> And to Adam he said, "Because you have . . .eaten of the tree of which I commanded you, 'You shall not eat of it,' cursed is the ground because of you. . . . By the sweat of your face you shall eat bread, till you return to the ground, for out of it you were taken; for you are dust, and to dust you shall return." (Genesis 3:17-19)

Jesus suffered not only the guilt of people's sins, he also took on himself the full brunt of God's curse. The Old Testament prophet Isaiah expressed it like this:

> Surely *he has borne our griefs and carried our sorrows*; yet we esteemed him stricken, smitten by God, and afflicted. But he was pierced for our transgressions; he was crushed for our iniquities; upon him was the chastisement that brought us peace, and with his wounds we are healed. All we like sheep have gone astray; we have turned—every one—to his own way; and the LORD has laid on him the iniquity of us all. (Isaiah 53:4-6)

Through faith in what Jesus did for us we have the life that Adam and Eve lost: "But in fact Christ has been raised from the dead, the firstfruits of those who have fallen asleep. For as by a man came death, by a man has come also the resurrection of the dead" (1 Corinthians 15:20,21). When Jesus returns, he will destroy our ultimate enemy, death. Paul wrote, "Then comes the end, when he delivers the kingdom to God the Father after destroying every rule and every authority and power. For he must reign until he has put all his enemies under his feet. The last enemy to be destroyed is death" (1 Corinthians 15:24-26).

Jesus restored peace between God and everything he created

After Adam and Eve sinned, there was "enmity" or hostility between God and mankind. God's just anger over sin rested on us. For this reason we could not look peaceably at God.

Jesus restored God's peace. Because of Jesus' life and death, God is again at peace with us, and this gives us courage to live at peace with him. Paul explained this using the word "reconciliation":

> Therefore, if anyone is in Christ, he is a new creation. The old has passed away; behold, the new has come. All this is from God, who through Christ reconciled us to himself and gave us the ministry of reconciliation; that is, in Christ God was reconciling the world to himself, not counting their trespasses against them, and entrusting to us the message of reconciliation. Therefore, we are ambassadors for Christ, God making his appeal through us. We implore you on behalf of Christ, be reconciled

to God. For our sake he made him to be sin who knew no sin, so that in him we might become the righteousness of God. (2 Corinthians 5:17- 21 NIV84)

Since God is at peace with us, we can face all our sins for what they are, offenses against him. We have the courage to do this because we can seek God's forgiveness in Christ and live at peace with him in the light of that forgiveness.

Jesus not only created peace between God and humanity, he also created peace between God and the rest of creation: "For in him all the fullness of God was pleased to dwell, and through him to reconcile to himself all things, whether on earth or in heaven, making peace by the blood of his cross" (Colossians 1:19,20). This is reflected in Romans 8. All creation, Paul says, awaits the day when God will usher mankind into the complete freedom of the new heaven and earth. And all of creation knows they will join Christians in that freedom:

> The creation waits in eager expectation for the sons of God to be revealed. For the creation was subjected to frustration, not by its own choice, but by the will of the one who subjected it, in hope that the creation itself will be liberated from its bondage to decay and brought into the glorious freedom of the children of God. (Romans 8:19-21 NIV84)

Jesus will restore the world to its original condition

There are four chapters in Scripture where everything is perfect. Genesis 1 and 2 are two of them. Revelation 21 and 22 are the other two. The chapters in between tell us how God overcame the tragedy of Genesis 3 and made Revelation 21 and 22 possible.

According to Jesus, who created the world, our present world is not moving forward toward a brighter future through the process of evolution or the efforts of mankind. After Adam and Eve fell into sin, God immediately changed the world by sending suffering and death into it. Someday, just as quickly, he will change it back to what it was before. Jesus told his disciples, "I tell you the truth, at the *renewal of all things*, when the Son of Man sits on his glorious throne, you who have followed me will also sit on twelve thrones, judging the twelve tribes of Israel" (Matthew 19:28,29). Peter said to the people of Jerusalem:

> Repent, then, and turn to God, so that your sins may be wiped out, that times of refreshing may come from the Lord, and that he may send the Christ, who has been appointed for you—even Jesus. He must remain in heaven until the time comes for God *to restore everything*, as he promised long ago through his holy prophets. (Acts 3:19-21)

Scripture describes the new, restored heaven and earth. In the last chapters of Revelation, Jesus lets John see it: "The old order of things has passed away" (Revelation 21:4); "I am making everything new!" (21:5). The old order will be replaced with what we all yearn for: "He will wipe every tear from their eyes. There will be no more death or mourning or crying or pain" (21:4).

Revelation 21 and 22 symbolize the restored creation. These chapters use symbols from the first creation in Genesis 1 and 2. This reflects the fact that God's creation will be restored to how it had originally been created.

As in the original Garden of Eden, "the dwelling place of God is with man. He will dwell with them" (21:3). It will be a perfect place. Its residents will be "those who are written in the Lamb's book of life" (21:27). In the original garden, there were rivers. In the new creation there will be a river flowing out from God's throne. The river contains the water of life. It is flowing down the center of the street in the city, accessible to everyone (22:1,2). The Tree of Life is there too. In fact, there are two of them, one on each side of the river. They will bear 12 crops of fruit each year. All will once again have access to the Tree of Life (22:2,3). God's servants will serve him perfectly, as he created them to do (22:3). There will be no more need of the sun because God himself will be his people's light (22:5).

The perfection of the first creation will be restored: "No longer will there be any curse" (22:3 NIV). This last statement is important. It calls the difficulties that came into the lives of Adam and Eve after they sinned *a curse*—a curse imposed by God himself at the beginning. The new creation and all who live in it will be free from the difficulties God imposed. The gates of the city (the city being a symbol of God's people), will never have to be locked shut; the enemies of God will have no power there (21:8,25).

Paul had this in mind when he described the suffering of this present world in Romans 8. We quote those verses again, this time in the ESV translation:

> For I consider that the sufferings of this present time are not worth comparing with the glory that is to be revealed to us. For the creation waits with eager longing for the revealing of the sons of God. For the creation was subjected to futility, not willingly, but because of him who subjected it, in hope that the creation itself will be set free from its bondage to corruption and obtain the freedom of the glory of the children of God. For we know that the whole creation has been groaning together in the pains of childbirth until now. And not only the creation, but we ourselves, who have the firstfruits of the Spirit, groan inwardly as we wait eagerly for adoption as sons, the redemption of our bodies. (Romans 8:18-23)

Jesus is the greatest expression of God's love

In chapter 3 we focused on the fact that God is love. When we look at Jesus, we see the greatest expression of God's love; we see the love of God in action. John tells us,

> For God so loved the world, that he gave his only Son, that whoever believes in him should not perish but have eternal life. For God did not send his Son into the world to condemn the world, but in order that the world might be saved through him. (John 3:16,17)

In our current state, we would all be condemned and perish eternally. John the Baptist said, "Whoever believes in the Son has eternal life; whoever does not obey the Son shall not see life, but the wrath of God remains on him" (John 3:36). God, in justice, will bring his wrath on all who remain in their sins, but he does not want to do that. In love he sent Jesus to save the world.

Whoever has faith in Jesus' work for them will be saved. Faith is well defined in Scripture. Paul declared his message to all: "I have declared to both Jews and Greeks that they must turn to God in repentance and have faith in our Lord Jesus" (Acts 20:21 NIV84). Paul explained the gift we have received through faith in Christ:

> But when the kindness and love of God our Savior appeared, he saved us, not because of righteous things we had done, but because of his mercy. He saved us through the washing of rebirth and renewal by the Holy Spirit, whom he poured out on us generously through Jesus Christ our Savior, so that, having been justified by his grace, we might become heirs having the hope of eternal life. (Titus 3:4-7 NIV)

Paul also prays "that you, being rooted and established in love, may have power, together with all the saints, to grasp how wide and long and high and deep is the love of Christ, and to know this love that surpasses knowledge--that you may be filled to the measure of all the fullness of God" (Ephesians 3:16-19).

The Son of God became the Son of Man

Jesus came to save people. Jesus sometimes called himself "the Son of Man." In order to save us, God's Son became a human being, a descendant of Adam: "But when the fullness of time had come, God sent forth his Son, born of woman, born under the law, to redeem those who were under the law, so that we might receive adoption as sons" (Galatians 4:4,5). Human beings are under God's law. Human beings receive adoption as God's sons and daughters.

Paul narrowed the scope of who fell and who will be restored in Christ: "For as by a man came death, by a man has come also the resurrection of the dead. For as in Adam all die, so also in Christ shall all be made alive" (1 Corinthians 15:21,22). The writer of Hebrews also emphasizes whom Jesus came to save. He did not come to save the angels who fell but human beings: "For surely it is not angels that he helps, but he helps the offspring of Abraham" (Hebrews 2:16).

Jesus became a human being in every way. The writer of Hebrews wrote: "Both the one who makes men holy and those who are made holy are of the same family. So Jesus is not ashamed to call them brothers. . . . Therefore he had to be made like his brothers in every respect, so that he might become a merciful and faithful high priest in the service of God, to make propitiation[231] for the sins of the people" (Hebrews 2:11,16,17). Genesis 1 and 2 make a clear distinction between mankind and the other living beings. In saying that Jesus became "like his brothers" and "shared in their humanity," the writer is drawing a boundary around the part of God's creation that Jesus came to save, namely "mankind."

Jesus came to suffer for our sins and to fulfill God's law in our place

Right and wrong are real things. Acts that go against God's will are sin. Sin is the cause of death. God's judgment over sin is real and it is just. These truths are repeated again and again in Scripture. Jesus came to earth because they are true.

We know they are true. We are moral beings. We know that it's wrong to do some things and right to do other things. We sense guilt when we do wrong and satisfaction when we do right. But regardless of how satisfied we sometimes feel, the burden of guilt we endure for the wrongs we do must be satisfied. That's why the Son of God became the Son of Man.

In one way or another, all the laws God gave the Old Testament people of Israel impressed on them that they had inherited the sin of Adam and Eve. Not only that, but some of those laws, especially the laws of sacrifice, impressed on the people that God would fulfill the promise he gave to Adam and Eve. He would send someone to sacrifice himself for them.

Paul spoke of Jesus' death in terms of the Old Testament "Passover" sacrifice and celebration. He encouraged the Christians in Corinth, "Cleanse out the old leaven [sin] that you may be a new lump, [bread with no leaven in it] as you really are unleavened [by being forgiven in Christ]. For Christ, our Passover lamb, has been sacrificed [on a cross]. Let us therefore celebrate the festival [our

---

[231] Propitiation is an act that makes up for the wrong a person did.

new life of freedom in Christ], not with the old leaven, the leaven of malice and evil, but with the unleavened bread of sincerity and truth" (1 Corinthians 5:7,8).

The Israelites had priests who performed their sacrifices. Jesus fulfilled the Old Testament laws relating to the priesthood. The writer of Hebrews explains,

> For it was indeed fitting that we should have such a high priest, holy, innocent, unstained, separated from sinners, and exalted above the heavens. He has no need, like those high priests, to offer sacrifices daily, first for his own sins and then for those of the people, since he did this once for all when he offered up himself. (Hebrews 7:26,27)

Paul described Jesus' work: "Christ redeemed us from the curse of the law by becoming a curse for us—for it is written, 'Cursed is everyone who is hanged on a tree'" (Galatians 3:13), and so did Peter: "He himself bore our sins in his body on the tree, that we might die to sin and live to righteousness. By his wounds you have been healed" (1 Peter 2:24).

Jesus also came to do what Adam and Eve failed to do. He came in order "to fulfill all righteousness" (Matthew 3:16). Jesus began his ministry by being baptized, which was something God wanted all the people to do. After his baptism, Jesus was driven out into the desert to be tempted by the Devil. He responded to Satan's temptations with a firm resolve to follow his Father's will.

God's law cannot be swept under the carpet. The people of Jesus' day were prone to tone down the Laws of God and adjust them according to which parts of them they could keep and which parts they found impossible to keep. In the Sermon on the Mount, Jesus explained the breadth and depth of the Ten Commandments. Jesus taught the ironclad nature of God's law as revealed in the Old Testament and that he himself had come to fulfill that law in our place: He said,

> Do not think that I have come to abolish the Law or the Prophets; *I have not come to abolish them but to fulfill them.* For truly, I say to you, until heaven and earth pass away, not an iota, not a dot, will pass from the Law until all is accomplished. Therefore whoever relaxes one of the least of these commandments and teaches others to do the same will be called least in the kingdom of heaven, but whoever does them and teaches them will be called great in the kingdom of heaven. (Matthew 5:17-19)

The Old Testament people had many religious rituals and rules for life that Scripture says we no longer have to follow (Colossians 2:16,17). But God's definition of right and wrong as summarized in the Ten Commandments remains God's will for all people of all time. Paul says, "For the commandments, You shall not commit adultery, You shall not murder, You shall not steal, You shall not covet, and any other commandment, are summed up in this word: 'You shall love your neighbor as yourself.' Love does no wrong to a neighbor; therefore love is the fulfilling of the law" (Romans 13:9-10).

All people, including those who have never seen a Bible, know the basics of God's law. Paul says: "When Gentiles [non Jews], who do not have the law, by nature do what the law requires, they are a law to themselves, even though they do not have the law. They show that the work of the law is written on their hearts" (Romans 2:14-15).

Any attempt to combine the law revealed in the Old Testament with some variation of evolved human altruism, makes God's revealed law into a sham. It does what Jesus said he would never do, namely, "abolish" the law. And it also turns into a sham Jesus' mission to die for our guilt and keep God's law for human beings who cannot keep it themselves. Jesus accepted his father's right to judge sin. He took the full brunt of God's judgment for sin on himself. Isaiah prophesied:

> He was pierced for our transgressions; he was crushed for our iniquities; upon him was the chastisement that brought us peace, and with his wounds we are healed. All we like sheep have gone astray; we have turned—every one—to his own way; and the LORD has laid on him the iniquity of us all. (Isaiah 53:5-6)

Jesus came to give us freedom

"So if *the Son* sets you free, you will be free indeed" (John 8:36).

Theistic evolutionists have a difficult time reconciling the goodness of God with the violence, struggle, and death necessary for natural selection to occur. But they feel they can justify God's use of evolution by arguing that human freedom is an indispensable component of human nature and only a process like evolution can make human beings free. We began discussing this claim in chapter 3. But it warrants further discussion because it has become the theistic evolutionists' trump card.

Theistic evolutionists claim that the method God used to create Adam and Eve as described in Genesis 2 did not give them the chance to become free. Adam and Eve lived in an environment where they did not have any choices. They were "programmed" to act in a certain way. This gives them another reason to dismiss Genesis 1 and 2.

Evolution, it is claimed, allowed human beings to develop in a *noncoercive environment*. Such an environment enabled them to assess options and choose between them. The result was human freedom. Applied to the Christian life it boils down to this: If a person only knows how to do God's will, then that person is a robot. But if one knows how to do both good and bad, then he or she can analyze the situation and choose the God-pleasing course. By growing to make informed decisions about right and wrong, people learned to serve God and their fellow man willingly and freely, which is what God wants.

So we have two ways to view ourselves: *robots* in a traditional reading of Genesis 1 and 2 or *free human beings* in an evolutionary reading of those chapters. But are these the only options? To start, consider the following illustration. It limps, but it makes an important point that will help us answer the question.

Suppose you have a good sum of money to invest, and you want to invest it wisely. You divide your money between two investors. The first says, "I have some ideas, and I want to meet every month to hear your ideas, and together we'll make some decisions about where to invest your money. But I will never force you to follow my advice. You have the final word." You look forward to the meetings and the chance to work together with him to make the right choices.

You take the other half of your money to another investor. The investor tells you to check back in six months. In the meantime, you are to follow his directions precisely. You cannot go off on your own and start modifying his investment choices. You must do as he tells you.

After the six-month trial period is over, you meet with the first investor with whom you have worked closely over these months. "We didn't do too bad," he says. "We lost money on these investments, but made some with these. Overall, we got a 5 percent yield. Let's keep working on it. I think we can do a little better." You've enjoyed working with him, but you hold off giving him your entire portfolio until you've spoken to the second investor.

You haven't seen him in six months. You've gotten his instructions via email. You often questioned his advice. His ideas often seemed counterintuitive. But worse, you agreed to act under his thumb with no say in the matter. You expected a short visit. But when you walked into his office, he pulled out your portfolio and calmly said, "Well, we made 30 percent. Not bad, but I think we can do better."

You hired him. From that moment on you gave yourself completely into his hands, followed his instructions to the letter, and let him do whatever he wanted with your money.

Here is the question: Under which investor were you truly free? Did you become a robot and surrender your freedom by giving yourself into the hands of the second investor? Did you feel limited as a human being because you didn't have the right to make your own choices? Did you feel hamstrung because you couldn't see the bigger picture?

Please don't take this illustration too far. It is intended to make one point: A person can be completely free even while completely submitting to someone else. The choice is not between being free and being a robot. It is between being free to do whatever *we* want to do, or being able to freely submit to the God of love who created us, who directs our paths, and blesses us in every way.

This is the kind of freedom God graciously gave Adam and Eve in the Garden of Eden. They were given a beautiful and flawless place in which to live. They had been created in God's image, which is not a matter of coercion any more than God is coerced to follow his own will. Adam and Eve knew what their Creator wanted them to do. They knew his love, and they loved him in return. They submitted to him willingly.

Satan's temptation was designed to take away their freedom. There was a higher wisdom, Satan claimed, that God was selfishly keeping from them. Only if Adam and Eve saw the big picture—only if they knew evil in the same way as they knew good—could they become more than robots. Only then could they gain the ability to make their own choices. Only with that knowledge could they step out and experience life to the fullest—become truly human.

But look what that "freedom" got them. Their knowledge and will became corrupt. All they could do now was choose which sin they wanted to commit. The good acts they might choose were marred by bad motives. And unless God had restored their freedom to love him by promising a Savior, that's the only freedom they ever would have known.

How is this any different than the freedom provided by evolution? The freedom promised in evolution allows us to make choices, but our choices can never rise above the constraints imposed by the self-centered behavior required by natural selection. If evil is part of the process through which we were created and not a foreign element introduced after the fact, evil is a part of our lives and we are stuck with it. In spite of all the talk about the noncoercive nature of natural selection, we are, in fact, coerced to follow the path it lays out for us. And on that path we are never free from temptation and sin, not to mention tears, death, mourning, crying, and pain—and after this life God's judgment on sin. Freedom from all that is found only in Christ.

When God created Adam and Eve, they were hardly robots. Since they were created in God's image, nothing could threaten their relationship with him. They could serve God unfettered by self-centered motives. They could care for God's creation motivated by nothing but love. There was no need to compete for scarce resources because they and the rest of creation had everything they needed to "be fruitful and multiply and fill the earth" (Genesis 1:28).

Those who claim that Adam and Eve were robots seem to overlook what actually happened. Adam and Eve *could* be tempted to sin, and they chose that path. It's only when they sinned that they lost the freedom in which they were created; they were no longer free to serve God as they had before.

If Adam and Eve had been robots, then Christians today are robots, which we are not. The Christian life is a life of willing service to God—yielding all our heart and soul and strength and mind to the One who has blessed us and continues to bless us with all things. By faith in the work of God's Son, believers "have it all"—just as Adam and Eve had it all.

Jesus is at the heart of this kind of freedom. Our freedom began when our sins were forgiven. Paul wrote: "God demonstrates his own love for us in this: While we were still sinners, Christ died for us" (Romans 5:8 NIV). The Old Testament prophet Jeremiah looked forward to the freedom people would find when they came to know and believe that God, in Christ, had forgiven their sins: "For this is the covenant that I will make with the house of Israel after those days, declares the LORD: I will put my law within them, and I will write it on their hearts. And I will be their God, and they shall be my people. . . . For I will forgive their iniquity, and I will remember their sin no more" (Jeremiah 31:33,34).

Speaking about Jesus, Peter said that God "exalted him at his right hand as Leader and Savior, to *give* repentance to Israel and forgiveness of sins" (Acts 5:31). The right to repent is a gift from God. It is God giving us the freedom to look at the horror of the wrongs we do and accept the fact that we deserve to be punished for them. We have that freedom because Christ was punished in our place and we are free from punishment.

We are free to love God. John wrote, "This is love: not that we loved God, but that he loved us and sent his Son as an atoning sacrifice for our sins" (1 John 4:10 NIV). Knowing God's love for us in Christ enables us to love each other unselfishly: "Beloved, if God so loved us, we also ought to love one another. No one has ever seen God; if we love one another, God abides in us and his love is perfected in us" (1 John 4:11,12).

The apostle Paul said that God's love in Christ frees us to live for him: "For the love of Christ controls us, because we have concluded this: that one has died for all, therefore all have died; and he died for all, that those who live might no longer live for themselves but for him who for their sake died and was raised" (2 Corinthians 5:14,15). Because Paul was free in Christ, he loved to call himself a "slave" of Christ (Romans 1:1[232]).

Jesus explained the meaning of freedom to people who were looking for alternate ways to be free:

> Jesus said to the Jews who had believed him, "If you abide in my word, you are truly my disciples, and you will know the truth, and the truth will set you free." They answered him, "We are offspring of Abraham and have never been enslaved to anyone. How is it that you say, 'You will

---

[232] The word is often translated "servant" but it is the normal Greek word for "slave."

become free'?" Jesus answered them, "Truly, truly, I say to you, everyone who practices sin is a slave to sin. The slave does not remain in the house forever; the son remains forever. So if the Son sets you free, you will be free indeed." (John 8:31-36)

In one sense we will never be completely free this side of heaven. Paul lamented, "I know that in me, that is, in my sinful flesh, dwells no good thing" (Romans 7:18). But our source of freedom remains constant, and a life of service to God is never a pipe dream. Paul encourages us,

What shall we say then? Are we to continue in sin that grace may abound? By no means! How can we who died to sin still live in it? Do you not know that all of us who have been baptized into Christ Jesus were baptized into his death? We were buried therefore with him by baptism into death, in order that, just as Christ was raised from the dead by the glory of the Father, we too might walk in newness of life. (Romans 6:1-4)

The freedom credited to evolution is the pipe dream. Nowhere in Scripture is there any idea that freedom can be gained if we simply have the ability to choose between the options. Quite the opposite.

Our freedom in Christ is God's gift. And because it is a gift, we are free from the fear that we will stumble and God will change his mind and take it away.

He was in the world, and though the world was made through him, the world did not recognize him. He came to that which was his own, but his own did not receive him. Yet to all who received him, to those who believed in his name, he gave the right to become children of God—children born not of natural descent, nor of human decision or a husband's will, but born of God. (John 1:10-13 NIV84).

Jesus gives his Spirit to those who repent and rest in God's forgiveness. And the Spirit gives us freedom to live as God wants us to live. Paul contrasted the works Christians are freed to do by God's Spirit with the works people who don't know God's love and grace are constrained to do:

The acts of the sinful nature are obvious: sexual immorality, impurity and debauchery; idolatry and witchcraft. . . . But the fruit of the Spirit is love, joy, peace, patience, kindness, goodness, faithfulness, gentleness and self-control. Against such things there is no law. Those who belong to Christ Jesus have crucified the sinful nature with its passions and desires. (Galatians 5:19,20,22-24)

In evolution, living beings have no choice but to seek their own good, to fight, and to survive at the expense of the weak. Followers of Christ, however, have the freedom to suffer lack and be wronged. Paul encourages us, "But join with me in suffering for the gospel, by the power of God, who has saved us and called us to a holy life—not because of anything we have done but because of his own purpose and grace" (2 Timothy 1:8,9). Jesus assures us that God can make up richly for anything we might give up for his sake: "Everyone who has left houses or brothers or sisters or father or mother or children or lands, for my name's sake, will receive a hundredfold and will inherit eternal life" (Matthew 19:29). Without these promises, we are slaves to the things of this world. With them, we are free to lose whatever God takes away.

Death began with Adam; it came to an end with Christ's death and resurrection; it will be put out of commission once and for all when Christ returns. In the creation/evolution debate, death easily turns into an academic discussion. But in the New Testament, it's a life and death matter.

> If only for this life we have hope in Christ, we are to be pitied more than all men. But Christ has indeed been raised from the dead, the firstfruits of those who have fallen asleep. For since death came through a man, the resurrection of the dead comes also through a man. For as in Adam all die, so in Christ all will be made alive. (1 Corinthians 15:19-22)

When we think of the new bodies we will receive in heaven, we are freed from worry about the weakness and pain we feel in our present bodies:

> If there is a natural body, there is also a spiritual body. So it is written: "The first man Adam became a living being"; the last Adam, a life-giving spirit. . . . And just as we have borne the likeness of the earthly man, so shall we bear the likeness of the man from heaven. (1 Corinthians 15:44-49)

In this hope we are free from the fear of death. And our lives are filled with purpose and meaning:

> "Where, O death, is your victory? Where, O death, is your sting?" The sting of death is sin, and the power of sin is the law. But thanks be to God! He gives us the victory through our Lord Jesus Christ. Therefore, my dear brothers, stand firm. Let nothing move you. Always give yourselves fully to the work of the Lord, because you know that your labor in the Lord is not in vain. (1 Corinthians 15:55-58 NIV84)

This is true freedom, and in Christ we have it. God's goal is to give us freedom from Satan's evil, from the guilt of our sins, and from eternal death. None of this makes any sense in the history of the universe as taught by evolution. All of it is God's solution to the problem that started in Genesis 3.

166

What Jesus Did for the World

According to Theistic Evolutionists

There are too many elephants in the room. There is little room left for Jesus. In the rest of this chapter, we'll see what theistic evolutionists do with him.

Academic calm often replaces Christian passion

Saint Paul was a man of great learning with a passion for Scripture and for Christ. He often used his learning to prove from Scripture that Jesus was the Christ: "And I, when I came to you, brothers, did not come proclaiming to you the testimony of God with lofty speech or wisdom. For I decided to know nothing among you except Jesus Christ and him crucified" (1 Corinthians 2:1).

One could wish that all theistic evolutionists shared that conviction and zeal. But their passion seems to be driven only by what keeps Scripture open to evolution. The conflicting interpretations of key Scripture passages relevant to creation create a swamp of unanswered questions that is easy to get bogged down in. Worse, the struggle at interpreting what appear to be clear statements of fact gives the impression that Scripture can't be read with confidence. Much of the Old Testament is supposedly made up of mythology or reflects ancient ideas that are impossible to apply today.

The rapid-fire volley of scientific arguments against creation, the claim that all areas of modern scientific research depend on evolution to make sense, and the idea that Scripture teaches ancient and obsolete beliefs about the universe create an academic environment that brings average readers to their knees, ready to listen to any speculation the author might throw their way.

Theistic evolutionists should learn from the creationists who wear their passion for Scripture on their sleeves as the following Christian writers do. These writers have seen the elephants for a long time:

- "Anyone who thinks that 'evolution is just a scientific theory' is living in a make-believe world or on another planet. Every sin condemned by the Bible is condoned by evolutionists as being an appropriate evolutionary adaptive behavior for some group." [233]

- "Any theory that somehow sanctions the existence of evil in God's good creation fails to do justice to sin's fundamentally outrageous

---

[233] Marvin Lubenow, *Bones of Contention,* (Grand Rapids: Baker Books, 2004), p. 74, Kindle.

and blasphemous character, and in some subtle and sophisticated sense lays the blame for sin on the Creator rather than on ourselves in Adam." [234]

- To modify the origin of mankind along theistic evolutionary lines and interpret Scripture accordingly "would fatally de-historicize it, forcing a different account of the origin of evil that would require an altogether different means of salvation."[235]

- "The logical implication of theistic evolution is that God made the world in a fallen state. . . . If there is no fall, there is no basis for the propitiatory death of Christ, or the gospel itself for that matter."[236]

- *"Evolutionists would say death and struggle led to man's existence. The Bible says man's rebellious actions led to death. These statements cannot both be true. One denies the other; they are diametrically opposed."* [237]

One rarely finds that kind of "line in the sand" mentality driving the theistic evolutionary discussion, unless it serves to promote evolution.

A few make fine statements of faith, but then they take them back

Once in a while an author will make a fine confession of faith. For example, Denis Alexander introduces his book like this: "I have written this book mainly for people who believe, as I do, that the Bible is the inspired Word of God from cover to cover. . . . So it is good for Christians as they read this book to remember that we are saved by the finished work of Christ on the Cross for our sins, and nothing can be added to our salvation other than what Christ has accomplished for us." [238] A good confession! But as we read on, we begin to wonder what Alexander meant by it.

Alexander says that the Bible is the inspired Word of God from cover to cover. He writes, "Sooner or later (generally sooner) discussions about creation and

[234] Andrew Kulikovsky, *Creation, Fall, Restoration: A Biblical Theology of Creation* (Ross-shire, Scotland: Mentor, 2009), p. 214, quoting A. M. Wolters, *Creation Regained* (Carlisle, Paternoster, 1996), pp. 48,49.

[235] Michael Reeves, "Adam and Eve," in *Should Christians Embrace Evolution?*, ed. Norman C. Nevin, p. 46.

[236] Andrew Kulikovsky, *Creation, Fall, Restoration*, p. 120.

[237] Ken Ham, *The Lie* (Green Forest, AR: Master Books, revised edition, 2012), loc. 1914, Kindle (emphasis author's).

[238] Denis Alexander, *Creation or Evolution: Do We Have to Choose?*, p. 11.

evolution come down to how Christians interpret the Bible."[239] Alexander says that "we have to think about how we interpret the Bible."[240] What then follows are the standard theistic evolutionary statements about how difficult it is to understand the Bible. Before it can be translated, we must discover the kind of language used in Genesis 1-3, the audience to whom it was written, the purpose of the text, and how ancient Near Eastern material helps us interpret Scripture. We are reminded that the original writers were not scribes through whom God merely dictated his Word, that we should not approach Scripture with the traditional Western mind-set, and that "Western readers, in particular, are not very practiced at reading ancient literature and have a tendency to interpret with a wooden literalism."[241]

In his book *Did Adam and Eve Really Exist?* C. John Collins spends several pages clearly describing Alexander's views on Adam and Eve and the fall into sin:

> Alexander presents the case for the biological continuity between humans and their animal ancestors, rejecting any idea of a special creative action that bestowed the image of God on the first human beings. . . . The consequence of Alexander's view is that death is a "natural" end of the life of every human being.
>
> When Alexander treats human death as something "natural," he never considers whether the "fall" has changed circumstances. . . . Even though he properly recognizes that death is an enemy in the New Testament, his overall discussion does not take seriously the human reaction to death as something unwelcome, as something we are right to grieve.[242]

Alexander's otherwise fine Christian confession of faith has been mutilated by the presuppositions of evolution.

Some outright deny the seriousness of sin and the need for forgiveness

Some theistic evolutionists follow the path to its logical conclusion. For example, in regard to the fall into sin, Price and Souminen sarcastically write,

> First . . .there was no such event; it is an ancient myth with evident pagan parallels. Second, those actions that have been labeled as "sin" do not arise from any subsequent corruption of our nature, but from our very nature itself as the descendants of reproductive survivors in a harsh

---

[239] Denis Alexander, *Creation or Evolution: Do We Have to Choose?*, p. 16.

[240] Denis Alexander, *Creation or Evolution: Do We Have to Choose?*, p. 16.

[241] Denis Alexander, *Creation or Evolution: Do We Have to Choose?*, p. 22.

[242] C. John Collins, *Did Adam and Eve Really Exist?*, pp. 125-127.

and brutal world. All of those "sinful" traits that Christian clergy have condemned from their pulpits . . . have evolutionary explanations that make a whole lot more sense than the story that Christian theologians dreamed up.[243]

Price and Souminen criticize those who explain Christ's death in scriptural terms: "What they do not seem to see is that the death of Jesus cannot be understood as a solution unless there is a prior problem to solve." Evolution takes away the problem and "replaces the whole Adam 'problem' with a scientific explanation."[244] Price and Souminen agree with Philip Johnson, pioneer of the intelligent design movement, who in the following citation is simply stating the obvious:

> The story of salvation by the cross makes no sense against a background of evolutionary naturalism. The evolutionary story is a story of humanity's climb from animal beginnings to rationality, not a story of a fall from perfection. . . . It is a story about learning to rely entirely on human intelligence, not a story of the helplessness of that intelligence in the face of the inescapable fact of sin.[245]

The natural move from Savior to Influencer

Those who discuss why Jesus came to earth—and not many do, at least not in much detail—view Jesus as a moral influence rather than as a Savior.

C. John Collins believes in a literal Adam and Eve. The biblical story, he says, "must include the notion of sin." But after quoting Peter's reminder to Christians that they were ransomed from sin "with the precious blood of Christ, like that of a lamb without blemish or spot" (1 Peter 1:19), Collins adds, "I am not arguing here that we must make this the only, *not even necessarily primary,* model for understanding the cross, only that it be included."[246] But if we realize that God is just in judging and punishing sin, how can God's pardon in Christ not be our greatest treasure?

Collins' position aside, we note Henri Blocher's comment about those who either downplay the account of the fall or who regard Adam and Eve as myth-

---

[243] Robert Price and Edwin Suominen, *Evolving Out of Eden,* p. 190.

[244] Robert Price and Edwin Suominen, *Evolving Out of Eden,* p. 187.

[245] Robert Price and Edwin Suominen, *Evolving Out of Eden,* p. 187. They are quoting Philip Johnson in *Relics of Eden* by Daniel Fairbanks (Amherst, NY: Prometheus Books, 2007), p. 161.

[246] C. John Collins, *Did Adam and Eve Really Exist?,* p. 42 (emphasis added).

ological characters. He writes that these authors "share a characteristic of being little concerned with individual guilt."[247]

Is this surprising? If God used sinful actions and death to create human beings, why should human beings worry about sinful actions they commit? What right does God have for punishing human beings for what he himself does? Accordingly, in theistic evolutionary literature, there is little emphasis on Christ as our substitute and more talk about Christ as a moral influence and inspiration.

This is the historic position of liberal Christianity. What follows are statements of various liberal authors who downplay and even reject Scripture's emphasis on Christ as our substitute. But as more and more Evangelical denominations accept evolution, the formerly liberal position is finding its way into historically conservative circles.

Ted Peters and Martinez Hewlett show how evolution influences Christians to view the work of Christ. They note the teaching of liberal Episcopal bishop Shelby Spong. According to Spong, Darwin

> forced us to acknowledge that there never was a finished and perfect creation. . . . Spong denies that we are fallen sinners; we do not start out innocent and then drop into sin. Rather, we start out sinful and progress to something better. We start out less than human, and we progress toward becoming fully human. Spong changes the story of salvation accordingly. Instead of Jesus Christ returning us to a lost innocence, Jesus models what we can become as we evolve further.[248]

Also on the liberal side is Patricia Williams. We noted her views on sociobiology and sin. Important for her views on Jesus' work, she writes, "God understands the worst of us, yet forgives us without requiring payment. Atonement doctrines based on restitution misunderstand God's free acceptance of us."[249] In spite of the fact that Scripture from one end to the other tells us that God accepts us through faith in Jesus' sacrificial work, Williams finds evolution a better way to interpret Jesus: "Sociobiology makes sense of God's readiness to accept and forgive, for it says that the very capacities and talents that make us human are the capacities and talents that enable us to be evil."[250]

She explains why God sent Jesus:

---

[247] Henri Blocher, "The Theology of the Fall and the Origins of Evil," in *Darwin, Creation and the Fall*, ed. R. J. Berry and T. A. Noble, pp. 152,153.

[248] Ted Peters and Martinez Hewlett, *Can You Believe in God and Evolution?*, p. 105.

[249] Patricia Williams, *Doing Without Adam and Eve: Sociobiology and Original Sin*, p. 192.

[250] Patricia Williams, *Doing Without Adam and Eve: Sociobiology and Original Sin*, p. 192.

God's response to our situation is not to destroy the good characteristics that are also the sources of our suffering and sin. Rather, God shows complete understanding of us and, through that understanding, forgiveness. . . . God's response to our rejection is to seek unity—at-one-ment—with us. One way God does this is to show what the at-one-ment of God and humanity looks like through showing us Jesus. The atonement is not an action Jesus performs. It is the message Jesus incarnates and enacts. Jesus has power to transform our lives. Because he is human, he is like us, setting an example we can emulate. . . . Being divine and human, he is a bridge between us and God, a mediator and a liberator. His presence with us here and now helps us overcome our evolved bondage to sin and death. His power is power to transform."[251]

Richard Mortimer analyzes Williams' work. On the basis of Williams' sociobiological explanation of human development, "Jesus did not die to atone for our sin, but gave us teachings and lived, and died, to show us how to live as God's creatures in God's world, beloved and accepted by him and, furthermore, he gives his presence to help and transform us."

Mortimer adds—and this is significant—

Williams' revisionism should not be dismissed lightly; she is not, we suggest, pioneering an eccentric view from the margins. Rather, she is responding to a shift in outlook that has substantially already happened in Western culture. Human nature is seen neither as fatally corrupted, nor deeply alienated, nor even . . . as naturally good—it is simply a ragbag to be lived with, enjoyed, and patched up when things go wrong.[252]

Joel Green, Methodist minister and professor of New Testament interpretation at Fuller Theological Seminary, concludes his book on human nature with these words: "One of the pivotal implications of this diagnosis of the human situation is its explanatory value for the virtual absence in Paul of the language of 'forgiveness of sins.' . . . Nor does Paul develop much the notion of 'repentance.'" Rather, "What Paul promises in Romans 5-6 is not 'remission of sin' but liberation from our enslavement to sin and decay and participation in a new humanity whose home is the new life ushered in by means of the faithfulness of Jesus Christ whose death on the cross comprises one of the most profound visual representations of the character of God."[253]

---

[251] Patricia Williams, *Doing Without Adam and Eve: Sociobiology and Original Sin*, pp. 197, 198.

[252] Richard Mortimer, "Blocher, Original Sin and Evolution," in *Darwin, Creation and the Fall*, ed. R. J. Berry and T. A. Noble, p. 192.

[253] Joel Green, *Body, Soul, and Human Life: The Nature of Humanity in the Bible* (Grand Rap-

Christopher Southgate clearly expresses the moral influence idea: "God's ultimate self-giving in Christ makes possible a self-transcendence in humans that evolution of itself would not make possible." When human beings believe in Christ and contemplate his example and sufferings, the "final phase of creation" will begin "in which the evolutionary process itself will be transformed and healed."[254]

According to Southgate, the futility to which God subjected creation (Romans 8:19-23) is "the futility of the evolutionary process."[255] Yet once evolution, as futile as the process might be, had enabled mankind's self-awareness and transcendence over the animals to become sufficiently complex, "God was able—through the incarnation of the divine Son within a creature—to inaugurate the process of redemption."[256] The death and resurrection of Christ initiated "a new era of possibilities."[257] Once this happened, human beings "can find their liberty, and in doing so be transformed from one degree of glory to another (2 Corinthians 3:18), and the creation itself will find liberation."[258]

Quoting Andrew Elphinstone, Southgate explains, "The whole evolutionary process will receive its final significance as the long process of scaffolding which produced man will at some point be finally and honorably dismantled."[259] The logical conclusion is that human beings receive "a very high, God-given calling to be 'co-creators,' or even 'co-redeemers' with God of the unfolding creation."[260]

All theistic evolutionists must interpret Romans 8:18-23 in a similar way. Read in a straightforward way, that passage speaks of a fallen creation. They interpret it something like this: Mankind failed to rise to their full potential. Their "sinful" actions included various practices that brought suffering into the lives of the other living creatures and that harmed the land. But someday we

---

ids: Baker, 2008), pp. 102,103, Kindle. What filter Green uses on Paul's writings to make this claim is beyond me.

[254] Christopher Southgate, *The Groaning of Creation: God, Evolution, and the Problem of Evil*, p. 76.

[255] Christopher Southgate, *The Groaning of Creation: God, Evolution, and the Problem of Evil*, p. 94.

[256] Christopher Southgate, *The Groaning of Creation: God, Evolution, and the Problem of Evil*, p. 94.

[257] Christopher Southgate, *The Groaning of Creation: God, Evolution, and the Problem of Evil*, p. 95.

[258] Christopher Southgate, *The Groaning of Creation: God, Evolution, and the Problem of Evil*, p. 95.

[259] Christopher Southgate, *The Groaning of Creation: God, Evolution, and the Problem of* [Evil], p. 37, quoting Andrew Elphinstone, *Freedom, Suffering, and Love*, p. 65.

[260] Christopher Southgate, *The Groaning of Creation: God, Evolution, and the Problem of Evil*, p. 104.

will change, which Christ, by his example, will help us do. When we experience that freedom—when our true potential is revealed—the creation will be freed from the bondage to corruption *we* have imposed on it, and we will live in the freedom to which we have evolved with Christ's help.[261]

George Murphy, another theistic evolutionist, states what he believes to be the human problem and how God will solve it. He writes,

> Consider then the first small group of hominins who had evolved to be capable of self-consciousness and communication. . . . These humans are able in some way to receive and to some degree comprehend God's Word, to trust God, to know God's will for them and to obey it. They are at the beginning of a road along which God wants to lead them and their descendants to fully mature humanity and complete fellowship with God.[262]

According to Murphy, the events described in Genesis 1-11, beginning with Adam and Eve, symbolize a gradual departure of human beings from this goal. Humanity took the wrong road and moved away from God. The fall into sin is "a metaphor for the human condition and should not be pressed too far."[263] Mankind could have reached God's goal through the process of evolution. Being on the path of evolution, however, is not the problem, nor is it sinful. The problem is that mankind got on "the *wrong* road, the one 'that leads to destruction' (Matt. 7:13)."[264] By getting on the wrong road, Murphy means engaging in obviously evil

---

[261] R. J. Berry, "Did Darwin Dethrone Humankind?," in *Darwin, Creation and the Fall,* ed. R. J. Berry and T. A. Noble, lists some of these views on pages 69-71. Quoting Derek Kidner, "It seems from Romans 8:19-23 and from what is known of the pre-human world that there was a state of travail from the first which man was empowered to 'subdue' until he relapsed into disorder himself." Quoting Charles Cranfield, "The magnificent theater of the universe . . . is cheated of its true fulfilment so long as man, the chief actor in the great drama of God's praise, fails to contribute his rational part." The various parts of creation "are prevented from being fully that which they were created to be, so long as man's part is missing, just as all the other players in a concerto would be frustrated of their purpose if the soloist were to fail to play this part." Henri Blocher holds a similar position: ". . . but in his [mankind's] insatiable greed . . . and in his short-sighted selfishness, he polluted the earth and destroys it. He turns a garden into a desert (cf. Rev 11:18). That is the main thrust of the curse of Genesis 3." Also see Malcolm Jeeves and R. J. Berry, *Science, Life, and Christian Belief,* p. 235: "Paul's point in Romans 8 is that as long as we refuse (or fail) to play the part assigned to us by God (that is, to act as his stewards or vice-regents here on earth), so long is the entire world of nature frustrated and dislocated; an untended garden is one which is overrun by thorns and thistles."

[262] George L. Murphy, "Christology, Evolution, and the Cross," in *Perspectives on an Evolving Creation,* p. 382.

[263] George L. Murphy, "Christology, Evolution, and the Cross," in *Perspectives on an Evolving Creation,* p. 382.

[264] George L. Murphy, "Christology, Evolution, and the Cross," in *Perspectives on an Evolving Creation,* p. 383.

actions like Cain murdering his brother Abel, Lamech's "exaltation in unbounded vengeance, the wickedness and corruption that lead to the Flood," and the other events recorded in the early chapters of Genesis. Murphy logically concludes, "If this is the human problem, then salvation must mean being put back on the right road."[265] "With the call of Abram, God begins a program of getting humanity back on the right road. . . . Finally Jesus appears, inviting people to follow him."[266]

This is how theistic evolutionists integrate Christ into the process of evolution. I'm sure that not all theistic evolutionists would accept everything these authors are saying. However, one thing is true: Theistic evolutionists from historically conservative churches who might accept Jesus' substitutionary sacrifice in their own personal faith are not stepping up to defend it in their books or carefully explaining how it might fit with the process of evolution.

The problem of evolved creatures living in heaven

Scripture and evolution diverge on eternity.

Evolution and Scripture explain the origin of the world in contradictory ways. Evolution teaches that the world is evolving toward a more perfect condition. Scripture teaches that the world was created perfect but has been living in sin and under a curse since Adam and Eve fell into sin. Someday God will *restore* it.

We have seen that these two beginning points force Christianity and evolution to go in opposite directions. They go in opposite directions on one more topic, the meaning of heaven. Robert John Russell admits the difficultly in reconciling Scripture and evolution on "eschatology" (the technical term for what will happen when Jesus returns and afterward). In fact, in his opinion, "the challenge of relating evolution and creation pales in comparison with that of relating eschatology and cosmology." In other words, fitting together what evolution and Scripture teach about the last times is even more difficult than fitting together what they say about the origin of the universe. While this topic is overlooked by many theistic evolutionists, Russell says that it "leads to what I consider as the most fundamental challenge: how to make Christian eschatology intelligible in light of the Big Bang cosmology, with its 'freeze or fry' scenarios for the future of the universe." Nevertheless, he encourages action: "It is time we faced these challenges."[267]

---

[265] George L. Murphy, "Christology, Evolution, and the Cross," in *Perspectives on an Evolving Creation*, p. 383.

[266] George L. Murphy, "Christology, Evolution, and the Cross," in *Perspectives on an Evolving Creation*, p. 383.

[267] Robert John Russell, "Special Providence and Genetic Mutation," in *Perspectives on an*

Catholic theologian James Wiseman makes the same point. The scientific study of where the universe is heading "raises the theological question of how the predicted demise of the universe [according to evolution] might correlate with the traditional doctrine of Christian eschatology with its promise of 'a new heaven and a new earth.'"[268]

Wiseman notes that some see "the somber predictions of scientific cosmology to be an ironclad refutation of that doctrine [that is, the Christian teaching about the last times] and of the hope that it inspires."[269] He quotes Ted Peters: "[If] the law of entropy has the last laugh and the cosmos drifts into a state of irrecoverable equilibrium . . . then we would have proof that our faith has been in vain."[270]

So how can the doomsday scenarios of evolution be fit together with the absolute hope of the new heaven and earth that Christians look forward to in Christ? Many evolutionists simply reinterpret Scripture. James Wiseman says that to interpret Scripture "as predicting an eventual transformation of the physical universe seems quite unwarranted."[271] Wiseman argues that Scripture's promises of a new heaven and earth in Revelation 21:4 should be read as an encouragement to Christians suffering persecution in Rome—that God will continue to show them his love even in the worst of situations.

Martinez and Hewlett write in rather abstract terms: "The task is to interpret the ancient Bible in light of modern science to paint a picture of reality in which all things are oriented toward the God of grace and salvation."[272] But is it really that easy to reinterpret Scripture so that evolution and God's grace and salvation are reconciled?

Can creatures created through evolution find heaven a natural place to live?

Theistic evolutionists must deal with another topic about heaven. It is a somewhat abstract topic, but an important one. Will creatures who evolved through natural selection be able to live in a place like heaven? Stating the question a little differently: Can evolved creatures live in a world that is unnatural for them? Here is the point: Scripture says *that suffering and death are unnatural* and came into the world from outside it. Therefore, creatures who were created as perfect beings will find heaven a very natural place to live. Evolution, on the other hand,

---

Evolving Creation, ed. Keith Miller, p. 368.

[268] James A. Wiseman, *Theology and Modern Science* (New York: Continuum, 2002), p. 98.

[269] James A. Wiseman, *Theology and Modern Science*, p. 98.

[270] James A. Wiseman, *Theology and Modern Science*, p. 101.

[271] James A. Wiseman, *Theology and Modern Science*, p. 106.

[272] Ted Peters and Martinez Hewlett, *Can You Believe in God AND Evolution?*, p. 125.

teaches that *the suffering and death we see around us* are natural. If that is so, a perfect heaven would be an unnatural place for evolved creatures to live.

Martinez and Hewlett state the problem like this: "Exactly how the laws of nature could be modified to eliminate the suffering of sentient beings is difficult for our scientifically informed imaginations to conceive."[273]

Consider the question from something we learn from Scripture: The formerly perfect world became imperfect, and it was consigned to live under God's curse. In order to put the world under his curse, God made many changes in the world. These included changes to human physiology and emotions, changes to the animal world, and changes to the earth itself and the universe around us. The changes were extensive. Of course, secular evolutionists reject all this.

However, when theistic evolutionists—at least those theistic evolutionists who believe that heaven will be a perfect place—reject such changes, they should realize that they must confess the same thing, only in reverse. In other words, they must explain the changes God will have to make in beings who were created to struggle, compete, and die—changes that will enable them to live in a place where they will have no need to compete, where they will live forever in peace with other creatures. We think of Paul's words regarding human beings who are living in our fallen state: "I tell you this, brothers: flesh and blood cannot inherit the kingdom of God, nor does the perishable inherit the imperishable. Behold! I tell you a mystery. We shall not all sleep, but we shall all be changed. . . . For the trumpet will sound, and the dead will be raised imperishable, and we shall be changed" (1 Corinthians 15:50-52) Of course, it's not just living creatures who will have to be changed; the changes God made after the fall into sin will pale in comparison to the changes he will make when he creates a new heaven and earth.

Christopher Southgate sees the problem. He uses leopards as an example. Leopards evolved to be predators, he says, both physically and mentally. The outcome of their evolution is their very selves. Can their very selves be changed to enable them to live in a perfect world?

Isaiah prophesied that in the new heavens and earth, "The wolf shall dwell with the lamb, and the leopard shall lie down with the young goat, and the calf and the lion and the fattened calf together; and a little child shall lead them" (Isaiah 11:6). Southgate reacts to this: "It is very hard to see how the leopardness of leopards could be fulfilled in eschatological coexistence with kids."[274] Isaiah's

---

[273] Ted Peters and Martinez Hewlett, *Can You Believe in God AND Evolution?*, p. 125.

[274] Christopher Southgate, *The Groaning of Creation*, p. 86. "Protological" refers to the leopards' beginnings, in this context to their evolutionary history.

prophecy about leopards lying down with kids is, in Thomas Derr's words, "hope without details."[275]

Southgate concludes, "Since this was the world the God of all creativity and all compassion chose for the creation of creatures, we must presume that this was the only type of world that would do for that process." In heaven, however, God will do something he was not able to do on earth, namely, allow leopards to remain what he created them to be through the process of evolution, yet be able to live with their prey without causing them harm.[276] It is clear they will have to be changed in some way.

Will people be truly free in heaven?

Theistic evolutionists claim that only creation by evolution provides creatures with an environment in which they can make choices, become free, and avoid becoming robots. But this claim forces them to view the promise of a new heaven and earth as a mixed blessing. In a new and perfect heaven and earth as described in Scripture, God will be taking away the so-called freedom of evolution and resume complete control over what happens there.

Will human beings be robots in heaven? Martinez and Hewlett quote influential theistic evolutionist John Polkinghorne's solution to the problem. Polkinghorne says that the laws of nature operating in this life will have to be replaced. He describes the sequence of events leading up to a Christian's entry into an eternity of life with God like this: "For it is conceivable that the divinely ordained laws of nature appropriate *to a world making itself through its own evolving history* should give way to a differently constituted form of 'matter,' appropriate to a universe *'freely returned' from independence to an existence of integration with its Creator*."[277]

This is a very clever way of describing life in heaven under God while preserving the freedom that is supposed to be such an important outcome of human evolution. The "divinely ordained laws of nature," that were appropriate during the eons when the creation was "making itself" through the process of evolution, will someday give way to "a differently constituted form of matter." The present universe will "freely" give up its independence and begin "an existence of integration with its Creator."

---

[275] Christopher Southgate, *The Groaning of Creation*, p. 86.

[276] Christopher Southgate, *The Groaning of Creation*, p. 90. Southgate will also argue that passages referring to a restoration of all things need not be taken literally, p. 90 footnote 33.

[277] Ted Peters and Martinez Hewlett, *Can You Believe in God AND Evolution?*, p. 125 (emphasis added).

The significant phrase in the Polkinghorne quotation is "freely returned." According to Polkinghorne, evolution has given *us* freedom, and in freedom *we* will choose to give up our independence and *we* will choose to begin an existence in which we become integrated with God and submit ourselves completely to his will.

Certainly, not all theistic evolutionists would express themselves like this or agree with Polkinghorne. But Polkinghorne is attempting to weave together the rhetoric that evolution is good because it frees us from God's absolute control together with the fact that in heaven we will put ourselves completely under his absolute control. It is similar to the problem Southgate wrestled with in trying to explain a leopard's life in heaven.

All theistic evolutionists should come up with a way to solve this problem, that is, to relate the highly touted freedom that comes through natural selection with the lack of that kind of freedom in heaven.

But the problem really lies in the meaning of freedom. Is true freedom the freedom to do what *we* might want to do, or is it the freedom to do what *God* wants us to do. Freedom as defined by evolution is the first. Scripture says it's the second: "Live as people who are free, not using your freedom as a cover-up for evil, but living as servants of God" (1Peter 2:16).

Is the creation finished?

Christians know that the creation was finished on the sixth day: "Thus the heavens and the earth were finished, and all the host of them" (Genesis 2:1). Secular evolutionists see the universe as unfinished; it continues to evolve. Theistic evolutionists find themselves struggling to find a middle road between these two positions.

Any attempt to combine Genesis 2:1 and evolution is futile. Creation is either finished or it is still evolving. Any claim that evolution has stopped is a denial of the process itself. Those who look for a point in history when creation might be considered finished may as well accept the straightforward way of reading Genesis 2:1: God finished creating the world "in the beginning."

Nevertheless, some theistic evolutionists attempt to combine God's words in Genesis 2:1 with evolution. Philosopher Robert John Russell speculates that creation will only be finished in heaven: "The long sweep of evolution may suggest not only an unfinished and continuing divine creation but even more radically a creation whose theological status as 'good' may be fully realized only in the eschatological future."[278]

---

[278] Robert John Russell, "Special Providence and Genetic Mutation," in *Perspectives on an Evolving Creation*, ed. Keith Miller, p. 368.

Peters and Hewlett suggest that we may be living somewhere in the sixth and final day of creation, still awaiting God's verdict:

> Could we think of the creation week of seven days as inclusive of the entire history of the creation from big bang to whatever will become of the universe in the future? . . . Could we see ourselves today standing between the initial moment when God opened his divine mouth to say, "Let there be . . ." and the final moment when God declares that "behold, it is very good"? Could we still be looking forward to the Sabbath day, to God's first day of rest yet in the future?[279]

They conclude: "Like a cake in the oven, we and all of reality in the universe are not done yet. We're not ready, but we will be. The world in which we live is still being created. *And when it is finally created, it will be redeemed.* It'll be ready for a divine feast."[280] In Scripture redemption refers to people being reunited with God. It seems, then, that God created a universe that from the start needs to be united with him—an odd thought, but totally consistent with theistic evolutionary claims.

Gregory Cootsona expresses it like this:

> Admittedly we are simply beginning musicians, most of the time out of tune and cacophonous. But we are tuning our instruments for a heavenly orchestra. There the goodness of creation, in the form of universal reference to the one true, good God will be brought to its full expression only at the point of eschatological consummation, when God creates a new heaven and new earth. *But that final chapter of God's creation awaits a few more chapters of this creation.*"[281]

Denis Alexander agrees: "This great programme of creation is finally brought to completion with John's vision of a new heaven and a new earth, for the first heaven and earth had passed away, and there was no longer any sea."[282]

Of course, all of this is speculation. It only diverts attention from the elephants in the room.

---

[279] Ted Peters and Martinez Hewlett, *Can You Believe in God AND Evolution?*, pp. 130,131.

[280] Ted Peters and Martinez Hewlett, *Can You Believe in God AND Evolution?*, pp. 121,122 (emphasis added).

[281] Gregory Cootsona, *Creation and Last Things* (Louisville: Geneva Press, 2002), p. 21 (emphasis added).

[282] Denis Alexander, *Creation or Evolution: Do We Have to Choose?*, p. 35.

Elephants in the room

In the previous lessons, we identified a number of elephants in the room. To keep them in mind, we'll repeat them:

- **The basic framework of the world's history as taught in Scripture is wrong.**
- **The evil associated with creation by evolution came from God.**
- **God, whom Scripture says *is love*, used the evils of natural selection over billions of years to create living beings.**
- **The process of evolution—which locks mankind into a system of self-interest, competition, and death—leads to freedom.**
- **Scripture's description of the origin of mankind is wrong. It is impossible to construct a scenario that does justice to both Scripture and evolution.**
- **God must be evil because his image defined human beings, and he requires human beings to take part in the evils of natural selection.**
- **God commanded mankind to rule over the earth in love, and then he made it impossible for mankind to fulfill that command.**
- **The requirements of evolution, not the will of God, define morality.**
- **Sin cannot be equated with evil because natural selection requires it. At best, sin can only be defined as causing others more suffering than is necessary.**
- **Death is good and natural.**
- **God cannot judge evolving creatures for doing what he requires them to do.**

This chapter reveals two more related elephants:

- **Jesus did not save us from the guilt of sin, death, and God's judgment.**
- **Jesus gave us an example of love to inspire us to rise above the evils associated with natural selection.**

Elephants in the Room

Any defense of evolution drives all these elephants into the room. You can be the judge of whether Christ can exist in a room with these elephants lumbering about.

Conclusion

Christ in the Room

Christ and the Elephants cannot exist in the same room

A traveling dinosaur show came to town this weekend. It was billed as an amusement park and museum rolled into one. There were dozens of large dinosaurs for kids to look at, to touch, and even to ride.

The show combined entertainment and learning. Video presentations were repeated throughout the day. There was even a pit where the kids could play archaeologist containing buried fossils to find and take home. Evolutionary charts were presented attractively in various places throughout the hall. They were there to help parents talk with their kids about what they were seeing and about evolution in general.

Dinosaurs are fun. Kids are intrigued by them. Many have a favorite. Some of the kids were scared by the dinosaurs looming overhead, but they were still having a good time. There was not much to be sad about at the fairgrounds this weekend.

But when you watch the kids and their parents, there is a reason to feel sad. You can only hope that some of them have a book on dinosaurs at home written by a Christian author who wants kids to enjoy dinosaurs but also to learn about them with Scripture in mind. You feel sad for the creators of the event, many of whom are simply repeating what scientists have told them.

But you can only feel anger toward the one who is behind all this, Satan, who is using the lure of dinosaurs to sweep kids away from the haven of forgiveness in Christ.

You cannot help but admire Satan's creativity, though. He has managed to turn stuffy philosophy about the world's origins into a kid's game. What formerly had been served up in university classrooms to dozing students in terminology few could understand is now being fed to little ones from the earliest age.

Dinosaurs can be fun and exciting. But if they are presented in the context of evolution, the elephant errors described in this book will be finding their way into the minds of these children. The errors might not be noticed at first, but they will be there, creating a view of the world's history that is the opposite of what Scripture tells us really happened. They will be creating a disconnect between the God of love revealed in Scripture and the god who supposedly used evolution to create the world. As these children grow, the disconnect will become more and more apparent.

As long as parents and children think of themselves as evolving creatures, they will never have a clear understanding of what it means to be human. The fact that they are special beings, created in God's image with an immortal soul, dissipates when they see themselves plotted on the colorful charts next to the hominins from whom they are supposed to have evolved. The fact that their ancestors fell into sin becomes a notion of ancient mythology. They have no reason to conclude that they have a sinful nature. They have no need for God's forgiveness in order to have the hope of eternal life. They lose the ability to understand the new nature God gives Christians through the freedom we have in Christ. As these children grow to understand the process of natural selection, the foundation stones of the Christian faith—the nature of God, the meaning of right and wrong, and the idea that God holds people accountable for sin—vanish.

The problem is not just with dinosaur shows—or even *primarily* with dinosaur shows. Pastors who say God could have used evolution as his tool of creation force their people to deal with the impossible contradictions between Scripture and evolution listed in this book. As soon as they even imply that evolution is an option, they are opening the doors of their sanctuary, their Bible study rooms, and their youth group meetings, to the elephants. And as those elephants enter the room, there is less and less room for Christ.

Many people simply repeat what church leaders tell them and live in two worlds. They are content to live in the world of evolution when they sit in science classes or stand at the rim of the Grand Canyon reading the signs. And they are content to live in the world of Scripture when they are in church or when they stand at a precipice in their own lives and want to be sure they are at peace with God. But trying to live in both worlds may catch up with them.

The room belongs to Christ alone

The words of R. T. Kendall quoted earlier in this book bear repeating:

> We may think that our issue is unprecedented in weightiness in its threat to the Bible. We may fear that at long last the Bible will be disproved and Christianity made extinct. But there is nothing new under the sun. Every generation has its stigma by which the believer's faith is tested, and the issue is always that which appears to be the last blow to the Truth.[283]

---

[283] R. T. Kendall, "Faith and Creation," in *Should Christians Embrace Evolution?*, ed. Norman C. Nevin, (Phillipsburg, NJ: P&R Publishing, 2009), p. 109.

How true.

Who are we to have the luxury of living in a world that is naturally in tune with the Christian faith? Who gave our generation permission to reshape the message of Scripture so it does not conflict with certain ideas the world holds dear?

Creation scientists provide some useful arguments that can help Christians analyze the claims of the theory of evolution. But in the end, the only thing that can drive the evolutionary elephants out of the room is the message of God's love—the love that prompted him to create a perfect world, to save the world from Satan's evil through the sacrifice of his Son, and to give all people a doorway into a perfect, re-created world where we can live with him forever. God encourages us: "'Has not my hand made all these things, and so they came into being?' declares the LORD. 'These are the ones I look on with favor: those who are humble and contrite in spirit, and who tremble at my word'" (Isaiah 66:2 NIV).

Christ cannot easily be driven out. In spite of how the theory of evolution has blanketed the world, the Lord has kept certain truths alive in everyone's heart. We are all aware that he exists. We see his glory in the amazing world around us. We sense that we are God's offspring when we observe how he miraculously guides and shapes the course of our lives. We have a sense of the Creator's laws and we know the basic difference between right and wrong. We have a conscience that feels good or bad depending on whether we are doing what we know is right or what we know is wrong. And we know we are accountable to God when we sin.

Evolution may cloud over this knowledge, but it can never destroy it. This knowledge is a "fifth-column," so to speak, in people's hearts. It gives us confidence to know that God's judgment on sin will strike a responsive chord in all people. It paves the way for the message of God's love in Christ.

Paul wrote:

> And I, when I came to you, brothers, did not come proclaiming to you the testimony of God with lofty speech or wisdom. For I decided to know nothing among you except Jesus Christ and him crucified. And I was with you in weakness and in fear and much trembling, and my speech and my message were not in plausible words of wisdom, but in demonstration of the Spirit and of power, that your faith might not rest in the wisdom of men but in the power of God. (1 Corinthians 2:1-5)

Paul was content to go into the fray armed only with the message of Christ crucified for the sins of the world. He knew that people would believe his message through the power of the Holy Spirit, no matter what obstacles might stand in the way.

Paul also wrote,

> For the message of the cross is foolishness to those who are perishing, but it is God's power to us who are being saved. . . . For the Jews ask for signs and the Greeks seek wisdom, but we preach Christ crucified, a stumbling block to the Jews and foolishness to the Gentiles. Yet to those who are called, both Jews and Greeks, Christ is God's power and God's wisdom. (1 Corinthians 1:18,22-24 CSB)

The writer to the Hebrews put it clearly: "By faith *we* understand that the universe was created by the word of God, so that what is seen was not made out of things that are visible" (Hebrews 11:3). An important word here is "we," that is, the believers to whom he was writing. We who believe in Christ—which the world considers foolish—also believe in Scripture's description of the creation of the world—which at the present time the world also considers foolish. But the Spirit of the Lord, who brings people to faith in the forgiveness God's Son won for us through his life, death, and resurrection, is also at work leading believers to confess that the universe came into being as narrated in the first chapters of Genesis. Faith in what those chapters teach us about the origin of the universe sustains our understanding of where we came from and who we are. It sustains our understanding of where sin came from, how serious it is, and what God has done to free us from its guilt and power. Such faith forces the elephants out of the room and keeps Christ, our Savior, there—where he alone belongs.

Bibliography

Alexander, Denis. *Creation or Evolution: Do We Have to Choose?* Grand Rapids: Monarch Books, 2008.

Anderson, Martin. *The Adult Class Manual.* 1938. Fifty-Sixth Printing, Minneapolis: Augsburg Publishing House, 1980.

Barton, John. *Reading the Old Testament.* Louisville: Westminster John Knox Press, 1996.

Barton, John. "Verbal Inspiration," in *A Dictionary of Biblical Interpretation.* Edited by R. J. Coggins and J. L. Houldon. London: SCM Press, 1990.

Barton, Stephen C., and David Wilkinson, eds. *Reading Genesis After Darwin.* Oxford: Oxford University Press, 2009.

Batten, Don, and Jonathan Sarfati. *15 Reasons to Take Genesis as History.* Powder Springs, GA: Creation Book Publishers, 2006.

Becker, Siegbert W. *The Scriptures—Inspired of God.* Milwaukee: Northwestern Publishing House, 1971.

Berry, R. J., and T. A. Noble, eds. *Darwin, Creation and the Fall: Theological Challenges.* Nottingham: Apollos, 2009.

Blocher, Henri. *In the Beginning: The Opening Chapters of Genesis.* Downers Grove, IL: InterVarsity Press, 1984.

Blocher, Henri. *Original Sin: Illuminating the Riddle.* Downers Grove, IL: InterVarsity Press, 1997.

Bowler, Peter. *Monkey Trials and Gorilla Sermons: Evolution and Creation From Darwin to Intelligent Design.* Cambridge: Harvard, 2007.

Brown, Warren S., Nancey Murphy, and H. Newton Malony, eds. *Whatever Happened to the Soul?* Minneapolis: Fortress Press, 1998.

Brug, John. *A Commentary on Psalms 1-72.* Milwaukee: Northwestern Publishing House, 2005.

Campbell, Ted A. *The Religion of the Heart: A Study of European Religious Life in the Seventeenth and Eighteenth Centuries.* Columbia: University of South Carolina, 1991.

Cassirer, Ernst. *The Philosophy of the Enlightenment.* Princeton: Princeton University Press, 1951.

Chaffey, Tim, and Jason Lisle. *Old-Earth Creationism on Trial: The Verdict Is In.* Green Forest, AR: Master Books, 2008. Kindle.

Charles, Daryl J., ed. *Reading Genesis 1-2: An Evangelical Conversation.* Peabody, MA: Hendrickson Publishers, 2013. Kindle.

Christian Worship: A Lutheran Hymnal. Milwaukee: Northwestern Publishing House, 1993.

Christianity Today. *The Origins Debate: Evangelical Perspectives on Creation, Evolution, and Intelligent Design.* Carol Stream, IL: Christianity Today, 2012. Kindle.

Coggins, R. J., and J. L. Houlden, eds. *A Dictionary of Biblical Interpretation.* Philadelphia: Trinity Press International, 1990.

Colling, Richard G. *Random Designer.* Bourabonnais, IL: Browning Press, 2004.

Collins, C. John. *Did Adam and Eve Really Exist?* Wheaton: Crossway, 2011.

Collins, C. John. *Science and Faith,* Wheaton: Crossway, 2009.

Collins, Francis, S. *The Language of God.* New York: Free Press, 2006.

Cootsona, Gregory S. *Creation and Last Things.* Louisville: Geneva Press, 2002.

Davidson, G. R. *When Faith & Science Collide.* Oxford, MS: Malius Press, 2009.

Edwards, Denis. *The God of Evolution.* New York: Paulist Press, 1999.

Ehrman, Bart. *The New Testament of the Great Courses series, course guidebook.* Chantilly, VA: The Teaching Company, 2000.

Eichhorn, Johann Gottfried. *Introduction to the Study of the Old Testament.* Translated by George T. Gollop. 1803. London: Spottswoode and Co., 1988.

Enns, Peter. *The Evolution of Adam: What the Bible Does and Doesn't Say About Human Origins.* Grand Rapids: Brazos Press, 2012.

Falk, Darrel R. *Coming to Peace With Science.* Downers Grove, IL: InterVarsity Press, 2004.

Giberson, Karl W., and Francis S. Collins. *The Language of Science and Faith.* Downers Grove, IL: InterVarsity Press, 2011.

Gitt, Werner. *Did God Use Evolution?* Green Forest, AK: Master Books, 2006.

Green, Joel B. *Body, Soul, and Human Life: The Nature of Humanity in the Bible.* Grand Rapids: Baker, 2008.

Greenwood, Kyle. *Scripture and Cosmology: Reading the Bible Between the Ancient World and Modern Science.* Downers Grove, IL: IVP Academic, 2015.

Grudem, Wayne. *Systematic Theology: An Introduction to Biblical Doctrine.* Grand Rapids: Zondervan, 1994.

Gunkel, Herman. *The Legends of Genesis: The Biblical Saga and History.* Translated by W. H.Carruth, 1901. Chicago: Open Court, n.d. Kindle.

Ham, Ken. *The Lie: Evolution/Millions of Years.* Green Forest, AR: Master Books, 1987. Kindle.

Ham, Ken. *Why Won't They Listen: The Power of Creation Evangelism.* Green Forest, AR: Master Books, 2002.

Hamann, Henry P. *A Popular Guide to New Testament Criticism.* St. Louis: Concordia Publishing House, 1977.

Harrell, Daniel M. *Nature's Witness: How Evolution Can Inspire Faith.* Nashville: Abingdon, 2008. Kindle.

Harrisville, Roy A. *Pandora's Box Opened: An Examination and Defense of the Historical-Critical Method and Its Master Practitioners.* Grand Rapids: William B. Eerdmans, 2014.

Haught, John F. *Science and Faith: A New Introduction.* New York: Paulist Press, 2012. Kindle.

Heck, Joel. D. *In the Beginning, God.* St. Louis: Concordia Publishing House, 2011.

Hornig, Gottfried. *Die Anfaenge der historich-kritischen Theologie.* Goettingen: Vandenhoeck & Ruprecht, 1961.

Horowitz, Wayne. *Mesopotamian Cosmic Geography.* Winona Lake, IN: Eisenbrauns, 2011.

"Humanism." *Cambridge Dictionary of Philosophy.* Edited by Robert Audi. 2nd ed. Cambridge University Press, 1999.

Hunter, Cornelius G. *Darwin's God: Evolution and the Problem of Evil.* Grand Rapids: Baker, 2001.

Hurst, John F. *History of Rationalism,* New York: Carlton & Porter, 1867.

Hyers, Conrad. *The Meaning of Creation: Genesis and Modern Science.* Atlanta: John Knox Press, 1984.

Israel, Jonathan. *Radical Enlightenment: Philosophy and the Making of Modernity 1650-1750.* Oxford: Oxford University Press, 2001.

Jacob, Margaret C. *The Enlightenment: A Brief History With Documents.* Boston: Bedford/St. Martin's, 2001.

Jacob, Margaret C. *The Scientific Revolution: A Brief History With Documents.* Boston: Bedford/St. Martin's, 2010.

Jahn, Curtis. *A Lutheran Looks at Catholics.* Milwaukee: Northwestern Publishing House, 2014.

Jeeves, Malcolm A., and R. J. Berry. *Science, Life, and Christian Belief.* Grand Rapids: Baker, 1998.

Keegan, Terence J. *Interpreting the Bible: A Popular Introduction to Biblical Hermeneutics.* New York: Paulist Press, 1985.

Keel, Othmar. *The Symbolism of the Biblical World: Ancient Near Eastern Iconography and the Book of Psalms.* Winona Lake, IN: Eisenbrauns, 1997.

Keil, Carl F. and F. Delitzsch. *Commentary on the Old Testament, Vol. 1: The Pentateuch.* 1861. Reprint, Grand Rapids: William B. Eerdmans, 1976.

Kidner, Derek. *Genesis: Tyndale Old Testament Commentaries.* Downers Grove, IL: InterVarsity Press, 1967.

King, C. Wesley. *The Battle for Genesis 1 and 2: Creationism vs. Theistic Evolution.* Nicholasville, KY: Schmul, 2015.

Kraus, Hans-Joachim. *Geschichte der Historisch-Kritischen Erforschung des Alten Testaments.* Neukirchen Verlag, 1956.

Kulikovsky, Andrew S. *Creation, Fall, Restoration: A Biblical Theology of Creation.* Ross-shire, Scotland: Mentor, 2009.

Ladd, George Eldon. *The New Testament and Criticism.* Grand Rapids: William B. Eerdmans, 1967.

Lamoureux, Denis. *Evolutionary Creation.* Eugene, OR: Wipf & Stock, 2008.

Legaspi, Michael C. *The Death of Scripture and the Rise of Biblical Studies.* New York: Oxford University Press, 2010.

Lennox, John C. *Seven Days That Divide the World: The Beginning According to Genesis and Science.* Grand Rapids: Zondervan, 2011. EPub.

Leupold, H. C. *Exposition of Genesis.* Vol. 1. Grand Rapids: Baker, 1942.

Levine, Amy-Jill. *The Old Testament of the Great Courses series, course guidebook.* Chantilly, VA: The Teaching Company, 2001.

Lewis, C. S. *The Problem of Pain (Collected Letters of C.S. Lewis).* HarperCollins, 2009. Ebook.

Lubenow, Marvin L. *Bones of Contention.* Grand Rapids: Baker Books, 2004. (Kindle Version)

Luther, Martin. *Luther's Works.* Edited by Jaroslav Pelikan and Helmut T. Lehmann. American Edition. Vol 1. St. Louis: Concordia Publishing House; Philadelphia: Fortune Press, 1955-1986

Luther, Martin. *Luther's Works.* Edited by Jaroslav Pelikan and Helmut T. Lehmann. American Edition. Vol. 54. St. Louis: Concordia Publishing House; Philadelphia: Fortune Press, 1955-1956.

Madueme, Hans, and Michael Reeves, eds. *Adam, the Fall, and Original Sin.* Grand Rapids: Baker, 2014.

Mahoney, Jack. *Christianity in Evolution.* Washington, D.C.: Georgetown University Press, 2011. Kindle.

Maier, Gerhardt. *The End of the Historical-Critical Method.* Translated by Edwin W. Levernz and Rudolph F. Norden. St. Louis: Concordia Publishing House, 1974.

Meyer, Stephen C. *Darwin's Doubt.* New York: HarperCollins, 2013.

Miller, Johnny V., and John M. Soden. *In the Beginning . . . We Misunderstood: Interpreting Genesis 1 in Its Original Context.* Grand Rapids: Kregel, 2012.

Miller, Keith B., ed. *Perspectives on an Evolving Creation.* Grand Rapids: William B. Eerdmans, 2003.

Montague, George T. *Understanding the Bible: A Basic Introduction to Biblical Interpretation.* New York: Paulist Press, 2007. Kindle.

Moreland, J. P., Stephen C. Meyer, Christopher Shaw, Ann K. Gauger, and Wayne Grudem, eds. *Theistic Evolution.* Wheaton: Crossway, 2017.

Moreland, J. P., and John Mark Reynolds, eds. *Three Views on Creation and Evolution*. Grand Rapids: Zondervan, 1999.

Morris, Henry M. III. *After Eden: Understanding Creation, the Curse, and the Cross*. Green Forest, AK: Master Books, 2003.

Morris, Henry M. III. *Biblical Creationism: What Each Book of the Bible Teaches About Creation and the Flood*. Grand Rapids: Baker, 1993.

Morris, Henry M. III. *5 Reasons to Believe in Recent Creation*. Dallas: Institute for Creation Research, 2008.

Morris, John. *Is the Big Bang Biblical?* Green Forest, AK: Master Books, 2003.

Mortenson, Terry. *The Great Turning Point*. Green Forest, AR: Master Books, 2004. Kindle.

Mortenson, Terry and Ury, Thane H., eds. *Coming To Grips With Genesis: Biblical Authority and the Age of the Earth*. Green Forest, AR: Master Books, 2008. Kindle.

Munitz, Milton K. ed. *Theories of the Universe: From Babylonian Myth to Modern Science*. New York: Free Press, 1957.

Neill, Stephen. *The Interpretation of the New Testament, 1861-1961*. New York: Oxford, 1964.

Nevin, Norman C. *Should Christians Embrace Evolution?* Phillipsburg, NJ: P&R Publishing, 2009.

Osborn, Ronald E. *Death Before the Fall: Biblical Literalism and the Problem of Animal Suffering*. Downers Grove, IL: InterVarsity Press, 2014. Kindle.

Otis, John M. *Theistic Evolution: A Sinful Compromise*. Triumphant Publications Ministries, 2013.

Peters, Ted, and Martinez Hewlett. *Can You Believe in God and Evolution?* Nashville: Abingdon, 2008.

Phillips, Richard D., ed. *God, Adam, and You: Biblical Creation Defended and Applied*. Phillipsburg, NJ: P&R Publishing, 2015.

Pieper, Francis. *Christian Dogmatics*, Vol. 1. St. Louis: Concordia Publishing House, 1950.

Polkinghorne, John, and Nicholas. *Questions of Truth: Fifty-one Responses to Questions About God, Science, and Belief*. Louisville, KY: Westminster John Knox Press, 2009. Kindle.

Poythress, Vern S. *Redeeming Science: A God-Centered Approach*. Wheaton: Crossway, 2006.

Preus, Robert. *The Inspiration of Scripture: A Study of the Theology of the 17th-Century Lutheran Dogmaticians*. St. Louis: Concordia Publishing House, 1957.

Price, Robert M., and Edwin A. Suominen. *Evolving out of Eden: Christian Responses to Evolution*. Valley, WA: Tellectual Press, 2013. Kindle.

Principe, Lawrence. *History of Science: Antiquity to 1700 of the Great Courses series, course guidebook.* Chantilly, VA: The Teaching Company, 2001.

Pritchard, James, ed., *The Ancient Near East: Anthology of Texts & Pictures.* Princeton: Princeton University Press, 2011.

Purcell, Brendan. *From Big Bang to Big Mystery: Human Origins in the Light of Creation and Evolution.* Hyde Park, NY: New City Press, 2012. Kindle.

Ratzinger, Joseph (Pope Benedict XVI), *"In the Beginning. . .": A Catholic Understanding of the Story of Creation and the Fall.* Translated by Boniface Ramsey. Grand Rapids: William B. Eerdmans, 1995. Kindle.

Rau, Gerald. *Mapping the Origins Debate.* Downers Grove, IL: IVP Academic, 2012.

Razmerita, Gheorghe. *Theistic Evolution's Struggle for Survival: An Analysis and Evaluation of the Appeal of Theistic Evolutionist Systems to Dual Anthropology.* Saabrucken, Germany: VDM Verlag Dr. Mueller Aktiengesellschaft & Co., 2009.

Ruggles Clive. *An Encyclopedia of Cosmologies and Myth.* Santa Barbara, CA: ABE-CLIO, 2005.

Ruse, Michael. *Can a Darwinian Be a Cristian?* Cambridge: Cambridge University Press, 2001.

Russell, Robert John. *Cosmology: From Alpha to Omega.* Minneapolis: Fortress Press, 2008.

Sheehan, Jonathan. *The Enlightenment Bible.* Princeton: Princeton University Press, 2005.

Snoke, David. *A Biblical Case for an Old Earth.* Grand Rapids: Baker, 2006.

Sorkin, David. "Reclaiming Theology for the Enlightenment: The Case of Siegmund Jacob Baumgarten (1706-1757)." *Central European History, Vol. 36, No. 4,* (2003), p. x.

Southgate, Christopher. *The Groaning of Creation: God, Evolution, and the Problem of Evil.* Louisville: John Knox Press, 2008.

Stott, John R. *The Message of Romans: God's Good News for the World.* Downers Grove, IL: IVP Academic, 1994.

Swarbrick, Mark W. *Theistic Evolution: Did God Create Through Evolution?* West Conshohocken, PA: Infinity Publishing, 2006.

VanDoodewaard, William. *The Quest for the Historical Adam: Genesis, Hermeneutics, and Human Origins.* Grand Rapids: Reformation Heritage Books, 2015.

Wallmann, Johannes. *Kirchengeschichte Deutschlands.* Tuebingen: J. C. B. Mohr, 1988.

Walton, John. *The Lost World of Genesis One: Ancient Cosmology and the Origins Debate.* Downers Grove, IL: InterVarsity Press, 2009.

Ward, Keith. *The Big Questions in Science and Religion*. West Conshohocken, PA: Templeton Press, 2008.

Warren, William. *The Earliest Cosmologies: The Universe as Pictured in Thought by Ancient Hebrews, Babylonians, Egyptians, Greeks, Iranians, and Indo-Aryans*. New York: Eaton and Mains, 1909, reprinted in 2012 by Forgotten Books.

Wellhausen, Julius. *Prolegomena to the History of Ancient Israel*. Translated by J. Sutherland Black and Allan Menzies. 1885. N.p.: Evinity Publishing, 2009. Kindle.

Whorton, Mark S. *Peril in Paradise*. Waynesboro, GA: Authentic Media, 2015.

Williams, Patricia A. *Doing Without Adam and Eve: Sociobiology and Original Sin*. Minneapolis: Fortress Press, 2001.

Wiseman, James A. *Theology and Modern Science: Quest for Coherence*. New York: Continuum, 2002.

Witham, Larry A. *Where Darwin Meets the Bible: Creationists and Evolutionists in America*. Oxford: Oxford University Press, 2002.

Wright, J. Edward. *The Early History of Heaven*. Oxford: Oxford University Press, 2000.

Wright, N. T. "Romans," in *The New Interpreter's Bible: A Commentary in Twelve Volumes. Edited by Leander* Keck. Nashville: Abingdon, 2002.

(This is the full bibliography for this book and for the second book of the set, *One More Elephant: Evolution Versus the Text of Scripture*.)

Appendix 1: Early Systems

The gap theory: In the early days of evolutionary thinking, two systems were developed to merge Scripture with the growing idea that the earth is very old. They were developed in the early 1800s—at a time when most churches read Scripture in a straightforward way. People needed a system that was faithful to the words of Scripture but which left room for the findings of natural philosophers, especially their conclusions about the fossil evidence.

One of these was the gap theory, devised in the early 1800s. Its purpose was to reconcile fossil evidence with the six-day creation described in Genesis 1. It teaches a gap between Genesis 1:2 and 1:3. The first two verses of Genesis 1 are interpreted to say that God created an initial world (verse 1), which was ruined through Satan's evil influence after he was cast out of heaven and rendered the first creation "void and without form," verse 2).

To accommodate fossil evidence, the gap theory teaches that in the first world living creatures evolved along the lines of current evolutionary theory. Proponents accept the current geologic column and the dating of fossils discovered in the various rock strata, but they say that the fossils were a product of the evolution of the first world. After God destroyed the first world, he then re-created the world in six 24-hour days as described in the rest of Genesis 1.

The gap theory was promoted in the *Scofield Reference Bible* (revised version of 1917) and became very popular during the first half of the 20th century, particularly among Fundamentalists. It lost much of its popularity in the second half of the 20th century after many Christians began to explain fossils in terms of the flood.

Gap theory proponents admit that there is little or no information in Scripture about the first world. The theory is based on speculation. One argument seems fairly standard. When God created Adam and Eve he told them to "be fruitful, and multiply, and replenish the earth" (Genesis 1:28 KJV). Since God told Adam and Eve to "replenish" the earth (taken in the sense of to "re-fill" it), the original earth must have been filled with human beings. The Hebrew word, however, simply means "to fill."

By this, gap theory proponents are admitting that human fossil evidence is valid and shows slow, gradual development over time. Although they believe that Genesis teaches that mankind was created in their mature state, they also believe that humans evolved in the first world. Logically, then, they must admit to a form of theistic evolution, at least in the first world. This, in turn, makes them participants in at least some of the modern theistic evolutionary arguments present in this book.

The day-age idea: The second early way of combining human fossil evidence with Scripture was the day-age view. It claims that the Genesis "day" was a long period of time, affording ample time for humans to have evolved.

The day-age theory is filled with all the difficulties present in any attempt to merge the sequence of events in Genesis 1 with the sequence required by evolution. One of the most obvious is the creation of the sun, moon, and stars on the fourth day, following the creation of light on the first day and the creation of vegetation on the third. Some explain this difficulty by claiming that clouds kept the sun from becoming visible until the fourth day. Others claim that the six days of Genesis are simply a framework for describing creation rather than a literal progression of days. Others claim that the days overlapped greatly. None of these, however, satisfy either Scripture or the theory of evolution. More important, none of them deal with the theological issues covered in this book. All forms of evolution strike at the basic teachings of Scripture and the gospel message.

Progressive creationism: Progressive creationism is another attempt to reconcile Scripture with evolution. It had its origins in the early 19th century. Progressive creationists accept microevolution (the ability of the "kinds" of Genesis 1 to adapt to the environment) but not macroevolution (the ability of an original organism to be the source of all the species in existence today). They teach that God created animals and mankind in a series of creative acts. That is, God would create one form of a living being, destroy that form through a natural catastrophe, and then create a more advanced form. This continued until living beings arrived in their present form.

This theory has the benefit of explaining human fossil evidence without having to trace the precise way one species evolved into the next. This is especially important for trying to explain the existence of modern humans with no intermediate hominin species still living in the world. Hominins, it is taught, were animals, and only in the most recent iteration did God give the species a soul and make them human.

Since progressive creationism rejects macroevolution, it does away with the suffering and death evolution entails. However, the suffering and death of the catastrophes is linked directly to God, who caused these catastrophes so he could create the next iteration of a species.

Appendix 2: Scripture on the Relation of Man and Animals

What follows in this appendix is merely "food for thought." It is offered in light of the claim by evolutionists that animals have some very "human" abilities and qualities. They use this to prove that mankind evolved from animals. It is also offered in view of the counterclaim that it only seems as if animals have these abilities and qualities and that animals operate by pure instinct.

Is it Scriptural to say that only humans have the ability to reason, while animals act only on some kind of preprogrammed behavior we call "instinct"?

In Scripture there are a few places where animals are spoken of in a negative way. In Psalm 73:22 Asaph, when he questioned God's ways, compared himself to an animal: "I was brutish and ignorant; I was like a beast toward you." Here, the contrast between mankind and animals is in a lack of understanding but not necessarily a complete inability to reason.

A word used in reference to animals is "irrational." Peter and Jude use this word to compare unbelievers to animals. Peter wrote, "But these, like *irrational animals, creatures of instinct*, born to be caught and destroyed, blaspheming about matters of which they are ignorant, will also be destroyed in their destruction" (2 Peter 2:12). Jude wrote, "But these people blaspheme all that they do not understand, and they are destroyed by all that they, *like unreasoning animals, understand instinctively*" (Jude 1:10).

The Greek word translated "irrational" and "unreasoning" is rare in the New Testament. Governor Festus thought it "unreasonable" to send Paul to Caesar without specifying the charges against him (Acts 25:27). It is interesting how the Greek Septuagint translates Exodus 6:12. In the Hebrew Moses said he was a man of "uncircumcised" lips, which is how the ESV translates: "How then shall Pharaoh listen to me, for I am of *uncircumcised* lips?" The Septuagint, however, uses the word Peter and Jude use in the New Testament, the one mentioned in the last paragraph, and has Moses saying: "I am unreasoning." In this case the word does not indicate a lack of reason, just that Moses was not using it very well.

The Greek word translated "instinctively" in these passages simply means "by nature," that is, animals (and the unbelievers Peter and Jude are talking about) do what comes naturally to them. It refers only to their unthinking sinful behavior; it is not saying that they have no ability to decide on (reason out) a course of action.

In the context, these words tell us that there is an important distinction between animals and mankind. But they do not rule out an animal's ability to reason. Anyone with a pet knows that a pet can adapt to its environment and learn some basic skills. In fact, some pets of the same species learn better than others; we even call them "smarter." Scripture supports this idea. It describes the serpent as "crafty" (ESV). In the context of a perfect creation, the word *clever* or *subtle* might be better translations. Nevertheless, Satan chose to use the serpent in tempting Adam and Eve because of its God-given ability.

Do animals have the ability to love, or does it just seem that way as they react to stimulants that give them pleasure? Might not our ability to relate to and love a pet stem from a similar ability on their part? Animals cannot use language as we can. But they certainly have their own ways of telling us what they want.

If we take the words "irrational" and "instinct" to imply that animals are robots and their choices are based only on unreasoning instinct, we might be reading too much into the words used to describe them. Might it not be best to say that God gave animals the ability to use their minds, make decisions, and have emotions *at the level and in the context of what he made them to be*? And we can also admit that God gave certain animals abilities to do certain things human beings cannot do. Is this "instinct" or a special form of reasoning appropriate to each according to their role in creation?

We might also consider passages like Leviticus 17:11: "For the life of the flesh is in the blood, and I have given it for you on the altar to make atonement for your souls, for it is the blood that makes atonement by the life." This principle is the foundation of the whole Old Testament sacrificial system. The sins of an Israelite person would be atoned for, or "covered over," by the blood—the life—of an animal sacrifice. In reference to the Israelite who was atoned for by the life of the animal, translators usually use "soul" (as in the ESV translation above) or simply "yourselves." But the Hebrew uses the same word NEPHESH for both the spirit of the animal being sacrificed and the spirit of the person finding atonement through the sacrifice. An Israelite would have heard God say that the animal's NEPHESH was given in place of his or her own NEPHESH. Regardless of the differences between mankind and animals, the animal's life could serve as a sacrifice for the life of a human being (at least under the Israelite Old Testament law).

Perhaps one more thought is in order. In our age of describing, dividing, and classifying, we might lose sight of something that every part of creation shares. The psalmist calls on the entire creation—animate and inanimate—to praise the Lord:

Praise the LORD from the earth, you great sea creatures and all deeps,
fire and hail, snow and mist, stormy wind fulfilling his word!
Mountains and all hills, fruit trees and all cedars!
Beasts and all livestock, creeping things and flying birds!

Kings of the earth and all peoples, princes and all rulers of the earth!
(Psalm 148:7-11)

Obviously, human beings can praise the Lord in many ways animals cannot. Nevertheless, Scripture ascribes to everything God has made the ability to praise him. We might not be able to say how the mountains and hills, the fruit trees and cedars, or the animals can praise the Lord. But Scripture says that they do.

We did not evolve along with the animals, but we were created on the same day the land animals were created. They, like we, were created from the earth. When a biologist gives examples of animals reasoning out problems or showing human-like love, Scripture does not seem to rule out such behavior. Yet Scripture does make it clear that animals and mankind were separate acts of creation and, as any biologist knows, are far different in their qualities and abilities, not to mention the fact that mankind was created in God's image.

Scripture Index

Made in the USA
Monee, IL
26 October 2021